03

Civic Space/Cyberspace

Civic Space/Cyberspace

The American Public Library in the Information Age

Redmond Kathleen Molz and Phyllis Dain

The MIT Press
Cambridge, Massachusetts
London, England

This book was set in Sabon by Crane Composition, Inc. and was printed and bound in the United States of America.

Library of Congress Cataloging-in-Publication Data

Molz, Redmond Kathleen, 1928–
  Civic Space / cyberspace: the American public library in the information age / Redmond Kathleen Molz and Phyllis Dain.
    p. cm.
  Includes bibliographical references and index.
  ISBN 0-262-13346-6 (hc: alk. paper)
  1. Public libraries—United States. 2. Public libraries—United States—Special collections—Computer network resources. I. Dain, Phyllis. II. Title.
Z731.M639   1998
027.473—dc21   98-16614
                                                                        CIP

Contents

Preface

This book chronicles two journeys: the first entailed a number of visits across the country to see and discuss the current state of public librarianship, and the second ventured into cyberspace and the ever-evolving dimensions of the information age. Explorers in the second of these terrains are many and their writings abound in bookstores and libraries, but outside the realm of professional literature for librarians there are few chroniclers of the first of these undertakings, an overview of the contemporary tax-supported public library in the United States. Established in the nineteenth century, brought to fruition in the twentieth, and about to enter a new millennium, the public library has for over 150 years proffered books, periodicals, and other media to countless users, answered innumerable patron inquiries, sponsored a litany of story hours and lectures, and afforded a multiplicity of viewpoints a voice and a hearing even in the silence of the stacks.

Although often ignored in analyses of contemporary American institutional life, the public library has of late been the subject of some scrutiny, largely stimulated by the advent of the Internet and other electronic media. While some commentators see a lessening of the dominance of print and the subsequent conversion of the library to electronic means of information delivery, others decry the potential loss of the literate experience exemplified by the very presence of the many volumes available on library shelves. Writing in the March 1997 issue of *Harper's Magazine*, Sallie Tisdale laments the undermining of the print-based public library that had so absorbed her as a child: "In the last few years I have gone to the library to study or browse or look something up, and instead have found myself listening to radios, crying babies, a cappella love songs, puppet shows, juggling demonstrations, CD-ROM games, and cellular telephone calls. . . . Silence, even a mild sense of repose, is long gone." On the other hand, librarian Peter R. Young in the fall 1996 issue of *Daedalus* celebrates the postmodern digital environment, which "requires that librarians add value to the use of information. Librarians working in digital information structures are creators of information through the assembly, organization, and generation of new knowledge. The authentication and validation of knowledge resources present new opportunities to the postmodern librarian."

The traditional challenges involved in the library's promotion of reading and the book to successive generations of learners and the new opportunities afforded it in the dissemination of electronic information are the subject of this book. We conceived of this book as an essay based on our observations, our reading of numerous documents and reports, and our long-held interest as both teachers and researchers in the place of the public library in the social and civic structure. We focus on major trends and issues and take a broad national view of the public library as an American institution. In a work of this sort and with our limited resources, we could not cover all aspects of the public library and from all vantage points, and our site visits and interviews focused mainly on metropolitan areas, where the great majority of Americans now live. The book does not derive from a scientific survey of our own or from the kind of lengthy and comprehensive research investigation characteristic of the Public Library Inquiry conducted at the close of World War II. Our work does not replicate the Inquiry's breadth, nor can it be considered an update of its conclusions. The findings expressed here, however, do suggest that an extensive research effort similar to the Inquiry be undertaken to study an institution that is used each year by two-thirds of the American population, a rather surprising indicator of its contemporary utility and viability.

Historical perspective plays a large part in these pages. In this regard, the viewpoint of *Thinking in Time: The Uses of History for Decision-Makers* by Richard E. Neustadt and Ernest R. May proved useful. Its authors, both Harvard academicians, argue that political leaders need to cultivate the habit of "seeing time as a stream," envisioning the present and future as emerging from the past and prefiguring how a new public policy, if adopted, would fit into the stream of history decades or even years later. For our purposes, "thinking in time" was one way to approach this examination of a venerable institution, now on the cusp of a revolution in communications media that many believe rivals the invention and development of printing.

The book illuminates two distinctive aspects of the public library: the first is the public library as a local institution empowered to sustain itself through taxation by the permissive legislation of the state; the second is the public library as a nationwide phenomenon, strongly identified with the national ethos of equality of educational opportunity. Historically, the public schools have also been instruments of social equalization, but the schools, unlike libraries, are almost totally responsive to their immediate environment, even though the standards for their services are mandated by the state. The public library, by contrast, has from its inception provided more than a local service. Out-of-town visitors freely browse through public library collections for which they pay no taxes; since 1917, an interlibrary loan code has made feasible a reciprocal lending of library materials from one location to another; some states encourage statewide library cards allowing the residents of the state to use any public library within its borders; and today the ubiquitous digitized catalog makes known the holdings of a given library collection to any surfer on the worldwide Internet. Speaking in 1936 before the American Library Association Council when the issue of federal aid for public libraries was being debated, one municipal librarian remarked that the proposed establishment of a minimum standard for library service sustained by federal revenues called up "all sorts of pictures of a coast-to-coast program, all-American, a sort of NBC network." The activities of the public library progressively leading it in the direction of a larger area of service and furthering its responsibilities for constituents beyond its immediate borders provide a contrapuntal theme to the book's consideration of the public library as a unit of local government, whether Denver or Salt Lake City or Los Angeles County. However local their origins, public libraries are also shaped by a host of policy actors on the national scene. All three branches of the federal government have influenced their course, as has the work of an increasing number of public-interest groups concerned with the emerging national information infrastructure. The delineation of that infrastructure and the role that public libraries are playing in it are topics to which the book gives special attention.

No one word can summarize our perceptions in observing the work of the public libraries that we visited, but a cluster of adjectives—eclectic, diverse, heterogeneous—comes to mind. The people who use these libraries and the purposes behind their use represent a kaleidoscope of contemporary American life—new immigrants seeking to learn English, students on the track of some school-related assignment, job seekers learning to write an acceptable résumé, persons in search of a "good read," and a new cadre of technophiles anxious to have their first experience with using computers. Critics who perceive that the social fabric of the United States is unraveling might take heart from what we saw—a social institution with multifaceted missions but an overall sense of direction and a strong commitment to the ideals of public service.

It would have been impossible to write this book without a grant from the H. W. Wilson Foundation, which underwrote our travel and most of our related expenses. We are grateful to the late Leo M. Wiens, president of the H. W. Wilson Company, and the other members of the Foundation's board. Robert Wedgeworth, university librarian, University of Illinois at Urbana–Champaign, has encouraged our work since it was first conceived at the late School of Library Service of Columbia University, where both of us were faculty members and he was dean. We appreciate his continued interest and support.

At Columbia's School of International and Public Affairs (where R. Kathleen Molz is now professor of public affairs), the then Dean of the School John G. Ruggie and Vice Dean Steven Cohen furthered the project with some very practical assistance, including clerical help and the assignment of teaching assistants. One of them, Pronita Gupta, was indefatigable in her pursuit of books and other materials from the holdings of the Columbia University Libraries.

Our work benefits from access to the resources of the New York Public Library and the generous provision of workspace in its Frederick Lewis Allen Room. Special thanks are owed for all sorts of assistance from the staff of the Leonia (New Jersey) Public Library, especially Director Harold Ficke and Assistant Director Deborah Bigelow, and to the Bergen County (New Jersey) Cooperative Library System, of which the Leonia Library is a member. The services now available in a small suburban community (where Phyllis Dain lives) exemplify the revolution wrought by technology—online countywide union catalog, quick interlibrary loan, Internet access, and online periodical and newspaper indexes and abstracts. All of these make feasible the research that in the past could have been done with difficulty even in large research libraries or not done at all in any library.

For arranging our invitation to attend the conference on "The Transformation of the Public Library: Access to Digital Information in a Networked World" held at the Library of Congress in 1995, we thank Eleanor Jo Rodger, president of Urban Libraries Council. Margaret Chaplan, librarian at the Labor and Industrial Relations Library of the University of Illinois at Urbana–Champaign, was helpful in searching for certain information sources. Ethel Himmel of Himmel & Wilson, Library Consultants, furnished recent information on the public library planning process. Claudette Tennant of the American Library Association's Washington Office reviewed the contents of the table dealing with federal library legislation.

We thank the MIT Press for its attention to our manuscript, with special appreciation to editors Douglas Sery and Deborah Cantor-Adams.

On a personal note, Norman Dain was always there with affectionate support, good advice, chauffeuring service, and critical reading of the text, and Bruce Dain was helpful and encouraging in many ways. Jean-Barry Molz, recently retired deputy director of the Baltimore County Public Library, served, as she has in the past, as proofreader par excellence but wisely and thoughtfully refrained from intruding her personal professional opinions on our own.

Most important to our work were the conversations we had with the many persons who agreed to be interviewed and whom we encountered on our visits to various libraries and other sites. Taking time out of their own busy professional schedules, they patiently submitted to all our questions, drove us around their communities to see libraries in both physical and virtual space, took us to lunch, plied us with coffee, and gave us piles of documents. In the list of site visits and interviews (see the appendix) we could not name all of the 160 or more persons with whom we spoke. But we are grateful to each of them for sharing with us their views and their visions of the public library in this new age of information.

A word on dates is in order. As our work on the contemporary scene progressed, we realized we were trying to hit a moving target, most especially, though not exclusively, in the constantly changing arena of national public policy on information and information technology. Our data are as up-to-date as possible, but, given the time lags in preparing a manuscript for publication, they cannot be up to the minute. On most important national policy issues, our information is current as of summer 1998; the currency of other data varies, largely depending on the availability of information at the time of writing. Nonetheless, it is inevitable that subsequent developments will alter the course of the events we describe. As a case in point, in September 1998, as the book was going to press, the Internet became the vehicle for the global distribution, by congressional vote, of the full, unedited text of the Independent Counsel's *Referral to the House of Representatives*, with all of its graphic particulars regarding President Clinton's conduct. White House concerns about the dangers of access by minors to pornographic sites on the Internet and efforts in Congress to mandate filtering technology in schools and public libraries accepting federal funds, all of which we discuss in chapter 4, take on a certain irony in light of what occurred in September. At the time of writing we could not, of course, predict the future, but we trust that the trajectory we trace of the public library from its past to its present remains informative and valid.

R. Kathleen Molz
Phyllis Dain
September 1998

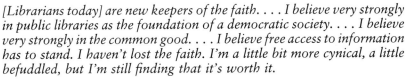

[Librarians today] are new keepers of the faith. . . . I believe very strongly in public libraries as the foundation of a democratic society. . . . I believe very strongly in the common good. . . . I believe free access to information has to stand. I haven't lost the faith. I'm a little bit more cynical, a little befuddled, but I'm still finding that it's worth it.

—*Librarian at the County of Los Angeles Public Library, July 1995*

Civic Space/Cyberspace

Introduction

Quintessentially American institutions, symbols of American faith in education, public libraries are both diverse and similar. As local structures in local sites, they are as different as the communities they serve—in size, scope, governance, funding, clientele, appearance. The nearly nine thousand institutional public library entities in the United States operate under fifty sets of state laws and thousands of local ordinances. Still, each library is familiar. Anyone walking into any one library building will have to learn the layout and the scope, but it is not hard to feel at home. Collections vary in emphasis and specialties, but the core is similar; proportions of print to nonprint materials may differ, but books, magazines, newspapers, and audiovisual media—plus, increasingly, videotapes and CD-ROMs— are likely to be found almost everywhere; children's rooms may be here or there or reference desks up front or in back, but they are bound to be somewhere; magazines and newspapers may be shelved in a separate room or not, but the current issues will still be displayed for browsing. Basic services and techniques, the organization of materials, and librarians' qualifications are fairly uniform. The old card catalogs are gone (or going) mostly everywhere, replaced by banks of computer terminals with more or less similar approaches to information not only about library holdings and their availability but all sorts of other things. Bibliographic standardization, together with librarians' cooperative enterprise and the new electronic technologies, can reveal what repository almost anywhere has which items and then obtain them, through fax, photocopy, modem, trucks, vans, and the United States mail. Perhaps more than most public agencies, libraries have joined together in national, regional, state, and local networks, consortia, or cooperatives to share resources, technology, and expertise. Public librarians all speak the same language: there is a more or less common understanding of what their libraries are—agencies offering to the public the means of acquiring information, knowledge, education, aesthetic experience, and entertainment. This consensus, though not without contradictions and complications through history and at any one time, derives from the evolution of a nationwide library ideology promulgated in professional education, professional literature, and the pronouncements and publications of the major professional organization, the American Library Association (ALA).

The commonalities are applied in the different environments where public libraries first appeared in the mid-nineteenth century. Local conditions have historically determined how much libraries could do, how, where, and for whom, and they continue to do so to this day. At the same time the emergence in the twentieth century of state and federal programs to aid and promote library service, in individual communities and through cooperative endeavors, brought to local library development monies, and, equally important, stimulation and standards.

The dualities present both problems and prospects for librarians. They are trying to offer full and free access to information and knowledge at a time of contradictory realities. Electronic technology and changing ways of life are eroding boundaries of space and time and transcending governmental jurisdictions, but the persistence of such jurisdictions, together with economic constraints, imposes limits on fulfilling visions of universal service. Still, the traditional public library—popular, nonpartisan, community based, and within real, not virtual, walls—carries important social value. It contributes to what social scientist Robert Putnam calls the "network of civic engagement" that anchors people to communities and fosters a sense of fellowship, civic participation, and democratic living.[1] As a civic space, devoted to cultural and educational purposes, the public library serves to reinforce social solidarity in an increasingly fragmented and market-driven culture. Some of the same social needs it was created to meet still exist but in different forms and in a very different environment: public libraries have both changed and remained the same. They arose as mediating institutions in a time of social transformation, then adapted to the needs of a modernizing world, and now, in a postmodern, postindustrial world, are navigating through changes whose impact we are only beginning to assess.

Creatures of the community and serving the entire community—people of all ages and conditions—public libraries have always mirrored trends in society at large. They can be viewed as microcosms of the macrocosm of American civilization, its social and governmental structures, economic conditions, political currents, and intellectual and cultural life. Not only are libraries best understood in relation to the larger society, but they can serve as lenses through which to see the effects of societal trends on community services, both historically and contemporaneously.

The first significant, influential tax-supported public libraries (with Boston leading the way in 1852) were organized in the growing antebellum and then post–Civil War northeastern and midwestern cities. The community leaders who founded public libraries conceived them first and foremost as educational agencies, supplementing the newly established public primary schools. In a representative republic extending the suffrage to all white male citizens and in a new and rapidly industrializing market economy, education was conceived as a civic necessity and a pathway to success. Public libraries would provide the intellectual wherewithal on which people could apply reading skills and further their education. The libraries had other purposes as well. They would be civilizing agents and objects of civic pride in a raw new country. Technological progress was making printed materials cheap and abundant, and a new American intelligentsia and scientific community demanded the intellectual and cultural accoutrements of the advanced civilization they hoped the United States would become. Libraries would preserve and transmit Western European culture and knowledge (and obviate the need for Americans to go to Europe to consult books) and, by collecting contemporary and historical records and publications, create an American archive for posterity. And (although not often expressed in the moralistic and utilitarian rhetoric of the time) libraries could offer means of (wholesome) amusement and diversion.

As the number of publications proliferated, librarians devised practical ways to organize the masses of printed matter for use—new cataloging and classifying systems and periodical indexes that remained standard until computers arrived in the 1960s. James Beniger, in *The Control Revolution:*

Technological and Economic Origins of the Information Society, calls nineteenth-century librarians "the first information scientists."[2]

Public libraries, like schools, came to be accepted as public responsibilities, civic goods benefiting the entire society and thus worthy of public support. This commitment was expressed in state laws as well as in library charters and educators' and librarians' speeches and writings. The legislation enabled rather than mandated communities to organize libraries. Until well into the twentieth century the states, while allowing and even encouraging municipal library service, did not substantially, if at all, fund it. Unlike schools, free public libraries have been voluntary in their establishment as well as use, and they were open in principle to the entire community, not just a portion of it. This made libraries popular and gave them a certain autonomy, but it left the library picture incomplete and uneven and left libraries without a clearly defined constituency.

The early public libraries, innovative as they were in their mere existence, had decided limitations. All adult residents (which would commonly include young people over fourteen years old) were theoretically welcome in public libraries, except until our own time African-Americans or other minorities subject to legal segregation or excluded by custom or inhibition. The libraries closed book shelves to browsing, offered limited opening hours, and restricted the number of books borrowed, especially fiction, which librarians, along with many other educated people, considered unserious and uneducational, if not morally and psychologically dangerous. Many librarians, taking to heart their professional obligations as educators and intellectual gatekeepers and believing in the power of words, accepted a role as moral, often narrow-minded, censors of reading materials. Nonetheless, interested, determined readers could find in urban public libraries the standard history and expressions of Western culture. Even when closely monitored, collections contained works that challenged the status quo and that offered alternative visions of human and social relationships that could stimulate and nurture original minds.

It was in the twentieth century that public libraries became the ubiquitous institutions that we now know. By the 1870s there were nearly three hundred public libraries in the United States, by 1900 almost a thousand, mostly in the North, and more than double that by 1923.[3] Not every American community had access to a public library by the 1920s and beyond, however, especially in rural areas, and there remained until midcentury and beyond sharp inequalities nationwide in library service and financial support. Still, the idea that a progressive city or town should have a tax-supported public library had taken hold.

Accelerating this trend was the unprecedented private-sector philanthropy emerging from industrial capitalism in the early twentieth century, exemplified by steel magnate Andrew Carnegie's largess. Neither the first giver of public libraries nor the last, Carnegie was the most famous and probably the most influential. In the current debates about private philanthropy versus publicly financed community services, it is too often forgotten that Carnegie's libraries represented partnership with government. Carnegie believed that the surplus of great fortunes, earned through superior ability, should be disbursed for the public good and thus redress the imbalances of modern industrial life and immunize against radical reform. Influenced by Social Darwinism, such philanthropy was not alms giving. Instead, it would allow talented and ambitious youths to acquire the knowledge and skill needed for success in the inevitable struggle for existence. The best place to do so was in public libraries, sites of self-education and civic enterprise. By 1917, when the awards ceased, Carnegie pledged more than $41 million for nearly two thousand public library buildings in the United States, all requiring the community to supply the land and promise perpetual operating support.

Many Americans of the time accepted the Progressive belief in the social power of knowledge and the positive potential of government, as well as the need to "Americanize" immigrants crowding into the country and to create a pool of educated workers to staff a modern economy. Expenditures for municipal services multiplied: in libraries in large cities local funding for operating expenses rose by two and a half times from 1902 to 1912 and nearly fivefold from 1912 to 1931, much more than price and wage rises.[4] Libraries in the major urban centers began to take their modern shape; they evolved into complex, multipurpose, multibranch, centrally controlled and coordinated systems. Managing this process were the librarians whom urban historian Jon Teaford calls "a fresh breed of professionals in American city government" who "asserted their authority and established their professional standing [and] . . . were seriously devoted to the task of making literature available to urban dwellers."[5] From the 1890s into the 1920s, municipalities, eager to show off their wealth and power and caught up in the City Beautiful movement that combined grand aesthetic design with city planning, built new monumental neoclassical/Renaissance/Beaux Arts central libraries in downtown Boston, Pittsburgh, Chicago, New York, Denver, San Francisco, Detroit, Cleveland, and St. Louis.

In 1910 Arthur Bostwick, a leading librarian of the "fresh breed," described the "modern library idea." It envisioned the public library as an active force, a "community center" striving to "bring book and reader together" and seeking to appeal to "the entire community, not merely to those who voluntarily entered its doors." Among the novel offerings of the "modern library" were unrestricted access to shelves, longer hours of opening, "cheerful and homelike library buildings," children's rooms, cooperation with schools, interlibrary loan, more useful catalogs and reading lists, lectures and exhibits, meeting rooms for neighborhood organizations, and deposit collections for homes, institutions, and workplaces—"the thousand and one activities that distinguish the modern library from its more passive predecessor."[6]

This "new" institution was responding to the powerful modernizing forces of industrialization, immigration, and urbanization. The United States was being transformed from an agricultural to an urban, industrial nation, with a corporate and bureaucratic rather than individualistic economic structure and a population more diverse than the previously predominantly Anglo-Saxon and Nordic stock. Social dislocations and resultant reform movements notwithstanding, American society seemed to be still on the ascent, with traditional culture still generally held worthwhile and worth transmitting to new generations and new arrivals. What was wrong could be fixed—through radical social surgery, palliative social medicine, or efficient organization, all of which had education as an ingredient. In the great northern and midwestern cities librarians, seeing themselves as active participants in the educational process that Americans variously believed would be an ameliorative, stabilizing, or egalitarian force in a changing world, labored, along with social workers and teachers, to bring knowledge, culture, and civic virtue to the people. At the same time central public library collections in several cities were growing into substantial research resources and information banks for the general public, including comprehensive sets of government documents, patents, and scholarly works and primary sources. Libraries began to promote their ability to answer questions out of their store of knowledge and serve as clearinghouses of information about the publications flowing out of the world's presses. The civic reform movements of the day also heightened the felt obligation of libraries, as public knowledge institutions in a republic, to provide information about government and its activities and services.

The library profession, and many libraries, with egregious lapses during World War I, were also liberalizing their moral and political outlook. By the 1920s, when old rigid mores and morals were breaking down in the United States, many librarians surrendered their role as outright and self-righteous censors (albeit some had always been cosmopolitan and fairly free thinking). A new generation devised the Library Bill of Rights, adopted by the American Library Association in 1939. The profession here endorsed three principles: book selection should not be influenced by writers' race, nationality, politics, or religion; reading matter should represent all sides of controversial issues; and meeting rooms should be available to all community groups on equal terms. Later revisions and interpretations took a strong libertarian stance against censorship and for unrestricted use of libraries and materials by all clients, children as well as adults. Whether this commitment to intellectual freedom has always been honored in practice is a question. As we will see, at various times and in various communities it has been seriously challenged, and some aspects remain complex and problematic. Nonetheless the Library Bill of Rights, affirming "all libraries as neutral forums for information and ideas," has come to serve as the library profession's credo.[7]

After suffering from the Great Depression of the 1930s, when budgets contracted and use expanded, and then the hiatus of the World War II years, public libraries shared in the remarkable overall postwar growth in the United States—in economic activity, population, education, and suburban development. Consistent historical as well as current statistics on libraries are hard to find, but we can see general nationwide trends. From 1945 to 1965 public library operating expenditures, mostly derived from local tax funds, multiplied fivefold. Capital outlays, mainly for constructing new buildings and refurbishing and extending old ones, went up more than eightfold in those years and from 1968 to 1986 by some twelve times. All these increases were far above inflation rates and cost rises.

Communities built modernistic, inviting, and often architecturally distin-guished public libraries; by the 1960s there was a discernible trend toward replacing old Carnegie libraries, while many others were renovated or expanded. This time there was no Andrew Carnegie around, and the money for construction and renovation came from the public purse—most sub-stantially and consistently from local bond issues and tax appropriations, to a small extent from state aid, and more significantly from federal aid.[8]

By the turn of the century the states had begun to be more actively involved in public library development, but their role was heightened by the movement, begun in the 1920s and accelerated during the New Deal and after the war, to equalize and upgrade library service throughout the country. Public library promoters campaigned for state aid and, for the first time, federal funds, which were first legislated in 1956. That and subse-quent congressional enactments offered libraries unprecedented federal subventions, largely through state library agencies, and encouraged more effective and efficient units of service through interlibrary cooperation.

All this library development did succeed eventually in bringing library service to most of the American population, and with the lowering of official racial barriers in the South, African-Americans could finally come in the front door. Public libraries evolved into the liberal, open, polymor-phous, and highly popular institutions found all over the country today—stocking all manner of media and imposing few restrictions on use. Not-withstanding the advent of radio, sound movies, and especially televi-sion—all initially seen as potential threats to books and reading—various national surveys, though not strictly comparable, showed substantial increases in use of public libraries, much more so than population growth.[9] Behind the aggregate figures, however, are variations through the years and among different localities and populations. Studies consistently show that library use tends on the whole to correlate with users' years of educa-tion, which correlates with socioeconomic class, and Americans on the whole tended after World War II to be better educated and more prosper-ous than previous generations. Beginning in the 1960s, profound changes in the class and ethnic mixes in American cities had a decided impact upon urban public libraries, which saw much of their constituency move to the expanding suburbs, where public libraries as well as schools were being developed to suit.

The story is familiar. In brief, many cities experienced middle-class "white flight" away from incoming poor white, black, and foreign-born residents. City downtowns might still be crowded with workers during the day, but at night and on weekends they were often deserted; retail stores followed residents out to the suburbs. The new outlying population centers encompassed corporate headquarters and other business establishments that found the suburbs, with their tax breaks, local workforce, and green acres, cheaper and more pleasant than central cities. The cities' tax bases eroded, but public services, including libraries, were needed more than ever by the leftover poor. Traditional library clienteles might have declined, but those users who remained, their children, and newcomers would still depend on the library as a quiet cultural haven, as a source of free information, and for help with homework and other pursuits. And with their large collections of retrospective and specialized publications and expert specialist librarians, the central libraries, like other older urban cultural institutions, could not be duplicated in the "edge cities," as writer Joel Garreau terms the new suburban-exurban conglomerations of people and industry.[10] The old central cities, north and south, were becoming cores of what have been called "citistates"[11]—a mix of multijurisdictional, urban, suburban, and exurban metropolitan communities in which by the 1980s most Americans lived, linked by roads, cars, telecommunications, and economic activity. However, traditional civic boundaries and jurisdictions, and therefore tax districts, remained for the most part the same, while political power, in terms of voting rolls, shifted to the suburbs.

The move from city to suburb and the decline of inner cities became intertwined with another profound demographic shift, a new internal migration, accelerated in the 1980s, from east to west, north to south. The entire country was becoming urbanized by the masses of people abandoning the Snowbelt—or the Rustbelt—for the Sunbelt (and certain areas in the Pacific Northwest), where new investment and new jobs in the growing postindustrial service, information, and high-technology economy, as well as in nonunion manufacturing, were to be found. Like their predecessors in the developing North and Midwest of the late nineteenth century, late twentieth-century southern and western communities built their public libraries—existing ones and new ones—into popular systems matching and even outdoing older libraries in scope and quality of service. All libraries were facing the "information explosion"—the spectacular increase in the amount and cost of published information and then a technological revolution making printed matter, profuse as it was, only one component of a complex communication world. In the 1970s double-digit inflation and then in the 1980s a tax revolt among property owners and the rise of a conservative antigovernment mood coincided with libraries' imperative to buy into the new technologies that would make their technical processes more efficient and their resources universally identifiable in massive digitized data bases. Entering the information age would be expensive; computers and telecommunications promised better and quicker but not necessarily cheaper operations and services. Eventually even the prosperous Sunbelt cities and the suburbs, many with handsome new public library buildings, began to feel the pinch.

Going into the 1990s, when library budgets eventually managed to keep pace with inflation and urban libraries experienced a certain revival, potent new trends emerged. The new immigration from Asia and Latin America was placing new demands on libraries, just as all public agencies were feeling political and fiscal threats to their budgets. Libraries would have to function in a society in which education counted more than ever but where public education was under attack, English as a second language was widespread, and traditional Eurocentric culture and traditional print culture were becoming endangered species. Furthermore, deepening class and color divisions portended a population divided into information haves and have-nots. Rapidly advancing computer and telecommunications technologies and a powerful information industry were transforming the forms and economics of information. National public policy for the so-called information highway was uncertain and overtaken by events—the evolution of the Internet, for example. The digital information revolution seemed to be pointing to a new, immaterial library without walls in the "city of bits" visualized by William Mitchell, dean of the School of Architecture and Planning at the Massachusetts Institute of Technology. In a book published in both print and digital form in 1995, he predicted that the façade of the library "is not to be constructed of stone and located on a street in Bloomsbury, but of pixels on thousands of screens scattered throughout the world. . . . there is nothing left to put a grand facade *on*."[12] Cyberspace would replace civic space—or would it?

1

The Mission: Consensus and Contradiction

Shaped by changing forces in the socioeconomic environment and by the emergence of new technologies in the transmission and preservation of the record, the mission of the public library, as perceived by its custodians, has been somewhat ambivalent and often dichotomous. During the nineteenth century the mission was relatively simple: by housing a collection of books the library was intended to educate and nourish the intellectual and civic life of the community. In brief, the public library was to be an institution devoted to the diffusion of knowledge. At the time of the founding of the leading public libraries during the middle and closing years of the nineteenth century, the majority of United States citizens did not attend secondary schools and had at most completed grammar school. New England, home of the public library movement, had the highest literacy rate in the country, and there the public library was regarded as "the crowning glory" of the public school system, facilitating the self-education of many people through their access to books and reading. Writing in 1876, the nation's centennial year and the founding year of the American Library Association, William Frederick Poole, himself an early librarian in Cincinnati and the founding public librarian in Chicago, made this observation: "In the public libraries which are growing up in our land, fully four fifths of the money appropriated for books is spent in works adapted to the wants of scholars. In the larger libraries the proportion is even greater."[1]

Unlike the benefactors of the public libraries who had little formal schooling, such as Ezra Cornell of Ithaca, Joshua Bates of Boston, and Andrew Carnegie himself, the directors of these nascent libraries were college educated, bibliographically inclined, and energetic in assembling their collections. Today a far greater distinction separates the careers of the academic and public librarian, but nineteenth-century library leaders frequently crisscrossed between the two types of institutions: Justin Winsor, librarian of the Boston Public Library, became librarian of Harvard; William F. Poole ended his career as the first librarian of the Newberry Library in Chicago, an endowed research collection devoted in large part to the humanities; Baltimore's first public library director was a medical doctor, who was succeeded by his son, a graduate of Johns Hopkins University with the degree of doctor of philosophy in history; and Charles Coffin Jewett, having failed to convince the administration of the Smithsonian Institution that it should build a great research library, left his position there to become the librarian of the Boston Public Library. These early librarians, equally at home in both the collegiate and public libraries, were academically trained men—and men should be emphasized—who came to their positions with an understanding of the scholarly apparatus, historical training (both Poole and Winsor served as presidents of the American Historical Association), and a profound interest in bibliographic matters. It was not until the Carnegie benefactions at the turn of the century that women entered the library profession in great numbers, administering the public libraries especially in smaller communities where many of them possessed few formal credentials for their positions—other than a respect for books and reading.

As one of the requisite three R's, reading at the time of the public libraries' establishment was perceived as the proverbial keystone in the arch of learning; and books, often beyond the purchasing power of the ordinary citizen, were construed as a social good the sharing of which was facilitated by the newly formed institutions. With almost missionary zeal, their librarians invoked the power of the book to lead readers upward in their ascent to the higher realms of knowledge. Even if, at the outset, lesser offerings on the literary altar were given preferment, it was assumed that readers would gradually achieve a refinement of taste and be induced to peruse the books the librarians themselves considered most useful and worthy of consideration. "When the habit of reading is once acquired," wrote William F. Poole, "the reader's taste, and hence the quality of his reading, progressively improves."[2] A similar comment by Poole's contemporary, William I. Fletcher, reiterates this conviction: "Let the library, then, contain just enough of the mere confectionery of literature to secure the interest in it of readers of the lowest—not depraved—tastes; but let this be so dealt out as may best make it serve its main purpose of a stepping stone to something better."[3] One notable naysayer to this postulate was none other than Melvil Dewey, originator of the Dewey Decimal Classification, who wrote in 1877: "It has been often said by our best authorities, and the doctrine seems to be gaining ground, that it is better to buy a second-rate book that is sure to be read, than a first-rate one that will stand idle on the shelves."[4] Historical evidence to support either of these stances is not easy to come by, but a spot inventory of the Boston Public Library made in the 1860s disclosed that all copies of the first volume of Bancroft's massive *History of the United States* were in circulation while six copies of the remaining volumes were sitting on the shelves. For some awestruck nineteenth-century readers, the weight of learning may have proved an incalculable burden.

The Dilemma of Building the Collection

From the outset of the public library movement, the formation of the collection posed a dilemma between two opposing camps: on the one hand, there was an appeal to popular culture, represented by the gradual inclusion of fiction and light recreational reading, and, on the other, there was the noble aim of the diffusion of knowledge, which was heavily dependent on the usefulness of reading, embodied in the standard classical works and those having practical, educative, and vocational value. In the same essay in which Fletcher recommended that librarians house some literary "confectionery," he also warned them to avoid not only the "Scylla of unlimited trash" but also the "Charybdis of too high a standard." In the amassing of materials and resources in either print or nonprint formats, public libraries, to this day, have never really resolved this dichotomy. Since the principal statistic used by public librarians to measure their services is the record of items borrowed, the raising of circulation figures became then and remains even now an important part of their agenda, both to increase their governmental appropriations as well as to certify their worth in community life. Although some public library leaders have recently predicted the demise of circulation figures as a measure of public library effectiveness, the fact remains that all statistical compilations of public libraries still refer to circulation as an index of their utility.

Notwithstanding their efforts to increase circulation, purposeful reading was always a goal held out by librarians to their publics, and the achievement of this has been in part facilitated by many activities, including the publication of book lists of estimable titles as well as their display, the sponsorship of programs dealing with literature and the arts, the invitation to local authors to share their own writing experience with their readers, and story hours for children. In the waning years of the nineteenth century and the early years of the twentieth, public librarians, especially those in the larger cities, devoted considerable activity to the Americanization of new immigrant populations. Although some resistance to the purchase of books in languages other than English was initially expressed, the librarians eventually conceded the value to their new clienteles of reading foreign-language materials. Collections of books in such languages as Chinese, German, Italian, Polish, and Yiddish found their way onto library shelves, and some branch libraries situated in neighborhoods with large immigrant populations were affectionately referred to by their users as the "Polish branch" or the "Russian branch," regardless of their official designations. Latter-day historians of the public library movement have sometimes castigated these efforts to Americanize the immigrant population as elitist in that their underlying purpose was one of social control. But to struggling newcomers to American shores, the issuance of informative library guidebooks dealing with such vital matters as education and employment and the provision of materials in their own language provided an unusual and welcome benefit, since most of the foreign-born readers had not enjoyed public library service in their homelands. Beginning in the 1920s, customized service through "reader's advisers" was promoted in many public libraries, enabling individual patrons to chart their personal reading (in English) around some specific topic of their interest. In addition, service to community institutions and groups and the sponsorship of public programs devoted to education and books became staples of the public library's efforts in adult education.

Many of these functions were discussed in *The American Public Library and the Diffusion of Knowledge*, a study published in 1924 after the Carnegie philanthropies for library buildings ceased in the period following World War I. Written by William S. Learned of the Carnegie Foundation for the Advancement of Teaching, the report proposed that the public library should serve as the intelligence service for its community "not only for 'polite' literature, but for every commercial and vocational field of information that it may prove practicable to enter."[5] Technical manuals for builders and plumbers, picture collections for artists, guidebooks for the traveler and motorist, books in important fields geared to the needs of students—all these were to be part of the library's holdings. This effort at matching the acquisition of library materials to the lifestyles and occupations of their clientele had another concomitant, as public libraries began to build special collections in subjects of particular interest to their local communities—for example, technology in Pittsburgh, western history in Denver, music in New York and Philadelphia, and to a greater or lesser degree, local history in innumerable public libraries throughout the nation. Fiction, traditionally looked on as frivolous, should be retained, wrote Learned, "because of its service in relaxation and entertainment."

The Library Faith

In spite of the increasing presence in their collections of bestsellers, mysteries, popular biographies, and other types of diversional reading, librarians held to their professed sense of purpose—in the words of political scientist Robert D. Leigh, "the conservation and organization of the world's resources of recorded thought and fact so as to make them available for present and future users." Over time librarians had transformed their concept of function into what Leigh called "the library faith. . . . a belief in the virtue of the printed word, especially of the book, the reading of which is held to be good in itself or from its reading flows that which is good."[6]

Leigh's analysis of this faith and its impact on the nation's public libraries was published in 1950 in the summary volume of the Public Library Inquiry, undertaken by the Social Science Research Council at the behest of the American Library Association and supported with funds from the Carnegie Corporation of New York. Begun in 1947, in the period immediately following the close of World War II, the Inquiry was an endeavor of several years, resulting in the publication of seven separate monographs issued by Columbia University Press and several additional reports and memoranda, all of which were published between 1949 and 1952. During these postwar years, profound changes were occurring in the United States, among them a greatly reshaped demographic pattern that witnessed the escalation of suburban life, a communications revolution that added television to the roster of mass media, and the emergence of a new electronic technology heralded in part by Vannevar Bush's article on memex, published in the July 1945 issue of the *Atlantic Monthly*, where it was likened in importance to Emerson's famous address on "The American Scholar." Bush coined the word *memex* to denote a scholar's workstation that would store books, records, and other forms of communication and that would be so mechanized that retrieval of these data could be done with exceeding speed and flexibility. In one sense, the personal computer connected to a telephone line and modem is a modern-day memex.

Writing in 1950 in her second edition of *Living with Books*, a buying guide for the development of library collections and a much-used text in American library schools, Helen Haines commented on what she termed as the "rounding century of the American public library movement." She characterized the ideal directing the public library during the past hundred years as "the use of books for spiritual and intellectual as well as for material and vocational profit, books for mental resource, reading for individual and personal joy—all elements in the diffusion, perhaps not of specific knowledge, but of culture in Matthew Arnold's sense."[7] Her opinion was reiterated a few years later by Ernestine Rose of the New York Public Library, who, in defining the public library's responsibilities, spoke "against the hypnotic influence of circulation figures and the tides of facile and superficial reading. . . . Libraries have an important job to do in the intellectual progress and continuing enlightenment which alone can lead to any widespread or meaningful use of our intellectual heritage."[8]

In sharp contrast to these rather optimistic depictions of the public library's role in the diffusion of culture were some of the sentiments expressed in the Public Library Inquiry, which Leigh had directed. Particularly shocking to the managerial cadre of the public libraries was the finding of Bernard Berelson, dean of the Graduate Library School at the University of Chicago, in his Inquiry monograph, *The Library's Public*, that the concept of "service to everyone" was a professional myth, obscuring the reality that the actual users of the public library constituted a primarily middle-class and better-educated clientele. If library users, he noted, were defined as those using a library at least once a year, then the percentage of adults (those over twenty-one) would be approximately 18 percent of the total population, while the percentage of children and young people would be somewhat under 50 percent. In response to some of his librarian critics who were uncomfortable with what they perceived as his depiction of an undemocratic service to an elitist community, Berelson struck squarely at the disparity between "the professed and the practiced objectives" for the public library: "Thus, just as many lawyers will tell you that their objective is to see justice done, whereas they are actually out to win cases, so many librarians will tell you that education is their objective, when they are busy trying to increase circulation."[9]

As the first generation of baby-boomers graduated from secondary schools and entered college during the early years of the 1960s, public library circulation rose dramatically throughout the country, exceeding in many cases the previous high record of the Great Depression years. The rise of this new generation placed a considerable burden on public library resources. In 1950 the five- to nineteen-year-old age group amounted to 35 million, in 1960 it amounted to nearly 50 million, and it was then estimated that by 1970 this population group would reach about 60 million. Student use of public libraries increased exponentially, owing not only to the sheer increase in the numbers of young people, but also to newer practices in the nation's schools, which sent many high school students to the public libraries for so-called research problems, requiring sophisticated materials often beyond the scope of secondary school library collections. College-age students also added to the increased clientele. As they returned to their homes for holidays and vacations, these students made frequent use of their local public libraries for the writing of term papers and theses. So great was the drain on library collections and staff, in particular those in the fields of literature and history, that in July 1963 the American Library Association sponsored a special conference devoted to the student use of libraries.[10]

It must be remembered that prior to the 1965 enactment of the Elementary and Secondary Education Act and the Higher Education Act, both of which made specific allocations to the libraries of schools and academic institutions, the public library was often the most convenient source within a given community for homework assistance and a range of reference materials, including bound issues of older periodicals. Reflecting on the momentum of the student-use issue, Lowell Martin, a long-time public library consultant, reminisced that during the early 1950s the library profession was concerned with "Why Johnny doesn't read?" Now, in the 1960s, he said, "it may be that with student reading today, we are witnessing the first mass utilization of books in our culture, and the appearance, for the first time, of a mass library audience."[11]

The Public Library Faces Demographic Change

The euphoria raised by the high circulation figures generated in part by student use was not to last very long. In 1963, the same year as the ALA conference, the National Book Committee, a consortium of librarians and publishers founded in 1954, in conjunction with the Joint Center for Urban Studies of the Massachusetts Institute of Technology and Harvard University, sponsored a three-day symposium in Dedham, Massachusetts, devoted to library functions in the changing metropolis. Some forty prominent urban specialists, social scientists, economists, and sociologists, plus representatives of the public libraries in ten major cities in the United States and one in Canada, attended. The problem for public libraries of increased student use was mentioned only in passing, mostly by the public library directors who were in attendance. What was uppermost in the minds of the social scientists was the predominant demographic change in the inner city as large numbers of middle-class residents moved to the suburbs. Sociologist Herbert J. Gans commented that the public library was *supplier oriented* rather than *user oriented*, and in low-income areas he considered "this middle-class library" unsatisfactory: "Here a library is needed that invites rather than rejects the poorly educated person, with book stock, staff, and catalogue system that are designed to help him read."[12] As the urban specialists perceived the situation, the public library, purporting to be an educational agency, was now finding itself serving a nonprint-oriented community. Its former readers were moving outside the central city, and in their place were nonlibrary users, some faced with a language barrier in that English was not their native tongue while others were confronted with so many cultural and economic disadvantages that the value of reading had little relevance to their lives.

In contrast to many of the speakers present, Dan Lacy, managing director of the American Book Publishers Council, eloquently argued that the urban public library in tandem with the urban schools could become the spokespersons for this new nonliterate class, interpreting their needs to the publishing industry and serving as instruments in the dissemination of materials that would aid in the transformation of the class itself. Noting that such a direction moved counter to the pressures placed on the public library to serve the highly literate segments of society, Lacy concluded his moving peroration in Dedham with this warning: "Yet a failure to discharge this responsibility could, by omission, contribute one more element to an already potentially explosive social situation."[13]

Although the Dedham attendees were divided about the future role of the urban public library—some argued for its continued service to the community's educational elite, and others suggested that it should be redirected toward the needs of the urban poor—the conference did illuminate the demographic and social movements of American urban life and in one sense served as a harbinger of future events. Inevitably, the high point of public library circulation achieved in large part by the intense use of students was dissipated as the later years of the 1960s revealed a plummeting of transactions, especially in the larger American communities. From 1965 to 1968, the aggregate public library circulation of both print and nonprint materials declined by 12 percent. In the smaller communities, those having between 25,000 and 34,999 people, there was actually an increase of 6 percent, but in the population group between 35,000 and 49,999, the decline was 1 percent, and in the group between 50,000 and 99,999 the decline was 8 percent. Hardest hit of all were the libraries in the largest communities, those with populations of over 100,000, where the decline was 16 percent (see table 1).

These declining circulation figures especially in the larger communities reflected the demographic changes articulated at the Dedham conference. In brief, many members of the historic client group of the public library—the reading-oriented, educated middle-class—had moved away to be replaced by a population less oriented to library use by experience, inclination, or opportunity. To alleviate this phenomenon, some inner-city libraries, in part inspired by President Johnson's War on Poverty, designed specific projects and initiated new services for the poor. Published in the fall of 1968, three issues of the *Christian Science Monitor* contained articles devoted to a nationwide account of "libraries that care." Acknowledging

Table 1
Library Transactions by Size of Community, 1965 to 1968

	1965	1968	Percent change
Transactions	634,624,000	560,214,022	–12%
Community			
100,000+	418,232,000	351,579,278	–16%
50,000 to 99,999	116,906,000	106,965,002	– 8%
35,000 to 49,999	54,184,000	53,629,222	– 1%
25,000 to 34,999	45,302,000	48,040,520	+ 6%

Source: U.S. Office of Education, National Center for Educational Statistics, *Statistics of Public Libraries Serving Communities with at Least 25,000 Inhabitants: 1965* (Washington, DC: U.S. Government Printing Office, 1968); U.S. Office of Education, National Center for Educational Statistics, *Statistics of Public Libraries Serving Areas with at Least 25,000 Inhabitants: 1968* (Washington, DC: U.S. Government Printing Office, 1970).

that the social activism of the inner-city public libraries was owed to their "we-care" librarians, the *Monitor* described their concern: "They have ventured into the inner-city in search of people to help—people who regard libraries as stuffy or forbidding places. 'We-care' librarians have taken a hard look at the library's role in the community, redirected its services, broadened its programs, and in many cases radically changed its methods."[14]

One of the outgrowths of this redirection effort was a resurgence of interest in community analysis, which acted as a stimulus in the initiation of information and referral (I and R) centers during the 1970s in the public libraries of such communities as Atlanta, Cleveland, Houston, Memphis, and Queens Borough in New York City. Usually credited as the innovator of this service was the Detroit Public Library, which created TIP (The Information Place) in 1971. Concentrating heavily on the provision of information about community agencies and services for inner-city residents, TIP was designed to address citizen needs in a city facing severe problems of urban blight. Each branch library created its own file identifying the organizations of particular relevance to their own communities and neighborhoods and providing information about the type of services offered, along with relevant data such as addresses, telephone numbers, service hours, and names of personnel. At the outset such files were manually maintained on index cards, but with the development of online computerized catalogs some libraries created a separate digitized database of community information that library patrons could read on the same terminals used for the display of the cataloging data.

Development of Public Library Systems

At the same time that many inner-city libraries were redirecting their programs in the neighborhoods, another development fostering the creation of larger units of service was occurring that affected library development in many previously underserved and unserved areas of the country. This trend, primarily affecting areas beyond the central city, brought into being aggregates of public libraries known in library parlance as *library systems*. To those outside the library profession, the phrase *library system* is often not clearly understood. The older municipal libraries with their downtown central buildings and satellite branches were and still are governed by a single board of trustees or commissioners and administered by one librarian. Examples of this type include Baltimore's Enoch Pratt Free Library, the Chicago Public Library, the Denver Public Library, the Seattle Public Library, and many others. These libraries are, of course, systems, but they are further designated as *consolidated* library systems in that the ultimate hierarchial authority to which the public library staff report consists of one unique administrative and policymaking entity. But library systems can also refer to aggregates of independent public libraries that band together in some form of federation or cooperative to provide services more economically and efficiently but do not lose their individual autonomy. Such systems, referred to as *cooperative* or *federated* library systems, are often governed by boards of trustees chosen from the boards of the member libraries. The decade of the 1960s closed with a landmark study devoted to larger units of service, *Public Library Systems in the United States*, prepared by Nelson Associates and published by the American Library Association in 1969.

The search for the optimally sized library unit had preoccupied professional thinking since the Great Depression. In his classic analysis of American library governance published in 1935, Carleton Joeckel of the University of Chicago had referred to the difficulties experienced by public libraries in effectively serving areas too small in population to sustain the necessary tax support to underwrite adequate services, and he advocated a restructuring of the local library movement to maximize revenue from a larger population group. In the document prepared for the ALA Committee on Postwar Planning, *A National Plan for Public Library Service*, which he coauthored with public library administrator Amy Winslow, Joeckel called for the development of federated library systems, through which individual libraries could participate in joint enterprises, such as reciprocity in circulation privileges among all the participating libraries, centralized purchasing and ordering of materials, and the provision of reference and referral services by the larger libraries in the federation. The rationale behind this proposal was a further extension of the public library's mission to reach all readers, regardless of their geographic location. "As the mechanism of cooperation becomes in reality a closely integrated system," the *National Plan* asserted, "the books and materials of many libraries in states and regions will become more nearly a fluid collection, standing ready to supply the needs of all serious readers, regardless of the particular political units in which they may happen to live."[15]

In 1956, the same year in which federal aid for public libraries was first enacted, the American Library Association published a compendium of standards for public libraries designed to be used by local boards and governmental officials. Clearly, the import of this document was its recognition of the value of library systems. It stated unequivocally this dictum: "Libraries working together, sharing their services and materials, can meet the full needs of their users. *This co-operative approach on the part of libraries is the most important single recommendation of this document.*"[16] The 1966 revision of the public library standards reiterated this premise and was entitled more precisely *Minimum Standards for Public Library Systems, 1966.*

By the time the Nelson study was published in 1969, the movement toward the development of library systems was already quite marked. The advent of federal aid had brought with it the need for statewide planning, and state plans energized to meet federal requirements were often concerned with the need for larger library units. These library systems took various forms, including an increasing use of the county rather than the municipality as the basic unit of service, the consolidation of city and county systems through merger, contractual agreements between larger libraries and smaller ones, and federation, a type of system recommended by Joeckel, which fostered cooperative activities among libraries while permitting each library to retain its individual identity, board structure, and local governance. Significant exemplars of this last type included the twenty-two public library systems of New York State, comprising over 700 local libraries situated in the state's sixty-two counties, and the eighteen cooperative systems established in 1965 by legislative mandate in Illinois that eventually encompassed that state's over 550 public libraries. Even though these cooperative library systems differ from state to state, their administrative pattern is somewhat similar: each system supports a staff responsible for coordinating services for the benefit of all the libraries in the system, but the policy governing the operation of each library within the system is still set by that library's board and carried out by its librarian. To signify the maintenance of their independence, libraries that belong to these cooperatives are usually designated as *member libraries* rather than as *branches*, the term more commonly used for the satellite agencies of consolidated public libraries. It is important to realize that these systemic changes in the organization of libraries were occurring at a time when electronic data processing was being developed, facilitating the computerized systematization of many bibliographic functions, including cataloging, the ordering of materials, and circulation. A study published in 1971, *Public Libraries in Cooperative Systems,* addressed the trend toward library automation in these new administrative entities: "The direction for the immediate future lies in a centralized bibliographic bank of resources of member libraries providing the means of remote control, query, and alteration from each member library."[17]

In addition to the formation of larger service units through the federation of many smaller municipal and town libraries, some of the rapidly growing suburban libraries were increasing their levels of support through more extensive county appropriations. These county libraries, which jurisdictionally resembled the consolidated libraries of the older municipalities in that they were administered by one board and one director, began to emerge as leading contenders among the nation's public libraries for top achievements in services rendered and items circulated. Although the municipal library, which historically had been the prevailing model of library governance, still remained dominant in terms of numbers, the county library became a viable force in public librarianship, evidenced today in the libraries of Broward County in Florida, Hennepin County in Minnesota, and Montgomery County in Maryland.

Restatement of the Public Library Mission

Beginning in 1970, a committee of ALA's Public Library Association (PLA) embarked on what appeared at the time to be a revision of the ALA-issued standards of 1966. Consuming the better part of an entire decade, this effort resulted in the development of a new approach toward the promulgation of nationwide standards, one that was input rather than output oriented and one that emphasized community characteristics, such as the demographics of the user population, rather than institutional ones, such as the number of volumes in the collection. Implementing this new course proved to be a rather formidable task, involving the design of a research project to test alternative approaches to the issue. Anticipating that the pursuit of this research would be a lengthy process, the PLA decided to issue a document that would serve both "as interim guidelines and as a bridge to the new approach to library standards." Published in 1979, *The Public Library Mission Statement and Its Imperatives for Service* began somewhat ominously with a simple statement: "The nation's public libraries are in serious trouble." Continuing in this vein, the compilers of the document noted that "for the most part, the public library of today is geared to the social needs of the nineteenth century which created it."[18]

Eschewing the nineteenth-century view of the public library as an agency of acculturation, Americanization, and standardization of lifestyle and values, the document's compilers called for a public library that recognizes cultural and ethnic differences and that encourages self-pride and appreciation of different cultural heritages. The document identified four distinctive roles for the public library: (1) a nontraditional educational agency mediating between the individual and the record, (2) a cultural agency fostering creativity, enjoyment of literature and the arts, and appreciation for America's pluralistic culture, (3) an information agency, and (4) a rehabilitation agency aiding handicapped persons to reach their full potential. In brief, the public library should undertake a program of activities to "meet the unique cultural, informational, educational, and rehabilitative needs of the community."

The document made relatively few references to electronic technology, although its drafters did acknowledge that unprecedented increases in the amount of information—fomented in part by the capacity of technology to preserve information in all of its formats, print, nonprint, and electronic—had created a new barrier to the human record based not on a scarcity of resources but on an abundance of them. The lack of reference to communications technology in the public library mission statement seems even more striking when it is compared with another policy document adopted by the ALA Council a few years earlier in 1975. At its annual conference that year, the Council pledged ALA's commitment to implementing the policy goals of "a national program for library and information services," proposed by the U.S. National Commission on Libraries and Information Science (NCLIS), an advisory group to both the president and Congress established in 1970. In its earliest draft, prepared in 1973, the NCLIS proposal had heavily emphasized the potential of the computer and communications revolution, calling for the creation of a national network in whose operation "the computer would become ultimately central" and in which "rapid and inexpensive telecommunications among libraries could turn out to be the greatest boon ever to the national distribution of knowledge for education and progress."[19] Even though the technological cast of the NCLIS document was somewhat tempered in its final version, the programmatic thrust of the national program that it described relied quite heavily on the benefits that would be realized for library users through "the potential of the information revolution now underway."[20]

The decade of the 1970s did not augur well for public libraries. With the election of President Nixon came the proposal that revenue sharing should displace the Great Society programs legislated during President's Johnson administration, and a battle ensued to preserve the massive educational funding of the Johnson years. On assuming office in 1969, Nixon dramatically revised Johnson's proposed education budget, cutting the federally supported library programs by 66 percent. Throughout Nixon's tenure, recommendations coming from his administration threatened retrenchment, rescission, and impoundment of federal library funds. The apogee of the administration's discontent with federal aid to libraries was reached when the U.S. Department of Health, Education, and Welfare announced that in fiscal year 1974 "Federal support will be discontinued" for all library programs. Nor was the situation much better at the local level, as the mid-1970s were confronted with the increasing burden of nationwide economic problems—escalating oil prices, rising food costs, high mortgage rates, continuing unemployment especially among ethnic minorities and youth, and the devaluation of the dollar. As inflation contributed to the shrinkage of local tax bases, public library budgets, particularly those in the larger cities, were severely cut, leading to the cancellation of subscriptions to popular periodicals, shortened hours of opening, reductions in staff, and the curtailment of many programs and services. In testimony before a Senate appropriations committee in 1978, Eileen D. Cooke, the ALA Washington lobbyist, noted that the overall inflation rate had risen by 36 percent since 1973; the cost of books since 1973, however, had risen 53 percent to an average of $18.03, while the cost of journal subscriptions had escalated by 52 percent to an average of $24.59. Inflation, she commented, continued to absorb dollars in wages and salaries and in the cost of energy needed to operate library buildings, most of which were not designed for energy efficiency. "These costs," she plaintively concluded, "are uncontrollable."[21]

Buffeted on many sides during these years by a plethora of problems, most of them stemming from the severe budgetary crisis of the 1970s, the public library, notwithstanding its efforts in the development of community information files, was often perceived by appropriating bodies as an agency that could not be truly responsive to the needs of the urban poor, while at the same time it was castigated as dilatory in adopting the newer technologies that would make it more viable in the provision of information services, *information* rapidly becoming the catchword of a service-based economy. Although the now ubiquitous paperback sold in a variety of locations from supermarkets to airports had cut into its role as a disseminator of popular literature, the public library was still regarded as heavily dependent on the medium of print, at a time when television had eroded the primacy of print as the most rapid purveyor of news and world events. Nonetheless, champions of the public library arose in many areas of the country, and one of them, New York attorney and library trustee Whitney North Seymour, Jr., organized in 1976 the National Citizens Emergency Committee to Save Our Public Libraries. Headquartered in New York City, the committee focused its attention on the need for improving library services through a national advocacy program. Its basic mission was to represent the concerns of the general public of library users at a time when libraries in Cleveland, Detroit, New York, Philadelphia, San Francisco, and many other communities, both large and small, were feeling the impact of new budget cuts.

The public library received another and perhaps unexpected impetus during the 1970s from a number of educational philosophers, calling for a deschooled society to lessen the bureaucratized nature of the public school system and restore the educational values and services needed by the nation. Writing at a time when conceptualizations of the open university, the university without walls, the external degree, and other alternatives to formal schooling abounded, John Holt, author of *Freedom and Beyond*, commented:

In any community, compare the local public library, which serves everybody, with the local public high schools, which serve only a four-year age span. In most places the schools are probably twenty to fifty times as large as the library and spend twenty to fifty times as much money. It is this kind of imbalance that we ought to change. Whatever money we put into institutions should go to those that are truly open, which anyone can use, without preconditions, and for his own purpose. Such institutions are what [Ivan] Illich, [Everett] Reimer, and others call networks, and the public library is only one very special and perhaps rather conventional example of these. Still it is worth looking at.[22]

Although the movement toward a deschooled society waned, it briefly lent increased attention to the public library—the "college around the corner," in the parlance of the educational reformers—and its role in non-traditional education.

Change in the publishing industry, already manifest in the late 1950s, was yet another factor that affected the dimensions of the public library during this period. With increased frequency, mergers were being fashioned between the older, family-held publishing houses of an earlier era, whose senior editorial and administrative personnel were not only known by librarians but were also influenced by them, particularly in the selection of children's books. Initially, these mergers took place among the publishing houses themselves, but later they occurred with companies outside the industry, pushing mainstream publishing activity further and further into the issuance of high-volume blockbusters while leaving to the smaller trade houses, university presses, and other scholarly venues the issuance of more specialized books. Among others, the houses of Scribner, Harper & Row, Doubleday, and Little, Brown were merged into more powerful corporate entities. A long-time holdout from this trend, the prestigious Farrar, Straus & Giroux, publisher of twenty Nobel laureates, finally succumbed and is owned today by a German publisher, Verlagsgruppe Georg von Holtzbrinck, which also owns Henry Holt and St. Martin's Press.

In the late 1970s, a representative of the Authors Guild sounded an alarm:

We have seen mergers in every imaginable permutation—hardcover houses merging with each other; hardcover houses merging with paperback houses; the combination thus formed being taken over, in turn, by huge entertainment complexes, involving radio-television networks and motion picture companies. And in some cases, perhaps most distressing of all, we have seen the business of choosing and purveying books, traditionally the province of more or less dedicated book men with one eye on profit and the other on literary and social values, falling under the control of businessmen with no prior interest in books—men, it has sometimes seemed to us, cursed like the Cyclops with having only a single eye, and that eye not trained on literary or social value but steadfastly on the bottom line of a company's financial statement.[23]

"Marketing" the Public Library

With an array of problems, including the steady erosion of their buying power and the changing dimensions of their principal suppliers, the publishers, public libraries cast about for new initiatives. One public library system, which had surmounted many of the difficulties vexing its peer institutions, began an aggressive campaign to "market" the public library. Founded in 1948, the Baltimore County Public Library serves residents living in a sprawling land mass surrounding the central city of Baltimore. From its beginnings, the county system, politically separate from that of the city, made no attempt to form a central library, maintaining only an administrative headquarters in the county seat. To provide its residents with access to such resources as government documents, patents, and the retrospective holdings of an older library, Baltimore County, in a statewide alliance of public library systems, contracted with the Enoch Pratt Free Library in Baltimore City. By 1968, reciprocal borrowing for all of the public library systems was instituted, permitting a resident in any one of Maryland's twenty-three counties and Baltimore City to take out and return materials in any public library throughout the state.

By the late 1970s, Baltimore County's public library, having undertaken a major reconsideration of where it was and where it was going, issued a document with the somewhat controversial title, *To Satisfy Demand*, which proclaimed: "Probably unique in this philosophy of a major public library system is its policy with regard to library collections. BCPL [Baltimore County Public Library] is committed to collecting, not a broad array of materials that librarians feel users *should* read or use, but those materials which most users *do* read or use; to provide these materials as soon after publication as possible; and to support the ensuing demand with sufficient copies to satisfy user requests promptly."[24] Its "demand" philosophy, seemingly at odds with the historic objectives of the public library to serve as an educative and cultural force in the community, nonetheless pushed the county system into the top echelon of library systems nationwide. In comparison with the forty-four large urban and suburban library systems reporting their 1974 data in the *Bowker Annual of Library and Book Trade Information*, Baltimore County's library ranked fourth in circulation of materials with a per capita figure of 10.2. In 1983, Baltimore County, with a per capita circulation of 13.85 for its some 660,000 residents, ranked first in the nation; in terms of total systemwide circulation, its annual circulation of 9,077,275 was exceeded only by the library systems of the City of Los Angeles and Los Angeles County, both of them communities serving populations in the millions.

These heightened records of use were all the more impressive since the demographic characteristics of Baltimore County's population, as reported in the 1970 census and used throughout the *To Satisfy Demand* document, were not such as to predicate heavy library use. With only 53 percent of the adult population (those twenty-five years and older) having graduated from high school, the educational levels of the county's residents were lower than those of all Maryland jurisdictions of more than 250,000 population, with the exception of Baltimore City, and fell near the average for the entire state. But Baltimore County's marketing strategy was not confined solely to the duplication of much-in-demand titles; the library consciously imitated the techniques of well-stocked and welcoming book-stores, using face-out shelving (that is, placing books on the shelves so the covers of the books, not their spines, face the reader), kiosks for paperback books, lighting above the shelves, and a more populist sign system—neon in some buildings—that used phrases such as *check out* for the *circulation* desk and *information* for the services rendered by librarians from what were usually called *reference* desks.

The "demand" philosophy of Baltimore County, sometimes referred to as "give 'em what they want,"[25] was not entirely well received by the library and publishing communities. In 1979, *Publishers Weekly*, the principal organ of the publishing industry, issued an article ominously entitled "The Selling of the Library,"[26] and the pros and cons of library marketing were argued and are still being argued in both the industry and library press. Although earlier library leaders, in particular John Cotton Dana, the turn-of-century librarian of the Newark Public Library, had held that the public library should maintain the ambience of an attractive bookstore, the Balti-more County experiment represented a rather dramatic paradigm shift, at least in terms of a publicly expressed viewpoint, in public library philoso-phy. It called into question some of the conventional wisdom held by the profession and defined its role for its service area as the principal "point of access for *all* needed information *of any kind*. With this recent develop-ment of total information services, BCPL is moving from a primarily mate-rials-oriented system to one where material resources in demand are matched by total information services."[27] In this latter regard, the county initiated AID (Accurate Information Desk), which was modeled on the Detroit Public Library's TIP program. Under the aegis of AID, staff mem-bers were expected to use resources beyond the library's collection and were encouraged to call or contact experts or specialists for answers to patron queries, thus ending reliance solely on published sources for library information service.

Many public librarians decried what they perceived as a pandering to the lowest common denominator of popular taste, among them Murray L. Bob, librarian of the Jamestown (New York) Public Library: "I have made what I said was a revolutionary statement: libraries have nothing to sell. Because libraries do not charge for their services, by definition they have nothing to sell. . . . Public libraries are publicly supported to serve as agencies of informal, self-motivated, self-regulated self-education; as adjuncts to agencies of formal education; as organized repositories of written and other forms of the culture's communication—all of this to be freely available to all, offering material useful or potentially useful to all, over the longest possible time."[28] Other librarians, however, were quick to assimilate some of Baltimore County's techniques, among them the computerized coding of circulation records so that each number in the Dewey Decimal Classification could be precisely identified with the number of times books classified by that number were in circulation. For example, if the circulation record for Dewey class number 643.7, Home Repair, or for 362.29, Drug Abuse, showed that all copies of the library's holdings in these two categories were consistently out on loan, the library's response would be to purchase additional titles or to duplicate more heavily those titles already in the collection. Conversely, if circulation records showed a low turnover of use for materials in selected Dewey classes, discard of materials in those classes would follow. It should be noted that turnover rates were established for minimum use, and these differed for Dewey classes so that no one class would be completely neglected. The turnover rate for books in the fields of religion, philosophy, or literary criticism was not expected to be as high as those for home repair, cooking, or crafts. This simple practice of inventory control, facilitated by the computerization of circulation data, was adopted by many public libraries.

In his examination of *The McDonaldization of Society*, sociologist George Ritzer finds that the efficiency-effectiveness syndrome of the McDonald's fast-food chain has elevated McDonald's into a powerful national and international symbol, so much so that many businesses are being given nicknames beginning with *Mc* to indicate their emulation of the McDonald's model. Examples include:

"*Mc*Dentists" and "*Mc*Doctors" (for drive-in clinics designed to deal quickly and efficiently with minor dental and medical problems), "*Mc*Child" Care Centers (for child-care centers like Kinder-Care), "*Mc*Stables" (for the nationwide racehorse training operation of Wayne Lucas), and "*Mc*Paper" (for the newspaper *USA TODAY* and its short news articles often called "News *Mc*Nuggets"). When *USA TODAY* began an aborted television program modeled after the newspaper, some began to call it "News *Mc*Rather."[29]

A 1990 essay in the *New Republic* suggested another coinage to be added to Ritzer's list—*Mc*Libraries. Expressing his displeasure at the conversion of libraries into merchandise marts, its author, himself a librarian, urged a return to the traditional balance between the public library's function as a leisure activity and its role as an educational resource. In particular, Baltimore County's philosophy was cited as a move toward the McDonaldization of the public library, and its director, Charles W. Robinson, was quoted as stating that public libraries should abandon their "elitist" pretensions and strive instead to become the "McDonald's of information and materials distribution." The essay further commented that "Robinson's own library, apparently, is such a McDonald's of the mind" and advanced this admonition: "Libraries receive tax money so that we may have a more informed citizenry, so that the general cultural level may be raised. If they are failing to fulfill these functions, government officials would be within their rights to apportion them fewer funds, not more."[30]

From the inception of the institution, the demand versus quality debate has occupied the public library profession and in all probability will never be completely resolved. What set Baltimore County apart from many of its peers was not so much its lack of missionary zeal in attempting to raise the cultural level of its suburban community, but rather its frank admission that the public footing the tax bill for its services should have some say in those that were provided. It is also interesting to note that the library espoused its position at a time when literary standards and cultural canons were coming under attack in American intellectual circles. Literary criticism was furthering its course in a variety of abstruse academic disciplines including, among others, hermeneutics, structuralism, deconstruction, and leftist cultural criticism, making "the field of literary studies in America during the Space Age seem a carnivalesque site," in which these somewhat esoteric schools of thought appeared to be "a series of interlocking sideshows."[31]

Then, too, as the century advanced and literary criticism became increasingly professionalized in university departments of English or comparative literature, the public intellectuals who had dominated the field at midcentury—critics such as Lionel Trilling or Edmund Wilson who wrote for that vanishing species, the "common reader"—held less sway in the literary environment. And when political correctness threatened the canon of established texts, older notions of good books or best books may have seemed increasingly anachronistic. Although few more disputatious defenders of the Western canon have emerged than Yale University critic Harold Bloom, it is he who nonetheless perceptively observes that "canons always do indirectly serve the social and political, and indeed the spiritual, concerns and aims of the wealthier classes of each generation of Western society. It seems clear that capital is necessary for the cultivation of aesthetic values."[32] As a consequence, Bloom admits, the relevance to life in the inner city of the cultural masterpieces that he celebrates is "inevitably rather remote." But it is precisely in the inner city that some of the nation's largest public libraries are located, and with their increasing population of low-income users or those for whom English is a second language, their custodians would appear remiss if they did not augment library collections in ways that would appeal to people lacking either the educational or monetary capital that encourages canonical appreciation.

In the contemporary culture wars, the public library has been somewhat buffeted, losing, on the one hand, part of its identity as a knowledge institution but, on the other, attracting new users by its more eclectic and pluralistic offerings. The provision of "open, non-judgmental access to collections and services without regard to race, citizenship, age, educational level, economic status, religion, or any other qualification or condition,"[33] as stated in the mission statement of Washington's King County Library System, may not ensure aesthetic distinction or canonical status, but it is, as a statement, reminiscent of the nineteenth-century dictum of Enoch Pratt, who stipulated that his Baltimore-based library "shall be open for all, rich and poor without distinction of race or color." The Pulitzer-Prize winning poet Karl Shapiro, who as a youth was employed in the Enoch Pratt Free Library, once wrote in its praise:

The availability of books of all levels, not simply the best or the greatest books, I see as a stimulus to the creative mind. Multiplicity is the criterion and it is the best one for this purpose. It is quite right for this library to treat the bulk of books as perishables; it is quite right to regard the bulk of printed matter as potting soil. Whatever else it does it makes things grow.[34]

The Public Library Planning Process

Although Baltimore County had its critics, the document that enunciated its philosophy, *To Satisfy Demand*, was partially reincarnated when in 1977 its principal author, Vernon E. Palmour, became the chief investigator of a research project to prepare a manual for community libraries engaged in long-range planning. At the behest of the Public Library Association, funds were granted by the U.S. Office of Education to support the project that brought into being *A Planning Process for Public Libraries*, cowritten by Palmour and two associates. This step-by-step description of the recommended process of planning from an initial assessment of community library needs to the setting of goals and objectives and their ultimate evaluation and measurement was published by the American Library Association in 1980. Included in the manual were examples of library objectives, a variety of sample surveys designed to elicit responses from both library users and nonusers, and techniques for the analysis of the survey data. With the issuance of *A Planning Process*, the decade-long endeavor of the Public Library Association to revise the 1966 public library standards came to its close. The older standards had attempted to prescribe acceptable measures for the size and scope of library collections, the numbers of staff, the hours of opening, and the characteristics of the physical plant. By contrast, the new approach represented a radical departure, emphasizing instead the individual community and its imperative to establish library performance measures appropriate to local conditions and needs. As the document's foreword made clear, "what public librarians need now are not rules for sameness [that is, another revision of nationwide public library standards] but tools which will help them analyze a situation, set objectives, make decisions and evaluate achievements."[35]

Although acknowledging that the public library's historic mission had included the provision of culture, education, information, and recreation to local communities, the manual's compilers urged that this broadly conceived approach be rendered in more specific terms as the provision of information services, materials, and programming that would be tailored to defined subgroups within the population, such as children, youth, adults and senior citizens, special groups, and even nonusers. One important step in the planning process was the determination of the library's role in the community: "The definition of role is critical to the planning process, since it forms the basis for everything that comes later. It is not a broad mission statement so much as an action statement that describes in global terms what the library is going to do during the planning period to serve the needs of its community. The goals and objectives which detail exactly what the library plans to do stem from it."[36]

The importance of role setting was again recognized and with a far greater degree of emphasis in the second major planning document issued by the ALA in 1987. *Planning and Role Setting for Public Libraries: A Manual of Options and Procedures* was a far simpler guide to library planning than its 1980 predecessor. Intended primarily for use by the small and medium-size public library, the document identified eight distinctive roles for library service, defining a role as a "shorthand way" of describing those factors important to library planners: What are we trying to do, whom are we serving, and what resources do we need to achieve our ends? The eight roles included those of a community activities center, community information center, formal education support center, independent learning center, popular materials library, preschoolers' door to learning, reference library, and research center. Although *Planning and Role Setting* credits Lowell Martin as the progenitor of the concept of library "roles," and indeed Martin did identify them in some of his library surveys, it should be noted that Leigh's 1950 summary report for the Public Library Inquiry defined "six fields of knowledge and interest to which the public library should devote its resources"—public affairs and citizenship, vocations, aesthetic appreciation, recreation, information, and research. With the exception of the specific mention of preschool children as a potential client group, almost all of the recommended roles in the ALA planning manual could be subsumed under Leigh's iteration. Throughout the 1970s and 1980s the public library profession became more and more committed to the definition of the library as a distinctive service agency largely responsive to its own immediate clientele. As one respondent wrote in reply to a poll of public librarians, published in 1972: "no set of goals could be universally applicable except in the broadest terms. *Each library must set its own goals based on its own community needs.*"[37]

Within a few years of the adoption of the second planning manual, an assessment of the opinions of the general public about the relative importance of the various roles played by the public library seemed in order. With funds from the U.S. Department of Education, the Gallup Organization and the University of Minnesota, under the direction of George D'Elia, undertook this assessment in 1992. A national probability sample (N = 1,001) was drawn from adults age eighteen years or older who could be reached by telephone. Since the number of African-Americans and Hispanics drawn from such a sample would be too few for cross-comparisons, supplemental samples of these two groups were also obtained. The role of educational support center was ranked as "very important" by 88 percent of the respondents, the learning center role was so ranked by 85 percent, and the educational opportunity for preschoolers by 83 percent. When comparisons were made among respondents with different household incomes and among those achieving different grade levels, however, the findings took on a different aspect. Respondents with household incomes below $15,000 and those with an eighth-grade education rated the educational roles of the library as "very important" more often than did those with incomes of $60,000 or more or those who had completed college. The data further revealed that African-Americans and Hispanics evaluated the importance of each of the roles of the public library more highly than did white respondents.[38]

At the same time as many public librarians embraced the concept of distinctive roles, some professional leaders expressed concerns about their value, believing that the delineation of too many roles further isolated the public library from the mainstream of tax support for education. The problem is not unlike the dilemma facing the public schools, which are expected to teach a myriad of subjects including driver education and are then accused of departing too far from their basic purposes. The very localism of the roles assigned to libraries, their critics believed, inhibits a consideration of the public library as an important instrument of change having broader implications and influence than those experienced by one particular community:

As community-based institutions, public libraries focus on local attitudes and opinions. Factors such as the current Public Library Association (PLA) planning process and increased competition for local funds further drive libraries to tailor their activities and services toward the needs of their community. This has resulted in an increasing trend in measuring attitudes and opinions at the community level. . . . However, by focusing only on local community concerns, librarians run the danger of becoming myopic—of failing to put their individual libraries into context.[39]

Adding to the problem of myopia, the multiplicity of public library roles also flies in the face of conventional organizational wisdom. As espoused by management guru Peter F. Drucker, the definition of mission is central to organizational survival: "An organization is defined by its task. The symphony orchestra does not attempt to cure the sick; it plays music. The hospital takes care of the sick but does not attempt to play Beethoven. Indeed, an organization is effective only if it concentrates on one task. . . . Society and community must be multidimensional; they are environments. An organization is a tool. And as with any other tool, the more specialized it is, the greater its capacity to perform its given task."[40]

The delineation of public library roles as conveyed in the 1987 edition of *Planning and Role Setting* has been revised by a committee of the Public Library Association. The new manual, *Planning for Results: A Public Library Transformation Process*, published in 1998, emphasizes the public library's ability and capacity to concentrate its resources and services in those areas where excellence can be achieved. The iteration of distinctive roles is being displaced "in favor of fourteen service responses that are community needs-based, situation-sensitive, and more specific, but at the same time more flexible, giving the library a new way in which to view its community."[41] The service responses identify areas in which the local library should concentrate its resources; the provision of basic literacy is an example of a service response, which suggests that the library provide an environment, materials, and tutorial assistance to enable patrons to reach their own literacy goals. In addition to the professional effort to revise the public library planning process, research designed to enhance the place of the public library in the national information infrastructure was undertaken with the support of the National Science Foundation. Recommended in the findings of this investigation, which were published in 1995, was the expanded use in libraries of more electronically derived information. Suggested new activities for the public library included its service as a hub linking and managing local information resources, as a center for making available local, state, and federal information that increasingly will be in electronic form, and as an electronic classroom providing lifelong learners with a range of educational opportunities.[42] The proposed expansion of their services is, of course, stimulated by the public library's claim to be an on-ramp to the information superhighway, especially for persons lacking home computers or the wherewithal to afford commercial online service. At the same time, however, they add to the library's already multifaceted activities, which Lowell Martin once categorized as "an overload of concerns and responsibilities," including but not limited to its functions as "the People's University, the student's auxiliary, the children's door to reading, the free bookstore, the information agency, the scholar's workshop and the community center."[43]

No one would seriously consider that the public library should ignore the potential of the additional benefits inherent in the Internet, but paramount among the considerations of librarians attempting these new or expanded technology-based roles is the question of cost. And cost looms large both in the economics of public library support and also in the fulfillment of its mission to provide equal access to public library resources and services. In a series of policy documents initially linked to its stance on intellectual freedom, the American Library Association has promulgated the concept of equitable and free access to information. Some of these policy documents have been issued as interpretations of the Library Bill of Rights, first enacted by the ALA Council in 1939 as its response to vigilante efforts to censor John Steinbeck's *The Grapes of Wrath* and remove it from public library collections. Two of these interpretations, "Economic Barriers to Information Access" and "Access to Electronic Information, Services, and Networks," were adopted by the ALA Council in 1993 and 1996, respectively. Both oppose the charging of fees as inimical to the concept of full freedom of expression and to the principle of equitable access to the informational content of a library that is publicly supported. Although the tenor of these documents is indeed forceful, the Association freely acknowledges that it has no powers of enforcement and that its policy statements can serve only as guidelines for local development. In 1996, an advisory statement, "Fees for Public Libraries: An Issue Statement," noted that "each public library must make its own decision about fees"[44] was accepted for discussion purposes by the board of directors of the Public Library Association. The statement, however, has never been promulgated as PLA policy.

Censorship from an Economic Perspective

The issue of charging fees in relation to the financial support of the public library will be addressed in the next chapter; what is relevant here is the issue of censorship as it relates to the assessment of user fees. The public library was, of course, never free: the public paid for its services collectively through tax support, and from their inception public libraries received gift funds and endowments. Yet in the popular mind, the public library was indeed free, as its name in the case of the Free Library of Philadelphia or the Enoch Pratt Free Library in Baltimore clearly implied. The issue, then, of assessing charges for the electronic services of the library, which could be rather appreciable, especially to a low-income family or household, seems to strike at the very rationales that brought the public library into being—namely, the sharing of materials for the betterment of the community intelligence.

In her book *Censorship: The Knot That Binds Power and Knowledge*, Sue Curry Jansen distinguishes between two types of censorial activity. The first, regulative censorship, refers to those exercises of power summoned up in defense of ideations imbued with auras of orthodoxy, such as religion, national security, or even personal purity. Through time, concepts inimical to the safeguard of such ideations have been suppressed on the grounds that they were either heretical, seditious, or obscene. Consequently, those espousing such heterodoxies could be identified and evaluated in measurable terms, such as the level of violence required to maintain control, the degree of tolerance for the unorthodox, or the severity of the purgation needed to remedy the situation. "Regulative censorships," Jansen notes, "can be amended or revolutionized in ways that raise or lower bodycounts, numbers of books banned or citizens ghettoed or gulaged."[45] Librarians are quite familiar with regulative censorship, having resisted in many cases efforts on the part of individuals or groups to remove materials from the collection. The latest of the pressure groups assailing libraries is an organization known as the Family Friendly Libraries, formed by Karen Jo Gounaud of Springfield (Virginia), with the assistance of such conservative enterprises as the American Family Association, Citizens for Community Values of Cincinnati, and Focus on the Family. In 1995, the September 18 issue of *Citizen*, the journal of Focus on the Family, featured Gounaud's work and contained an accusatory article about the no-censorship stance of public libraries, accompanied by a cartoon showing children reading *Playboy*, as well as books with such titles as "Anarchy Atlas," "Pipe Bombs Illustrated," and "My Pal Manson," in a library alcove clearly identified as the "A.L.A. [American Library Association] Reading Corner."[46]

In contrast to overt regulative censorship, Jansen identifies existential censorship, which is more pervasive and, because it is less easy to identify, more insidious. Elite interests, whether those controlled by the state or the market or, increasingly, by the alliance of both, display a form of monopolistic domination in which public access to some forms of knowledge and information is either subverted or denied. Jansen notes that the beginning of existential censorship can be traced at least in part to the ideation that knowledge produced in the public interest and often supported by public taxation has become a purchasable commodity subject to the regulation of the market and best handled through the control of the private sector. This viewpoint is represented by a new class of information capitalists and brokers representing commercial interests involved in the production and dissemination of information. During the decade of the 1980s, the commodification of government information grew apace, as the Reagan administration eliminated thousands of government publications, made profitability a criterion in decisions affecting the issuance of government information, increased the price of documents available through the Freedom of Information Act, tightened government classification schemes, and authorized a federal circular (OMB Circular A-130) that placed "maximum feasible reliance on the private sector" for the dissemination of government information.[47]

"Classic Liberal models of democracy," Jansen writes, "were premised upon the assumption that knowledge is a social resource, a public utility, or a collective good. For this reason, free public libraries have been regarded as cornerstones of democracy. Even the much criticized Utilitarian image of 'a free-market of ideas' protects the belief that access to knowledge is a right rather than a privilege; it assumes free entry of diverse ideas into a public marketplace which is open to all citizen/shoppers who seek knowledge."[48] That right, Jansen believes, is being currently threatened as "the marketplace of ideas" now becomes no longer a public utility but a private enterprise serving "only those who can afford to pay a price for the commodities it markets to citizen/shoppers." This threat and all that it portends is precisely the issue confronting the public library profession and underlies the stance of the professional association in opposing the assessment of fees, particularly for the services supplied by the newer technologies. The creation in 1983 by the American Library Association of a

Commission on Freedom and Equality of Access to Information was in part the Association's response to the efforts of the Reagan administration to privatize the dissemination of federal information. The Association's sponsorship of a summit meeting in February 1996, "Equity on the Information Superhighway," devoted to a discussion of the role of public libraries in affording equitable access to electronic information, was a response to the Clinton administration's advocacy of a nationwide network connecting schools, libraries, hospitals, and clinics by the year 2000.

There is no easy answer to the dilemma facing public libraries over the issue of access. Free public libraries, as Jansen says, "have been regarded as cornerstones of democracy." This rhetoric has infused the profession since the founding of public libraries in the late nineteenth and early twentieth centuries. Even today, the mission of the Brooklyn Public Library, as that of many others, is to ensure "the preservation and transmission of society's knowledge, history and culture . . . and, by providing free and open access to information, to help individuals become better citizens of their community and their nation."[49] The American Library Association defines the public's right to a free and open information society as "intellectual participation," and the ALA considers its responsibility for that participation as equal in importance to its defense of intellectual freedom.[50]

At the outset of this chapter, as at the outset of the public library movement, the Scylla and Charybdis of the public library's mission symbolized professional ambivalence toward a populist and pluralistic collection and one that was more directed to the pursuit of high culture. Over time, as other agencies—the adult education movement, the extension activities of universities, and the community colleges—rivaled the public library's once paramount claim to supporting lifelong learning, its collection became increasingly eclectic, developing into a kind of cafeteria that afforded books in foreign languages for new immigrants, materials for the home handyman, commercial information for those engaged in business, manuals for the test taker, books on hygiene and diet, and bestselling novels. Science fiction entered the public library in a big way after World War II, as did paperback books, films, now displaced by video cassettes, and long-playing records, themselves displaced by compact discs. Still in the collection were copies of the classics, often required for school assignments.

Except for the marginal fees charged for such conveniences as the reserving of a book or the provision of a photocopy, the costs of maintaining the collection and providing its resources to the public through circulation or reference was the responsibility of the library and ultimately of the taxpayers who supported it.

Today, the Scylla and Charybdis no longer typify the distinction, drawn by a nineteenth-century librarian, between a populist collection and one more directed to high culture; the rock and the whirlpool between which the public library steers its course represent a new set of dichotomies. Among them is the integration of interactive media into an environment previously dominated by a book-oriented culture and, more important, the need to overcome the divisiveness in the nation's social structure that sets apart the haves from the have-nots. The public libraries we visited have seemingly struck a balance between older and newer ways to transmit information. Although the now ubiquitous computer sits atop the reference desk or the reading room table and public library access to the Internet is increasing, a host of activities and services—children's story hours and summer reading games, book talks, the teaching of English to new immigrants, the circulation of books in large print—attest to the library's traditional emphasis on reading and literacy. In this regard, what is at issue is not so much the integration of older and newer technologies but the identification of new sources of funding to support them both. Some of the nation's greatest public libraries having substantive holdings of research materials, such as those of Boston, Cleveland, Denver, Detroit, Philadelphia, and New York, are located in cities that have deep pockets of poverty, both economic and intellectual. Beneficiaries of what the twelfth Librarian of Congress Daniel J. Boorstin once called the "community's small change," these libraries do not always compete favorably in the public coffers with civic departments devoted to more pressing social concerns, such as public safety or public health. Yet libraries are a safety net not only for learners without access to the collections of colleges and universities but also for many poor children, whose parents cannot afford to buy either books or computers. The African-American youngster in Queens, using the data on a CD-ROM to complete her homework assignment; the two boys of Southeast Asian origin, no more than seven or eight years old, in a Seattle branch, operating a computer as if they were professional programmers; and the Newark schoolchildren probing the holdings of its African-American history collection—all are witness to the continuation of the "library faith," embodying a value system that cannot be wholly approximated by cost-benefit analysis.

Evidence of this faith was apparent not only in our visits to public libraries but also in the interviews with library administrators. The creation of "a literate, enlightened, and learning-oriented society sustained by free and equal access to the universe of knowledge and information provided by libraries" was the expressed "vision" of one library system in Massachusetts.[51] An abbreviated version of this mission is posited by the Denver Public Library: "inform, educate, inspire, and entertain." Ambitious as these statements are, they are typical of the over-arching concerns of the present generation of public librarians. To some, their ambition to be all things to all people would seem an admixture of great naiveté and considerable hubris, but it is forged by people who care deeply about literacy, learning, and the dissemination of information whether it is conveyed in print or by electronic means. If librarians have been influenced at all by the present trend to "market" the public library, that influence is shown by their sometime adoption of the word *customer* rather than *patron* to designate their clientele. In the best business parlance, the customer is, of course, always right, but public librarians, in thinking of their users as customers, show that they strongly emphasize an ethos of public service.

Like the trajectory of its country's history, the public library in the United States has been shaped by contradiction and paradox. In the past, its aspirations to high culture were often countered by the pragmatic necessity of accepting other values and other tastes, as its links to the equality of educational opportunity and to the principle of universal service were questioned when in the 1950s their client group was defined as more elitist than populist. Today, the continuance of the concept of free and equitable access creates an additional ambivalence, as libraries struggle not only to provide the latest in electronic formats but also to enfranchise all of their users in "the republic of letters," to use Daniel Boorstin's phrase, a republic enacting no levy other than literacy for citizenship. To many people, the imposition of a fee for value-added library service, the latter being the most likely to accommodate such a charge, appears a contravention of the public library's basic mission. At the same time, and from another quarter, some critics of the public library assail it for adopting the kind of market mechanisms popularized in the "reinventing government" movement of the early 1990s. Whatever course they take in the future, public librarians can only acknowledge that their present-day Scylla is enshrouded in mist while the eddies of the Charybdis continue to swirl.

2

The Institution: Governance and Funding

The eventual viability of libraries in a new information age may be a vital question among library leaders and other interested persons, but the reality for the present—and, in the view of many commentators, for the near future, at the very least—is that they are still going enterprises and still cherished by communities, which remain their field of operations. Beyond the larger trends that affect libraries—the economy, technology, cultural currents, demographics, state and federal policies—each public library functions within a constellation of forces, interests, and power relationships that determine the particular shape that library services take and that affect the library's freedom of action. The common problems and prospects of all libraries and librarians' shared professional values are played out locally. That is where the money and the essential societal validation have been. The introduction of information technology for public use is occurring at the local level as public libraries offer access to the global Internet, plus other electronic resources, to people in their own neighborhood libraries or at home and workplaces.

Public libraries represent considerable investment of money, physical plant, material, and personnel.[1] According to the latest nationwide statistics, for fiscal year 1994, the fifty state library agencies and the District of Columbia reported to the U.S. National Center for Education Statistics (NCES) a total of public library operating expenditures of nearly $5 billion and capital outlays of more than $600 million. The largest libraries (serving five hundred thousand persons or more) had average operating expenses of $22 million each. Similar patterns were revealed in the 1996 statistical survey of the Public Library Association. Collections nationwide in 1994 totaled 672 million book and serial volumes, 24 million audio materials, and 9.3 million videotapes: nearly $730 million were spent on all such materials. The public library workforce in 1994 totaled nearly 113 thousand paid full-time equivalent staff, a third of whom were professional librarians.

Libraries cannot compete with radio or television, which can be found in practically all American homes (even more than have telephone service), or movie theaters, which had nearly 1.3 billion attendees in 1994. But in comparison with other cultural and recreational activities, the public library does well. Reports of library attendance in 1994 added up to nearly 822 million library visits (4.1 per capita), and nearly 1.6 billion items circulated (6.4 per capita), with ranges much higher and somewhat lower in different states. The PLA survey for 1996 showed that the proportion of the population having library cards ranged from an average of 44.4 in libraries serving the largest populations to 93.9 in those serving the smallest, and from 49.6 to 75.2 percent in between. A 1995 *U.S. News*/CNN poll found that 67 percent of American adults went to a public library at least once that year. The 1996 National Household Education Survey of the National Center for Education Statistics yielded a similar result for household members' use during the past year; it also found that in 44 percent of households someone used library services during the previous month. Public library visits top by more than 60 percent the combined attendance at baseball, basketball, and football games, art museums, and classical music concerts. If public libraries are, as critics and lamenters have suggested through the years, marginal institutions, they appear to be marginal only to the mass electronic media, whose appeal few, if any, other cultural, educational, or recreational offerings can approach.

Library service is offered at nearly nine thousand separate public libraries—that is, libraries operating under one administrative entity—and over 16 percent of these reported more than seven thousand branch library outlets. Library service is hence dispensed at nearly sixteen thousand stationary outlets, including central buildings, neighborhood branch buildings, storefronts, or other facilities, plus close to a thousand bookmobiles. Legal population service areas—"the number of people in the geographic area for which a public library has been established to offer services and from which (or on behalf of which) the library derives income, plus any areas served under contract for which the library is the primary service provider"—now cover nearly the entire United States population. In other words, very few people today are not within reach of public library service. How hard or easy it may be to get to the library or how well supported or adequate the library may be are other, and obviously important, questions, but it is safe to say that the issue today is not, as it was in the 1930s, enough libraries. The library profession and its supporters did reach their goal of universal access, and, for most people, access is available in larger, multi-outlet units of service. About 11 percent of public libraries serve nearly 71 percent of the legal service population areas. The rest of the libraries are quite small establishments whose distribution varies state by state, not necessarily related to population density but rather more to state library legislation and policy and the evolution of governance structures.[2]

The achievement of service coverage is particularly striking on a regional basis. Louis R. Wilson's classic 1938 study, *The Geography of Reading*, showed the development of libraries in southern, southwestern, and north-western states (all then still quite rural) lagging substantially behind that of the rest of the country, a finding corresponding to regional economic, educational, demographic, and cultural conditions, and, in the South, de jure racial segregation and its attendant deep rural poverty as well. States in regions categorized by the U.S. Census as South and West (as distinguished from Northeast and Midwest)[3] now offer library service to virtually all the population, although there are still disparities among states in any one region, with some states doing better than others.

The United States, sixty years after Wilson, is a predominantly metropolitan society. The South and West have grown tremendously in economic activity, population, cultural and educational institutions, and political significance, and the South is urbanized and desegregated. If regionally the South, and to a lesser extent the West, may not have fully caught up in library development to the Northeast and Midwest, which had a head start, both South and West have done so in particular metropolitan areas that mushroomed in recent decades. Among the top fifty public libraries (by population served) in the United States and Canada in 1995, more than two-thirds of the American libraries are in the South and West. The PLA 1996 sample survey documented a similar tendency among seventy-two public libraries serving five hundred thousand or more people. These include library entities, many of them leaders in the field, in places that have undergone spectacular development. For example, the South has the well-known libraries of Dallas, Houston, and San Antonio, in Texas; the city of Jacksonville and Broward and Orange Counties in Florida; Atlanta and Fulton County, Georgia; Charlotte and Mecklenburg County, North Carolina; and Baltimore, Montgomery, and Prince George's Counties in Maryland. In the West there are the libraries in the cities of Los Angeles, Sacramento, San Diego, San Francisco, and San Jose, and the counties of Contra Costa, Los Angeles, Orange, and San Bernardino in California; Las Vegas and Clark County, Nevada; Phoenix and Tucson, Arizona; and King County and Seattle, Washington.[4]

Interestingly, though, despite the wealth of Sun Belt metropolises, among the largest libraries surveyed in the PLA report (population over five hundred thousand), most of those falling below the median in per capita expenditures were in the South and West. The 1994 nationwide NCES compilations for per capita library operating expenditures, by state, indicated a similar pattern for all libraries in regard to both national average and median. Southern states, except for Maryland and Virginia (and the District of Columbia), tended to rank rather low.[5] The rankings should be viewed, however, with some reservation, as they may reflect regional and state disparities in labor costs, cost of living, and other local conditions, such as the financial reverses suffered by California counties in the early and mid-1990s.

Formal Governance and Its Implications

For reasons pertaining to the origin and history of libraries, as well as the complexity of the American governmental structure and state policy, public libraries have also varied in their formal organizational status and governance, state by state, area by area. Carleton Joeckel concluded in 1935 that the "keyword" was "opportunism"—the use of whatever means, structures, and relationships enabled libraries to give service. Given this overriding motive and all the different laws and historical precedents applying to libraries, he said, "the resultant picture, when viewed by the detached observer, is often illogical, irregular, and confused."[6]

The picture today is still complex, perhaps even more so and in different ways. Joeckel was writing before the advent of extensive interlibrary cooperation, before the post–World War II expansion of suburban communities and of county libraries, and before state library agencies took on new roles as dispensers of state and federal aid and monitors of library activity. Indeed, it was Joeckel's research that convinced him of the wisdom of large units of service, for which he then became a driving force and which became a guiding principle in librarianship. Although the federal programs from 1966 on encouraged interlibrary cooperation, no neat national network of public libraries emerged. The aim of library service for all was realized in an incremental, variegated, inequitable way—characteristically American—through a variety of formal consolidations and agreements, informal cooperation, and sharing of common goals rather than adherence to a national blueprint. This patchwork is also the product of inventive adaptations by libraries to the new metropolitanism as well as their ideology of cooperation and larger units of service.

The complications of library governance cannot be explored here in detail and, in fact, deserve separate study. The current governance situation can be here only briefly characterized and its broad dimensions indicated. A majority of public libraries are administered and financed under municipal governments; this type constitutes 55.4 percent of all libraries in the states and the District of Columbia and is represented in all but three states. Nearly 12 percent of public libraries operate under county or parish jurisdiction, and thirty-nine states had such libraries. Nearly 10 percent (in fourteen states) are nonprofit, nongovernmental association or corporation libraries, and most of these holdovers from the past are found in a few of the older states. Nearly 6 percent (in thirty states) are under multijurisdictional governance or intergovernmental agreement; 7.6 percent (in eighteen states) comprise "separate government units known as library districts." Almost 4 percent are part of a school district, a type found in nine states and concentrated in four, especially Ohio and New York. Just fewer than 1 percent are multitype—that is, combinations of academic and public libraries or school and public libraries, a category sparsely scattered in twenty states, mainly in Alaska. A little over 5 percent fall in the NCES category "other."[7] Within these rubrics there may be permutations and combinations, plus a certain amount of overlap because of differences in geographic and jurisdictional categories. For example, California is listed by NCES as having four of the major governance types, but a recent study, *Public Library Organization in California*, identifies seven major library governance structures in the state, with subsets that include contractual agreements among different library entities to provide service to more than one jurisdiction.[8]

The California situation, with its kaleidoscope of county libraries, independent city and town libraries, special districts and authorities, and contractual arrangements, is not unique in its variety. But each state, under whose legal aegis, in our federal system, libraries fall, is different. Most contain more than one NCES library governance category, and the majority have four or more. Hawaii is unique in having one public library system, run by the state, and two other states, Maryland and Wyoming, have county libraries almost exclusively.[9] After World War II Maryland consolidated all but one of its municipal and town libraries into library systems administered by the counties. Today twenty-three multibranch county libraries control all public library service in the state, with the exception of the city of Baltimore, which is served by the Enoch Pratt Free Library. Wyoming also has twenty-three county libraries plus one small independent town library administered as a branch of a county library.

The Wyoming system, with county libraries dating to the late nineteenth century, makes sense in the least populated, and rather untypical, state in the Union. The county scheme in Maryland, a state whose population is close to the national state average and sixth in population density and whose development more closely represents national trends, also makes sense, but of another kind. Maryland's county system can be seen as a clear reflection of post–World War II and then postindustrial living and working patterns. The county consolidation movement there concentrated on library service to people living in rapidly growing suburbs, some already with small libraries and newer suburbs with none. Consider Baltimore County, with a population now about the same as that of Baltimore City. Supported by both the state and the county, governed by a board of trustees, the system, influenced by a prescient consultants' report of 1957,[10] when the county was on the cusp of its great expansion, now comprises fifteen libraries. Some are within discrete communities like Towson (county seat and library headquarters), others are in shopping malls or on suburban thoroughfares near newly built housing developments and major highways, and all are linked by telecommunications and a book delivery system and offer reciprocal intrastate borrowing. In California, by contrast, which had actively led the county library movement launched at the turn of the nineteenth century to serve rural populations, county libraries also grew by the late twentieth century into leading organizations serving large populations, but alongside (and sometimes in association with) cities and towns with their own independent libraries. In Florida, a relative latecomer in library development and a postindustrial boom state, there are also mixed patterns. For example, the Broward County Library, a stellar system only some twenty years old in a fast-growing county that is among the largest in the nation, evolved from two municipal libraries into a multibranch system covering the entire county, with the flagship library in Fort Lauderdale, the county seat.

A recent trend around the country seems to be interest in the separate library district or what is also called the independent taxing district. In 1994 there were reported to NCES some 678 such districts, defined as "a district, authority, board or commission authorized by state law to provide library services." These library entities existed in eighteen states but were concentrated mainly in nine, and altogether they constituted a 29 percent increase over the number of such districts for 1993. The independent districts can encompass one or a group of communities, are usually not part of any other agency of government, and may receive public monies through some sort of formula or special tax levy. The library laws of at least twenty-one states seem to contain provision for separate district libraries, although in some states the category is not clear.[11] These libraries are only one kind, and a small proportion at that, of the 31,555 special districts in the United States, some devoted to a single function and others to more than one. They include, along with libraries (but not including school districts), districts for water, transportation, fire protection, environmental management, and health services and altogether account for some 37 percent of all 84,955 local and county government entities.[12] Political scientists and regionalists like Neal Peirce, who has delineated "citistates,"[13] or David Rusk, author of *Cities Without Suburbs*,[14] might deplore the proliferation of such districts as being inefficient and contributing to the fragmentation of American government. Libraries, however, seem to have on the whole done well under such independence.

In the predominant historic pattern of governance and financing, public libraries receive most of their local income from revenues of the local government under whose jurisdiction they operate. In some communities or states there may be a dedicated tax or portion of tax revenues set aside for libraries, and various other arrangements complicate the picture. Independent district status, by contrast, definitively gives public libraries a discrete source of income and one that, if set by formula, is stable. The libraries are thus spared having to fight for their budget each year before governing bodies and officials dealing also with other government agencies. They can instead appeal directly to the public with their own unique message, and they can cover more than one political jurisdiction. One librarian told us district status was "budget nirvana." On the down side, special districts have to go it alone without the support systems (or constraints) of local governments, they may have to compete for tax money with other special districts, and their existence can be seen as contributing to municipal decline.[15]

Prominent municipal libraries that have converted to independent district status include the Kansas City (Missouri) Public Library and Tulsa City-County Library System; another large library, Las Vegas-Clark County Library District, is a consolidated special district. A comparatively long-standing independent district library is the King County Library System of Washington, founded in 1942 in a state with no direct state aid program for libraries and in a region Peirce criticized for its proliferation of special districts. Now comprising thirty-nine libraries, many in new or renovated, beautifully designed and appointed buildings with latest technologies, King County Library grew along with the region, with its new edge cities outside Seattle and expanding outer communities in the mountains to the east. Up to now, because of the economic stability that its independent status and the county's prosperity has provided, the library system, in the heart of Microsoft country, has been able to flourish, although, of course, librarians do not have unlimited money to do everything they would want or need to do. And what will happen when the library system's cap on tax assessment is reached and if the property values on which that is based stop rising is a question.

Other states, many in the South, have regional library "systems," authorized by state law, in which discrete libraries join together through contracts or other means to provide service under the regional jurisdiction. Some states, like New York and Wisconsin—leaders in the post–World War II library movement that attempted to equalize public library service in cooperative arrangements other than formal reorganizations and consolidations—show a different pattern. Superimposed on existing library organizations (which in New York, for example, fall into every one of the eight NCES governance categories, and in Wisconsin, six) is a grid of "systems," commonly state sponsored and to an extent state funded, comprising autonomous libraries that may share, through the "systems," access to collections, consultants' services, cataloging data and processing, book processing, reference services, and electronic technology. Several states, such as Illinois, support, through a per capita funding formula, statewide cooperatives of different types of libraries—public, academic, school (private and public), and private special libraries. Membership is voluntary but necessary if public libraries want to receive state monies, interlibrary document delivery, discounted access to computer networks, and other services. Other cooperatives or consortia may be pragmatic arrangements more or less independent of state or county government. The *American Library Directory* lists hundreds of cooperative library organizations and systems across the United States, and NCES reported that 69 percent of public libraries were members in 1994 of "a system, federation, or cooperative service"—that is, they participated in formal or informal arrangements among autonomous libraries.[16]

Another institutional adaptation to metropolitan spread, with its frequent city-suburb dichotomy—where the older city might have had a well-established library system, and an adjacent or surrounding county, with a large and growing population and often a more vital economy, did not—is some sort of city-county combination. By consolidation, contractual agreement, or some other arrangement, the city library furnishes service for the county or there is an integrated city-county system, with residents in both jurisdictions eligible to use all the libraries. Such combinations are found in large and prominent public library systems in the country. There are, for example, the libraries serving both Atlanta and Fulton County, Buffalo and Erie County, Memphis and Shelby County,

Miami and Dade County, San Antonio and Bexar County, and Tucson and Pima County.

Not only is library governance an interesting example of the evolution of a local public service in a changing environment, but it has real relevance for that service. While ordinary citizens may not know or care about the details of library governance, the scope and quality of library service available to them may turn on issues of legal jurisdiction, decision-making power, and legal funding sources. The independent taxing district status is one example. Another is public libraries in California, where libraries that were under county auspices and supported almost wholly by ad valorem property taxes were hit very hard by the combined effect of sagging local economies and "reforms" (such as Proposition 13) that severely curtailed tax revenues and gave the state the power to allocate tax funds in the counties. A report of the Restructuring California Public Libraries Joint Task Force, issued presumably in 1995, which among other things recommended cost-benefit analyses of local library governance and its possible restructuring, proclaimed public libraries in California as "nearly bankrupt." They were reeling from more than a decade of budget reductions, which in fiscal year 1993 to 1994 alone amounted to a loss of $70 million.[17] The County of Los Angeles Public Library, highly respected and one of the country's largest consolidated systems, with eighty-seven outlets serving fifty-two out of eighty-eight cities plus almost all the unincorporated areas in the county, had in fiscal year 1993 to 1994 no public appropriations at all to buy books and other materials and in 1995 faced another devastating budget shortfall. Its drive to generate additional public monies through a special tax assessment met initial legal challenges from antitax advocates, but finally a special election in June 1997 yielded a vote of nearly 70 percent in favor of the measure.

By contrast, the separate Los Angeles Public Library is supported out of the general fund of the city of Los Angeles, which, like California cities generally, has considerably more fiscal flexibility than the counties and can generate revenue in various ways. The library, along with other municipal libraries in the state, has suffered financially but not quite as badly as the county libraries. In fact, in 1995 the city of Los Angeles awarded the library a 10 percent increase to buy books and two years later another, unexpected, substantial increase that would be spent on staff, hours of opening, and technology.

Other Local, State, and Federal Factors and Actors

If public libraries differ in their type of formal governance, they are similar in having boards of trustees that are composed usually of appointed or elected (mainly the former) local residents. Sometimes the board includes municipal officials ex officio, and in some cases it consists of county commissioners, county boards of supervisors, or appointees of county courts. Library as well as school boards generally survived twentieth-century municipal modernizations and reforms that replaced boards with salaried chiefs of public services. The vast majority of public libraries, including county libraries and those in independent taxing districts, still have boards.[18] Originally a legacy of laws following the British model for incorporated charitable institutions, board governance became further entrenched in the nineteenth century, when municipalities organized public services and city leaders entrusted oversight of certain quasi-autonomous municipal functions to special bodies. This was done partly to insulate municipal services from politics and presumably venal and philistine politicians. Trustees and librarians did succeed in keeping their institutions politically out of bounds and free from graft, but to the point of cultivating a somewhat unrealistic, sometimes counterproductive, and eventually anachronistic disdain for the political process. So concluded Joeckel and his colleagues at the University of Chicago and, later, political scientist Oliver Garceau in a study for the Public Library Inquiry in 1949.[19] They criticized boards as being outdated and inefficient, as being elite and unrepresentative or comprised of undistinguished mediocrities, and as tending to isolate the library from important local power groups.

Yet, as was also pointed out, boards have their uses. Theoretically, they speak for the community to the library and for the library to the community. As in nonprofit organizations generally, boards can be sources of moral and material support, providers of legal and other expertise, and guardians of private endowments; in libraries they can act also as buffers in censorship issues and as dedicated advocates in struggles for money and recognition. Depending on state law, local laws and regulations, custom, and informal power relationships, their roles can vary, however. Trustees may have real power to manage money, set policy, and speak for the library, they may be only advisory and function mainly as fundraisers and donors, or they may be just window dressing or historical holdovers.

For the years since 1949 we do not have extensive national studies of library board composition, status, and functioning, but we can speculate that, given the extensive postwar library development, library board membership has become more prestigious and that (as our field visits indicated) some boards, following general trends begun in the 1970s, are now somewhat more representative of their communities. In some cities there has been to some extent a changing of the guard to encompass new moneyed interests and new social and power networks as well as possibly more grassroots representation. Prominent businesspeople, professional people, and politicians have the contacts, the resources, and the voices to help the library get what it needs. At the same time, representatives of ordinary people, minority groups, trade unions, young people, and local activists can bring to library decision-making the outlooks of users (and nonusers) and can articulate their needs in support of library interests.

Formal library institutional status is one of several interrelated forces that control policy and decision-making and affect budgets and public image.[20] A key factor is the ability of chief librarians to understand and operate within whatever governance structure they find themselves and regardless of the library's position in the official hierarchy in the government on which they depend for funds. In the all-important, usually annual competition for public monies, that effectiveness translates into understanding who and what will help the library win approval of its proposed budget and into being able to articulate the library's mission and value and to garner support for that budget.[21] This is mainly though not entirely a local affair, since the preponderant source of public library monies in most states is local. Nationwide, 78.2 percent of all public library operating income in 1994 derived from local sources, 12.3 percent from state, 1.1 from federal, and 8.4 percent from other sources.[22]

Given current institutional and funding patterns, library directors and trustees must be close students of their local power structures and learn how to maneuver within them. The days of the stereotypical reclusive librarian, sequestered in his or her office, scornful of politics and politicians, are over (if they ever really existed to that degree). Congenial and productive relations with members of the official, governmental power structure are very important to the library's success in meeting its goals. This applies as well throughout the library staff, in central administration and out in the neighborhoods, and it involves understanding the governmental balance of power, which determines in part the political targets aimed at in behalf of the library. In some cities and counties a mayor or chief executive may be all powerful and the legislative body relatively weak. In Houston and Chicago, for example, the mayoralty is dominant; the mayor's picture hangs in every Chicago branch library. Elsewhere the legislature or a county commission may be the paramount force, or city managers or municipal department heads carry a good deal of weight.

Whether or not city or county council members are powerful as a group, they often have a good deal of influence in their home constituencies in which branch libraries exist. Libraries may not command a large proportion of a mammoth municipal budget (on a national scale, slightly less than 1 percent of total city expenditures in 1993 and third lowest of all categories in per capita expenditures),[23] but in their districts they often represent job opportunities and, more important, stand as objects of local pride and material evidence of municipal interest. That may be particularly true in poor areas with few public facilities besides schools. There have been instances in older cities in which local politicians scuttled or resisted well-founded plans to close or consolidate library branches or have insisted on constructing new ones in locations that did not really need them.

The political process involves much more than dealing with government per se. Community leaders and representatives are invited to serve on library advisory boards or committees, and library directors make it their business to keep up with community affairs; they serve on boards and committees of cultural, civic, and educational organizations and institutions and attend civic and business functions. The hard times of the 1970s and thereafter reaffirmed the value of cultivating sustained public support for libraries and developing political clout, among people in the neighborhoods as well as civic and business leaders. Furthermore, the decline of the party system in American politics and the political focus on local communities and interest groups all point to the importance of appeals to a wide variety of interests and to building coalitions with community organizations and stakeholders.

Public libraries also must and do pay attention to federal and especially state affairs. Like so many institutions in the complex American political system, libraries operate within state and federal contexts that exert both direct and indirect, and not unimportant, influence. Historically, the states varied in their concern for public libraries, and they still do, and each state's general fiscal and tax policies, as they affect local governments, impinge on libraries. Depending on their strength and their effectiveness as lobbying organizations, state library associations may also be influential in setting state library policies, as are the variously named and variously bureaucratically placed official state library commissions or agencies. In the early twentieth century a number of states became more activist in library development, but virtually all state library agencies gained importance by mid-century as never before when the advent of federal aid to libraries funneled funds through the states. The progress made by the library profession in achieving larger units of library service and broad service coverage occurred state by state, encouraged by federal legislation and spurred by a national library ideology. This phenomenon is discussed in some detail in the next chapter, which deals with the federal and state roles in public library development from a national policy perspective.

Most but not all states now have some sort of direct financial aid program for public libraries. Apart from the material help that state grants provide, conditions for such aid raised standards and expanded services in many communities. The average state contribution to public library operating income in all fifty states (and the District of Columbia) in 1994 was 12.3 percent of total income; because of several uncommonly high figures, a better measure is the median, 4 percent. The range of state support for public libraries varies a good deal and may be variable within each state as well. In Ohio, in which since 1986 a portion of the state income tax has been dedicated to public libraries, the state provided in 1994 72.8 percent of their income, and in Hawaii the contribution is virtually 100 percent (as it is for the similarly statewide elementary and secondary public school system there), except for small amounts from federal and "other" sources. Elsewhere, revenue from the state ranged from 32.1 percent in West Virginia and 26.1 percent in Georgia to 1 percent or less of total library income in Arizona, Nevada, Oregon, Texas, Vermont, Washington, and Wyoming and zero percent in New Hampshire and South Dakota.

There were regional differences as well. Strongest state support came in Southern states as a group, with only two out of sixteen, Oklahoma and Texas, falling below the median. That does not mean that libraries were very well financed in the South. Figures for expenditures per capita by public libraries show proportionately more states in the South than in other regions with low rankings (as do, though less so, figures for public school expenditures per pupil for 1995). Apart from Hawaii, and except for Alaska, which stood above the median, and California, at the median, Western states tended toward low or minimal state support for public libraries but did much better for public schools. All these disparities have origins in the uneven historical development of libraries and educational institutions and public policy toward them in regions, individual states, and communities, as well as diverse economic conditions.[24]

Direct aid for operating funds aside, all states offer various services to public libraries, most commonly the collection of library statistics, continuing education opportunities, and library planning, evaluation, and research. In 1994 almost every state library agency planned or monitored electronic network development, many funded or operated such networks and developed network content; thirty states also expended monies to help public libraries conduct programs promoting adult literacy, lifelong learning, and school readiness; and all but four gave aid from state revenues for public library construction. Statewide initiatives were cited in a 1996 national survey done for the National Commission on Libraries and Information Science (NCLIS) as the primary motivation for public library interest in the Internet, especially among smaller libraries; state library networks accounted for nearly a fifth (the highest percentage) of providers of Internet connectivity, followed by local and state governments.[25] Some states (Vermont and Nebraska, for example) run extensive online information networks involving libraries. The state of Ohio, where libraries have been traditionally well supported, supports OPLIN (Ohio Public Library Information Network), which serves every public library in the state and has been called a model system for statewide electronic access to information resources. In the enthusiasm for Internet access and computer literacy, states are including libraries in schemes to wire up educational institutions, and states have been investing funds to aid implementation of federally mandated discounts for telecommunications costs in libraries and schools (of which more in chapter 4).

All states administered federal grant monies under the Library Services and Construction Act (LSCA) programs, a role that will continue under the Library Services and Technology Act (LSTA), the new library legislation enacted by the 104th Congress in 1996 and which replaces LSCA. Local libraries have also benefited from other federal programs and services, such as preferential postage rates for books, the depository program for federal government publications, and the cataloging, bibliographic, and reference services of the Library of Congress and other national libraries.[26] The Library of Congress, though functioning primarily as a research library, also runs several special national services on a more popular level and has been trying to fashion a somewhat more populist role for itself. Its National Reference Service answers all kinds of questions from the general public but aims optimally to be a court of last resort for public and other libraries and regional reference centers; children's librarians are among the constituents of its Children's Literature Center; the Library's National Digital Library of Americana is aimed at the general public as well as researchers and educators; and its Center for the Book promotes reading and literacy nationwide and has stimulated and worked with state Centers for the Book, several of which are located in public libraries. For its bicentennial in the year 2000, the Library of Congress is highlighting the value of libraries of all kinds "in promoting knowledge, creativity and liberty in America."[27] People anywhere in the United States who are blind or have physical disabilities can get free Braille and recorded materials and playback equipment, postage free, through public libraries from the Library of Congress's National Library Service for the Blind and Physically Handicapped (NLS), which acquires the original materials, develops standards for and produces tape and other recordings, and monitors contracted production of recordings. In effect, the NLS is in its field a public library for the entire nation, one that in 1993 circulated nearly 22 million items.[28] Established by an act of Congress in 1931 and fairly well funded annually, the NLS also offers bibliographic services and reading guides for people who are blind or have physical disabilities and is a distinguished national and international center of information in its field and of research into new technologies and delivery systems for its constituency.

So far, in recent national public policy (which is discussed at length in subsequent chapters), efforts to democratize use of the "information highway" have been largely concerned with enabling local institutions—schools, community organizations, local governments, and individual libraries, for example—to provide public access to computers and telecommunications, albeit they are encouraged to act cooperatively. This is true of the new Library Services and Technology Act and of the Telecommunications Act of 1996, which earmarks telecommunications discounts for libraries and schools.

Notwithstanding the contribution of both the states and the federal government, the main operating arena for individual libraries remains local. Local funds are not only still the basic, predominant support for public libraries, but borrowing from the collections, still the major public use of libraries, is also mainly on site so far. Although interlibrary loans in public libraries have increased substantially in recent years, over the past twenty years borrowing from other libraries as a proportion of total circulation of library materials steadily accounted for only some one-half of 1 percent nationally.[29] Figures for fiscal year 1994 show a 8.7 percent rise over 1993 in the reported number of borrowed items (including copies of materials), which represents a slight increase in such borrowing as a proportion of total circulation.[30] Interlibrary loan is certainly important to users who need the materials, particularly those in the smaller communities, and no one library can supply all wants; the figures also presumably do not show the extent of interbranch lending within library entities. The rate of interlending may increase further as libraries make their holdings better known by digitizing their catalogs, participating in national computerized bibliographic networks, offering remote direct dialup access and Internet access to a variety of information sources as well as their own holdings, and enabling patrons to request materials online, without a visit to the library.[31] On the other hand, if libraries firmly establish themselves as preeminent places to access conveniently and freely a wide range of digitized information, with advanced, multimedia hardware and software that individuals find hard to upgrade at home, on-site use may rise and with it borrowing of traditional materials, which people evidently like to have at hand. One thing is sure: everything is in flux, and predictions are difficult to make.

In any case, the compilation of statistics of library use will be changing in order to show the magnitude of electronic connections made to and through the library and thus give a more complete picture of library performance. A joint NCES-NCLIS project, the Federal-State Cooperative System for Public Library Data (FSCS), has formulated standard input measures for electronic access that will be collected annually in each state. The standardization of measures of use data, a more complex task, has not yet been achieved and has been under study by FSCS, the Public Library Association, and state library agencies. So far the collection of use statistics is taking place minimally and only locally if anywhere, though everyone agrees that measuring volume of use of electronic services is very important.[32]

Budgetary Issues

In face of virtually infinite demands and opportunities for service in an expanding technological environment and contracting public sector, finding adequate funding, always a challenge for libraries, becomes imperative. The budgetary implications of the new technologies are not simple. There are various costs—for membership in networks, contracts with service providers and database vendors, telephone line use, installation and maintenance, staff training and new personnel, time spent helping users, upgrades of hardware and software, and computer paper and printing supplies. Ideally, new technology should represent new money to be added to, not replace, necessary expenditures for traditional services still in demand. The state and federal programs and other grants to enable libraries to connect to the Internet are a decided help, but they defray only part of the costs. Many communities also confront a fairly new expense—security systems to safeguard collections and guards to protect patrons and staff. The result of all this is a difficult balancing act of allocating limited or scarce resources.

It is true that public libraries on the whole have been moderately successful in their budget campaigns, at a time when all governmental expenditures have been under scrutiny and subject to cuts. On a national scale public library operating expenditures seem to have been keeping up with or even surpassing inflation rates. Public appropriations for public libraries as a group, following the business cycle, were higher in the 1980s than the late 1960s and the 1970s, and libraries did better in the 1980s than other municipal services. But libraries were not well supported, they had to meet higher costs for books and other budget items, and in certain localities they endured severe budgetary declines, to the point of threats of total closure.[33] As recession deepened in the early 1990s, stories of budget crises filled the library literature.

At this writing an improved national economy may spell better times ahead. According to *Library Journal*'s annual sample survey, public library operating budgets increased overall 6 percent from fiscal year 1994 to fiscal year 1995, and 6.4 percent from 1995 to 1996, approximately double the inflation rate; the report for fiscal year 1997 showed a 4.1 percent rise over the past year. Some of the increases seemed to be spent on technology (a rising expense that has tended to some extent to consume cuts in materials budgets but perhaps less so in fiscal year 1997 than previously). It is hard to know what proportion of all expenditures goes toward information technology, although libraries are beginning to add separate budget items for Internet costs.[34] A 1992 sampling of public library spending on collection materials indicated that electronic information products were purchased from the materials budget, but the impact on that budget was not noted. Such purchases would include CD-ROM and online reference sources, which public libraries increasingly acquire (to some extent as replacements for print versions).[35] In the 1996 NCLIS survey nearly a third of the public libraries reported that they did not know their current percentage of technology-related operating costs. A follow-up ALA-NCLIS survey done in spring 1997 affirmed the complexity and difficulty of calculating the costs of information technology, especially as some Internet costs were covered by other agencies, grants, or gifts. But the study indicated that such costs were considerable and expected to rise, that there were disparities among libraries and among legal service areas, that cost was a key factor in nonconnectivity to the Internet, and that libraries considered that they needed more and better equipped workstations.[36]

Overall operating budgets vary community by community as well as among regions and states, as tax revenues differ depending on the local economy, tax bases, property values, local budget priorities, and the impact of state limits on local budgets or tax rates. Libraries in certain cities, like Atlanta and Baltimore, still suffer extreme fiscal pressure (although public protest rescued them from the most drastic cuts). Reports of public referenda for library operating funds show that an average of 83 percent passed during the three years from 1994 to 1996. Only a relatively few (seventy-five in 1996, for example) libraries were involved, though interest in ballot measures for library expenditures is growing. But these and other surveys reveal that when the public is asked directly (and, notably, in well-run campaigns) to support libraries, they often respond positively and in majority votes well beyond 51 percent, and public opinion surveys yield strong responses in favor of more money for public libraries.[37]

There is, however, the countervailing impact of the trend toward smaller government and lower taxes, as well as increased competition for local public funds as the federal government reduces spending and implements "devolution"—the transfer of powers and responsibilities to lower levels of government. As the chief of the Census of Governments Branch of the U.S. Bureau of the Census points out, relationships among federal, state, and local components "are continuously in flux," with the most contentious decisions being the financial ones.[38] A recent example of these fluctuating relationships occurred in California, where local elections brought some budgetary relief to certain public libraries but where statewide voters passed Proposition 218, which amends the state constitution to require voter approval before local governments create or increase taxes, special assessments, and property-based fees. And in Oregon voters approved in 1996 an initiative to limit property taxes and give priority in state funding to public safety and public education, which may or may not be interpreted to encompass libraries. The Oregon situation had an immediate drastic effect on the budget for the Multnomah County Public Library (including Portland), which then had to wage a difficult—and just barely won—campaign to turn out the more than 50 percent of registered voters that are required for property tax funding measures and then to convince a majority of those voters to approve a library operating levy. Hard-fought victories have also been reported in several states in campaigns to maintain and, in Rhode Island, increase levels of library support.[39]

Libraries must meet not only ongoing operational costs but needs for physical plant as well. The actual number of new library buildings constructed has been on a downward slope in the 1990s, but additions and renovation projects were up (some to conform to the Americans for Disabilities Act guidelines), and community approval of capital projects submitted to referenda remains strong, even more so than for operating funds. From 1987 to 1996 more than 80 percent of 486 referenda for library buildings passed, with average majorities of 64 percent; in 1996 alone, 89 percent of such referenda passed, with an average majority of 67 percent of the votes.[40] And in the midst of fiscal difficulties and just when some futurists are predicting the demise of the physical library, cities have been putting up grand central public library buildings and renovating and expanding existing ones. There also seems to be something of a trend toward constructing new branches and refurbishing old ones—with as much care and attention paid to aesthetics for branches as for central buildings.

Although the bulk of the money for both operating and capital expenditures comes from the public purse, that has not been nearly enough. This is so especially for operating budgets. Building projects are financed, at least in part, by bond issues, not current revenues, and are finite and tangible, while operating budgets have results that are less easy to see and are always there, year after year. Indeed, in some cities with brand-new or restored buildings, book acquisition budgets have gone begging, and opening hours have been curtailed. Expenditures for books and other materials, often the only substantial discretionary item in operating budgets, tend to feel the brunt of fiscal stringency. We saw one city branch library, which had been designed by a famous architect in the 1980s and which contains an important special collection relevant to the city, that had practically no money to purchase new books or to provide proper security. At night the building was a sparkling attraction for tourist buses, but it was open for use only two evenings weekly; in the daytime, men from a nearby homeless shelter frequented it. Other library systems cannot afford to stock videotape collections in every branch. In New York City, when a municipal fiscal crisis resulted in drastic cuts to the budgets of the city's three public library systems (the New York, Queens Borough, and Brooklyn Public Libraries) in 1991 and 1992, public pressure forced restoration of enough funds to reopen branches five days a week and then six, but practically no money for new books was forthcoming. The libraries resorted to an Emergency Book Fund Campaign, sponsored by the Chase Manhattan Bank, but the dearth of appropriations for collections continued. Then in 1997, at the New York Public Library, Mrs. Vincent Astor, its great benefactor and honorary chair of the board, stepped in to help. She committed $5 million from the Vincent Astor Foundation to establish a book endowment to purchase fiction and poetry for the branch libraries and thus create for them something of a stable financial base independent of the vagaries of year-to-year municipal budgets. Subsequently, the municipality, taking advantage of higher tax revenues, added to its election-year budget for fiscal year 1998 substantially higher appropriations for all three library systems in the city.

Library budgets may have, furthermore, constraints more or less built into the budget. Requirements to prepare line-item operating budgets limit flexibility, and, as one director said, there is usually no venture capital to enable libraries to take risks. In those libraries with collective bargaining units, labor contracts, which must be honored regardless of fiscal vicissitudes, have an impact on salaries and wages, the preponderant proportion of operating budgets; contract provisions may also inhibit flexible deployment of personnel. Unionization of professional librarians and clerical support workers is a fairly new phenomenon in libraries. Up to about thirty years ago, when unions began seriously to organize public-sector white-collar employees, the relatively low salaries of public library workers in effect subsidized institutional budgets (and in some places probably still do).[41]

Fundraising

Librarians try to husband their wherewithal through planning and management techniques, but that approach has limits. And even the best-supported libraries do not have unlimited resources and as a rule cannot do everything they would like or perceive as necessary. As a result, public libraries are engaging in what a study of public library financial practices dubbed "revenue diversification."[42] In other words, they are scrambling to find additional monies from the private sector. Not only must public libraries continue to compete for public funds, but they are joining the ranks of the legions of nonprofit organizations and other public institutions (including even public schools) contending for "private" dollars. This involves libraries' reaching outward beyond their public appropriations as never before since the age of Carnegie to raise or earn money. They also save labor costs through the work of volunteers, whose presence in some libraries is indispensable.

The fundraising has been occurring in a changing and highly competitive philanthropic environment. Governmental cutbacks heightened needs in the nonprofit sector at the same time as corporate downsizing slowed corporate giving, and the rate of private philanthropy in general remained flat during the decade before the economic upturn and the bull market of the mid-1990s. There is tremendous new wealth in the United States, but the new generations of rich and super-rich people are just learning how to give away their surplus money, and their approach is different from their predecessors. Their philanthropic interests and their new foundations tend to be more specifically targeted and focused less on the arts and humanities and on established institutions and more on other objects.

Although the extent of private giving to public institutions is not yet well tracked, as far as libraries are concerned the NCES figures for 1994 show that nonpublic sources account for 8.4 percent of total public library operating income nationally, as compared to 1.1 percent from the federal government. These proportions seem to be a sharp reversal of those twenty-five years ago.[43] In fiscal year 1997, more than half of new public library buildings and renovations and additions had some nonpublic financing; gifts paid entirely for one new library and four renovations or additions. Of the total costs for all this construction, gifts accounted for 7.9 percent, corresponding to a range of 7 to over 8 percent for most of the previous six years.[44] Large libraries have launched campaigns for millions of dollars for capital projects and special programs both.

Although overwhelmingly supported by tax dollars and commonly connected if not entirely intermixed with local government, public libraries have always also been part of the independent, private, nonprofit, "third" sector of American society. Many libraries were founded as nongovernmental agencies, and even when they joined the public sector their boards frequently have operated quasi-autonomously. Legally, public libraries can accept gifts of money and securities, real property, physical plant and equipment, books and other documents, and art works; some libraries have endowments. Citizens, although conceiving of public libraries as public goods deserving tax support, are not averse to private fundraising for them. Libraries seem to be regarded not exactly as government, not as part of a supposedly bloated official power structure needing downsizing or privatizing, and generally not as a public sector failure. Indeed, by all accounts they are held in great affection by the public and have the reputation of being prudently managed. Their budgetary problems are influenced mainly by the general fiscal vicissitudes of local and state government, prevailing economic conditions, static or declining tax bases, and the relative smallness of libraries in that whole picture, especially compared with what are usually seen as more crucial public services, such as police, fire, and public health. That very smallness, though, means that citizens do not see libraries as eating up their tax dollars, and, as one public library director commented, libraries have not up to now offered businesspeople the prospect of enough profit to warrant taking them over. That situation can change, however, under certain circumstances (and with the advent of management firms). In a highly unusual move, the county of Riverside, California, contracted in 1997 for one year, with renewal options, with a private vendor of library systems and services to run a new entity, Riverside County Library System. The county libraries had for the previous eighty-five years been part of and administered by the Riverside City and County Public Library, under a contract the city chose not to renew, a decision that was influenced by the difficult fiscal situation in California counties as well as festering regional problems. A year later, the Jersey City (New Jersey) Public Library board voted to turn over management of the library for the next three years to the same private company, a move that also reflected local politics and library conditions but which, the *New York Times* suggested, "could reverberate throughout the nation's libraries, especially those facing budget squeezes."[45]

Public libraries receive nonpublic income from various sources, most substantially from fines and fees; book sales; vending machine charges (such as photocopying); endowments and library foundations; donations from corporations, nonlibrary foundations, and Friends of the Library; and most of all (and in line with philanthropic patterns generally), gifts and bequests from individuals. The Urban Libraries Council, an institutional membership organization of now more than a hundred public libraries, including most of the largest public libraries, sponsored a survey of fundraising activities of its members that was published in 1994. Three-fourths of the respondents were actively engaged in private fundraising, which had increased over the past ten years and was expected to continue to do so. Some 50 percent of the sample in *Library Journal*'s annual public library budget survey for 1996 reported fundraising activities, a decided rise over previous years. The 1997 report estimated that libraries had tripled the amount of dollars yielded from fundraising.[46]

The American Library Association started in 1995 its Fund for America's Libraries, an endowment with well known Americans on the board, to raise funds from the "philanthropic community" to promote and improve libraries through ALA activities. The Association received foundation grants to train directors and trustees of small to medium-size public libraries in fundraising through its new Library Fundraising Resource Center. The ALA has another national program, Library Advocacy Now!, that trains advocates for libraries on the local level. And the National Endowment for the Humanities in 1996 announced a project to help public libraries form, on a matching fund basis, endowments to support public programming in the humanities, preferably in collaboration with other groups.

Public libraries have not been generally a high priority for the philanthropic community as represented by the large foundations, but a few important foundations have been interested in libraries, and the Urban Libraries Council study reported a steady rise in foundation grants for public libraries from 1982 to 1991 in both total dollars and number of grants (except during three years affected by the 1987 stock-market downturn). The proportion of total foundation grant dollars and number of grants given to libraries remains small, however. The latest *Foundation Grants Index* reported that in 1995 giving for the purpose "Library Science/Libraries" (all types) amounted to 1.9 percent of total grant dollars and 1.1 percent of all grants. Specifically, for "Libraries" as institutional recipients the proportion of grant dollars and of total grants was .6 percent each. These figures are not broken down by type of library (such as public or university), so that those for public libraries would be lower yet. They also do not include small, local, but in toto not insubstantial foundation grants from both private and community foundations, and most library fundraising is local. In certain cases large foundations have given quite sizable grants—some in the millions and others in hundreds and tens of thousands of dollars. Local foundations commonly give small grants (less than $10,000). But large or small, a grant could mean a great deal for any one institution.[47]

Large libraries may have development officers and may also use outside professional fundraisers. Like museums, libraries also try to earn money as well as solicit it. Scarcely a new central city public library building is without a retail sales shop offering books and related wares, and older libraries have them as well. Other moneymaking ventures on library property include restaurants and coffee bars, parking sites, and rental fees for nonlibrary use of space. Libraries also sell products and services to other libraries. For example, the County of Los Angeles Public Library embarked on an arrangement to market through a commercial vendor "good reads," a CD-ROM user's guide to fiction that was originally created for in-house use. Twenty percent of the libraries sampled in a special PLA "Public Library Finance Survey" for 1993 reported sales of services. To save money, as differentiated from earning it, there is increasing use of outsourcing—contracting out (with both nonprofit and for profit enterprises) for operations traditionally done in-house. This practice is becoming an issue in the field, highlighted by the case of Hawaii's public library system's contract with a commercial vendor. The staff's concern about loss of quality and control, especially over book selection, as well as the impact on personnel, reached the Hawaii state legislature, sparked a state investigation and a government employees' lawsuit, and led to cancellation of the contract and subsequent litigation.[48] Debate on the issue within the library profession prompted the American Library Association Executive Board to appoint in 1997 a task force to study and make recommendations concerning outsourcing, subcontracting, and privatization of library services.

Friends of the Library groups, which originated in 1922 and have proliferated during the past twenty years, yielded, along with overdue fines and vending revenue, the most nonpublic income in 1994.[49] There are now some three thousand or more Friends groups, many, probably most, in public libraries, both librarywide and in neighborhood branches. They raise money, campaign for special library projects or annual budgets, protest budget cuts, and do volunteer work in libraries. In large municipal and county systems, Friends groups also offer local communities a way to become involved in library affairs. The PLA "Public Library Finance Survey" found that 84 percent of the sample libraries received funds through Friends groups.[50] A national organization, Friends of Libraries USA, founded in 1979 and now having twenty-eight hundred member groups and Hillary Rodham Clinton as honorary chair, fosters Friends groups, promotes library advocacy, and acts as a clearinghouse for news and guidance.

Another recent development, evident in the 1980s, is the formation of library foundations, especially in larger libraries. These are private non-profit incorporated entities, distinct from the library itself, that receive, hold, and manage private funds for library purposes. The PLA "Public Library Finance Survey" listed nearly a third of the libraries as having foundations (with nearly two-thirds of the foundations in libraries serving 100,000 people or more); 44 percent of the respondents in the Urban Libraries Council survey had foundations, and another 20 percent were planning to establish them.[51] The library foundations in San Francisco, Denver, and San Antonio were instrumental in raising millions of dollars to supplement public bond issues for the new central libraries there, and in Chicago the foundation funded badly needed book purchases. In Atlanta the library foundation mounted an eventually successful campaign for funds for a new central library, community libraries, and the Austin Avenue Research Library on African American Culture and History. The endowment of the Tulsa Library Trust, a pioneering public library foundation, grew in just over a decade from nearly $14,000 to nearly $5 million, the income from which has been used for special needs and projects of the Tulsa City-County Library. Broward County Library's foundation gave a million dollars to construct a special collections and rare books library in the main library in Fort Lauderdale and receives the monies raised to match the County Commission's pledge of $5 million to build a new African American Research Library and Cultural Center by 1999. In 1996 the Chicago Public Library Foundation launched a three-year, $10 million initiative, Project MIND (Meeting Information Needs Democratically), which aims to ensure that every branch library and therefore every community has state-of-the-art information technology, resources, and training. (At the same time the Chicago City Council approved a three-year, $50 million project to construct new branches, renovate existing ones, and give high technology capability to all.) In early 1998 the Seattle Public Library Foundation, which had initiated a campaign to revitalize book collections throughout the library system, received a $2.5 million matching grant from the Paul G. Allen Charitable Foundation. (Allen was a co-founder of the Microsoft Corporation.) The grant, which is earmarked for books, is expected to double the library's acquisitions budget over the next five years.

The pursuit of private monies by a public agency has its risks. With the intensification of such activity, which these days is generally encouraged or at least not opposed by local authorities, there is always the worry that, where not legally prohibited, the public budget will be reduced if substantial private funds come in. Reportedly, this has not often happened overtly, though instances have occurred. Research on the effect of changes in public funding for nonprofit organizations has indicated that when private philanthropy rises, public funding declines and vice versa.[52] Such statistical study of public libraries is beginning to be done and suggests that something of the sort may occur under certain circumstances, but the data are very limited so far.[53] Besides the issue of whether the public sector is encouraged to abdicate its responsibility and libraries are being regarded as objects of charity, private financial support for public libraries, especially for general purposes, presents the danger of overdependence on possibly unstable or erratic sources of funds.

Librarians are well aware of these potential liabilities and are always careful to emphasize private giving as a supplement to the public budget, not a substitute for it. Private donors, moreover, expect the public sector to fulfill its responsibility to the library, and the interest demonstrated by private giving, most often for special purposes and building projects rather than as supplements to tax funds, can reinforce the library's importance as a public service deserving of tax support. Indeed, some of the most successful fundraising projects have involved combinations of public and private monies, and there is much talk of public-private partnerships.

A creative financing arrangement among New York State, New York City, and private sources (an enterprise that Governor Mario Cuomo, running for reelection in 1994, touted as an accomplishment of his administration) enabled construction of the new $100 million high-technology Science, Industry and Business Library of the New York Public Library, which opened in 1996 in a renovated landmark former department store. Three-quarters of the cost of the library, designed by Gwathmey Siegel, came from the private sector, which was convinced of the value of such information sources to the economic and social health of the city. Also at the New York Public Library, an Adopt-A-Branch program was started in 1991 to attract private donations to supplement inadequate city support for capital improvements in rundown branches. The Chicago Public Library has a similar project whose most prominent example is the Chicago Bulls' adoption of the new Mabel Manning Branch. The opening of the attractively furnished building, which sits almost alone on a vacant lot in a poor neighborhood not far from the Bulls' arena, was a celebrity affair. Whether such programs will be viewed as stopgap measures during temporary hard times or as a permanent pattern is a question.

Although some library buildings carry his name, when Andrew Carnegie donated his millions to build public libraries across the English-speaking world nearly a hundred years ago, contrary to popular belief he made no condition that they do so. Today, library units may well be named for donors (whether requested by them or not), and their walls and floors may be bedecked with plaques honoring contributors. Is this (along with renting space for gala fundraising events) a form of commercialization of the library, or a time-honored American practice of rewarding philanthropy? In at least one reported case (Los Angeles Public Library), the city council officially pledged to rename branches after million-dollar donors, a policy that was soon disavowed and that few if any libraries would openly propose or endorse.[54] As for the restaurants, gift shops, and space rentals for dinners and receptions, they do not seem to have raised much criticism. On the contrary, in helping to make downtown libraries popular new gathering spots, they are welcome enhancements of the libraries' image and centrality.

Another potential problem is uneven community resources.[55] Libraries in poor cities and towns with low tax bases and therefore very thin public purses will lack a population able to organize and contribute to private library funds. Similarly, within a large library system in which neighborhood branches campaign individually for contributions, low-income communities do not have the wherewithal that more prosperous ones can draw on. Will libraries in the poorer neighborhoods, which may acutely need well-stocked and well-appointed libraries, fall behind? Or will central administrations step in, as they have in some places, to adjust the imbalances? The current trend toward equipping and wiring every library facility for electronic information access represents one way to equalize resources, but it is not as thoroughgoing as the development of systemwide fundraising campaigns that will address each branch's total needs, technological and otherwise.

Also of serious concern is the possibility that libraries' missions and commitments might be skewed by donations and donors or by support and advisory groups representing special interests or particular neighborhoods. Such tensions have not been unknown in the past; a cardinal principle in librarians' training is to avoid gifts with strings attached. Even without actual strings, subtle pressures may be felt to cater to certain donors or avoid offending them, or to use certain equipment or operating systems, which libraries will then have to maintain and upgrade. There also is the potential for power or turf struggles between library boards and support groups or between Friends groups and foundation boards. And what of public accountability for private funds used for public purposes? A related potentially sticky issue, one that has come up in regard to other institutions (and was raised years ago in a few communities about Carnegie's library donations), is the perception of the moral status or acceptability of specific donors. This point may apply particularly to corporate donors (tobacco companies, for example), as well as to libraries' investment portfolios.

San Francisco is an interesting, and probably cautionary, case in point of the use of Friends and foundations and the pitfalls of public-private collaborations. The Friends of the San Francisco Public Library, after a successful $109 million bond issue campaign in 1988 for a new, long-needed central library, formed the Library Foundation of San Francisco, which in receipts from seventeen thousand donors overshot by several million dollars its goal of $30 million to equip the new library (called the New Main). The foundation developed an innovative program that appealed not only to the usual corporate and foundation communities and to individual citizens but to the city's distinct constituencies, which the *New York Times*'s architecture critic, Herbert Muschamp, called the "rainbow of San Francisco communities." Ten "affinity groups"—including African-Americans, gays and lesbians, Chinese-Americans, Latin

Americans, Filipino-Americans, and environmental interests—raised millions of dollars for both the library in general and for special collections in their fields, several with their own rooms in the building.

This went on during a time of political turmoil, fiscal stringency, and harsh cuts in municipal social services. To balance the campaign for the New Main and stem the hemorrhaging of local branch budgets, the library director formed the Council of Neighborhood Libraries. Out of the struggles to build the New Main and simultaneously maintain and strengthen branch library service came a city charter amendment, overwhelmingly approved by the voters, to set aside for the library budget, for fifteen years, a certain proportion of the property tax. That the New Main finally went up and the budget referendum passed was, in the words of a leading Friend of the Library, "an act of political will." The monumental, very contemporary, high-technology New Main, designed by James Ingo Freed, the architect of the Holocaust Museum in Washington, DC, and Cathy Simon, garnered immense attention in San Francisco and publicity in the national media when it opened in April 1996, and it brought in droves of new library users.

The New Main also generated criticism that the local and national press picked up and that went much further than the building per se. Some San Francisco librarians and critics in the community leveled a variety of charges: the New Main's design wasted space and crowded out books; the Library Foundation was a closed corporation overly involved with both local business interests and library administration; the creation of the special collections indulged special interests at the expense of genuine space and user needs; attaching donors' names to sections of the library smacked of commercialism; the library was hostage to new technology; prior to the move thousands of books had been carelessly discarded; and the card catalog, replaced by an online version, was to be scrapped. Library officials denied these claims either as erroneous or as evidence of backward thinking and unrepresentative of the popular will, and they justified their actions as prudent and progressive management. The various issues coalesced into a cause célèbre in San Francisco and then beyond, thanks to an article in the *New Yorker* by the writer Nicholson Baker, a Berkeley resident and critic of online catalogs who became enmeshed in the affair. In January 1997, in the wake of a considerable operating budget shortfall, the library director was forced to resign, less than a year after the New Main's triumphant opening.[56]

The San Francisco situation can be seen as a conjuncture of feisty Bay Area politics, inadequate damage control by the library administration, and general trends in librarianship—automation, private fundraising, attention to multiculturalism and current community interests, and the construction of monumental new buildings equipped with the latest information technologies. Some of the criticisms suggest a certain nostalgia for an irretrievable past of politics, economics, and technology different from today's, and others reflect internal library conflicts and management-union relations in San Francisco. But serious ethical concerns not unique to San Francisco were raised, and the intense public discussion displayed a community interest in the library and its mission from which those worrying about the institution's marginality or imminent demise might take heart.

Issues of Equity

Among the broader policy issues touched on in the San Francisco controversy, and one filled with fiscal and ideological implications, was the assessment of fees for certain services (a practice that has grown significantly in the independent nonprofit sector in recent years[57]). As we observed earlier, library ideology, as expressed in the Library Bill of Rights and its interpretations and adopted by the American Library Association, avows the principle of free and equal access to all in a double sense—free of charge and free of censorship—and with no discrimination based on type of material or information. Traditionally, the few exceptions to services without direct charge—for example, for reserving books or borrowing from duplicate collections of current popular titles—involved nominal payments not seen as really inhibiting full library use. Later, photocopying charges could be justified by the argument that photocopying is fairly inexpensive and optional, a convenient substitute for manual copying of the library materials that anyone could freely use.

The newer technologies, however, are more costly to libraries and are not merely mechanical devices; they involve the quality and extent of access to collections and information. Some librarians remain committed to the principle of free access to everything. One prominent library leader declared that if a choice had to be made between providing a library service and charging for that service, it should not be offered. Others feel obliged to take pragmatic stances as they try to provide videotape and audio collections, CD-ROM services, fax document delivery, and computer printers, all often without commensurate increases in budgets or with budget cutbacks. More problematic are payments for electronic access to databases (many of the most important are still available only through payment of fees to vendors). The PLA "Public Library Finance Survey" for 1993 showed 73 percent of the respondents reporting income from fees (including "e.g., online searching, fax, reserves, nonresident cards"), as distinguished from fines, received by 86 percent, and income from vending machines (including photocopying), 86.6 percent.[58]

Most problematic is the imposition of fees for lengthy customized searches for corporate or individual clients, called value-added services, that go well beyond standard or basic information service. The Minneapolis Public Library has had a fee-based information service for some twenty-five years, Tulsa has had one since 1975, and fee-based information services have been more recently offered at the County of Los Angeles Public Library, the New York Public Library's Science, Industry and Business Library, and the Cleveland Public Library, among others. A 1996 PLA "Business Services Survey" found that nearly half of the responding libraries (predominantly the larger ones) offered information retrieval and search services for business topics; a third of the libraries doing so charged a fee. Among the latter were a number of prominent municipal and county institutions all over the country (including, in addition to those named above, the libraries of Boston, Charlotte and Mecklenburg County, Chicago, Dallas, Detroit, Houston, Indianapolis and Marion County, Jacksonville, the city of Los Angeles, Philadelphia, Pittsburgh, and Phoenix). Those that did not charge (in some cases possibly because of legal restrictions but in many no doubt on principle) included the libraries of Baltimore County, Brooklyn, Denver, Hennepin County (Minnesota), King County, Las Vegas and Clark County, Memphis and Shelby County, Newark (New Jersey), San Antonio, and Seattle.[59]

What is involved here is a new concept of equity of access, based on ability to pay for convenience or special services or both. Eleanor Jo Rodger, president of the Urban Libraries Council, has publicly advocated reconsideration of the fee issue in face of libraries' fiscal pressures, as did William Bowen, president of the Mellon Foundation, in a speech to world library leaders on "Funding the Global Library."[60] The 1995 California Joint Task Force report recommended that while fees could provide only a small proportion of libraries' income and were no substitute for stable public revenues, local libraries should "have the authority and ability to charge for services above the basic level . . . for entrepreneurial and convenience services." The following year an extensive California State Library report, *Entering the 21st Century: California's Public Libraries Face the Future,* recommended value-added fee-based services as one alternative funding source.[61]

This position is predicated on a continued scarcity of funds and the necessity therefore to use librarians' expertise to generate new monies and to enhance the library's importance in society as well. Offering fee-based services also enables libraries more fully to utilize for the community's benefit their resources and their staff's skills in ways that their budgets could not otherwise support. There are also economists who argue that since public libraries are used mainly by the middle class but taxation falls disproportionately more heavily on the lower class, library user fees are justified.[62] But the statistics on which such a conclusion is based indicate central tendencies, not every user's economic class, and libraries deal primarily with individuals. How then to treat the person who might need or want "value-added" service but can't afford the fees? Will there be a means test? Or will convenience be only for the well heeled and well established? Young people generally do not have very much spending money, and neither do low-income, less educated people, and some rural dwellers, all of whom tend also to have much less access to digital information and computers (and even telephones) than other groups.[63] The danger arises that the public library may abandon its traditional raison d'être—openness to all on an equal basis—and instead establish a class system mirroring and perpetuating societal inequalities, possibly even be sliding down the slippery slope of privatization.

In "Economic Barriers to Information Access," a 1993 interpretation of the Library Bill of Rights, the Council of the American Library Association acknowledged these concerns in affirming the public library's "essential mission" of providing "free and equal access to information for all people of the community the library serves," a mission that "must remain the first consideration for librarians and governing bodies faced with economic pressures and competition for funding." The statement declared that the ALA "opposes the charging of user fees for the provision of information by all libraries and information resources that receive their major support from public funds. All information resources that are provided directly or indirectly by the library, regardless of technology, format, or methods of delivery, should be readily, equally, and equitably accessible to all library users." Librarians were urged to "resist the temptation to impose user fees to alleviate financial pressures, at long-term cost to institutional integrity and public confidence in libraries" and find other ways to manage with inadequate budgets.[64] An interpretation relating specifically to electronic information and services, adopted in 1996, opposed user fees for information services provided by "all libraries and information services that receive their major support from public funds."[65] A draft of a subsequent explicatory document, obviously conceding the realities in the field, asserted that "whenever possible, all services should be without fees" but that "the higher priority is fee free service."[66]

At the same time the library profession has been promoting public libraries as prime community sites for free and equal citizen participation in the information age—a campaign that has begun to pay off in private philanthropy. Donors on a national scale are responding to the appeal of the concept of libraries as equalizing agencies.

The most spectacular reaction is that of William H. Gates III, chair and CEO of the Microsoft Corporation. Working with the ALA, the Microsoft Corporation began in late 1995 Libraries Online—a program to equip selected public libraries in inner cities and rural areas across the United States and Canada with computers, software, and technical support. In launching Libraries Online, his company's first large-scale philanthropic project, Gates, was, in the *New York Times*'s words, "taking a page from Andrew Carnegie's drive to help build public libraries across America during the age of steel [by helping to] connect some of those libraries to the information age."[67] In New York City, Microsoft's commitment in 1996 of $2.2 million dollars to the needy Brooklyn Public Library, announced at the library with much hoopla and by Gates himself, stimulated $5.5 million in additional contributions from the city and borough for wiring all fifty-eight branches.[68] Soon thereafter, on the occasion of his gift of cash, hardware, software, and technical support worth $1.1 million to the Los Angeles Public Library and the Los Angeles County School System in November 1996, Gates said, "Through our projects in schools and libraries around the country, we're seeing the power of technology to help people of all ages and backgrounds, particularly young people."[69]

In June 1997, on the basis of successful experience with community use of Libraries Online donations, Gates and his wife Melinda French Gates announced that they were creating the Gates Library Foundation, "dedicated to partnering with U.S. and Canadian public libraries to bring computers and digital information to the communities they serve." The foundation, which includes on its board Vartan Gregorian, president of the Carnegie Corporation and former president of Brown University and the New York Public Library, plans initially to spend $400 million over five years. Half this amount would be given in cash; the other half, in software. It is to be used in two ways—(1) to help libraries in the United States and Canada, with emphasis on those in low-income areas with the least access to information technology, acquire computers and provide Internet access and (2) to train and support library professionals in the use and management of digital information. Configurations of hardware and software will differ depending on need, but all computers received under the program will provide CD-ROM educational multimedia, basic word processing and spreadsheet applications, and access to the Internet. The foundation intends to supply ongoing technical assistance and training and to work with library systems, the library profession, and library supporters "to create the conditions that will build long-term sustainability into the project."[70] The first grant guidelines target high poverty states and communities; public libraries in Alabama are the first statewide beneficiaries of the project.

The new Gates fund, which the foundation president and board chair, former Microsoft executive Patty Stonesifer, sees as "catalyst and seed money," constitutes the largest single gift to American public libraries since Carnegie's and is expected to have a considerable impact on public access to technology in libraries throughout the country. (Translated into today's prices, Carnegie's aggregate gift amounts, in one economist's estimation, to almost twice as much as Gates's; more significantly, its share of the gross national product of Carnegie's day is twenty-seven times that of Gates's in 1997. An ALA estimate calculates the dollar value of Carnegie's gift as roughly 21 percent higher than Gates's in today's terms, and 18 percent higher if Gates's previous Libraries Online donation is included.[71])

Announcing the formation of the foundation, Melinda Gates said, "Our public libraries represent free and open access to information and knowledge. Bill and I are excited to be helping libraries ensure that children and adults from all walks of life will have access to the wealth of information and understanding that computers and digital information make possible." And the foundation's background statement concludes: "America's and Canada's public libraries are arriving at a critical point in their evolution. Beloved for free and egalitarian services, libraries find themselves challenged by diminishing budget dollars and their patrons' demand for increased access to digital information and resources. It is the dedicated goal of the Gates Library Foundation to work with libraries and community partners as a catalyst for practical and positive change as we enter a new century."[72]

Several years earlier Microsoft's chief rival at the time, Apple Computer, Inc., started Apple Library of Tomorrow (administered by Steve Cisler, a former public librarian) to support innovative research and demonstration projects in all types of libraries with donations of equipment and software produced by Apple and third-party manufacturers and publishers. (This project was discontinued in the fall of 1997 when Apple, in financial trouble, closed its library and reorganized its parent unit, the Advanced Technology Group, and Cisler left the company.) MCI is financing MCI LibraryLINK, a three-year partnership (running from 1995 through 1998) with the American Library Association to help selected public libraries advance their technological capabilities. The LibraryLINK Internet home page states that "over 40% of all Internet traffic in the U.S. is carried by MCI, which has the fastest commercial Internet backbone in the world."[73] More recently, regional Bell phone companies have begun to fund Internet access at public libraries through grants for equipment and training.

Questions arise not only about the dependability of corporate gift programs (given the Apple case), but whether there is an element of self-serving combined with a sense of social responsibility in this giving by interested parties. Bill Gates is quoted in answer to doubts about his motives: "Obviously, I'm somebody who believes that personal computers are empowering tools. People are entitled to disagree, but I would invite them to visit some of these libraries and see the impact on kids using this technology." In another interview he points out that the actual cash gifts ($200 million) were not for software. The second half of his library foundation's program did involve a direct gift of Microsoft software to the "library market," but anyone else was welcome to do the same, he said. "Clearly, this is a philanthropic gesture. Yes, I'm making it easier for libraries to get Microsoft software that is really standard software. That we're saying we're going to administer this program and give our software and help libraries buy the other things they need to link to the net—with no revenue going to Microsoft—is hard to criticize."[74] So far the issue does not seem to have caused special problems for libraries, which generally have not been loath to accept gifts from telecommunications and computer-related corporations for technology and electronic services.

A further aspect of equal access, and one also linked to library finances, is that of jurisdictional barriers to public services. This is an old issue that new technology can both obviate and aggravate. Libraries probably more than other street-level public institutions have worked to overcome institutional parochialism and promote equitable service through cooperative systems and arrangements. One might even say that they have been in the avant-garde of regionalism. Still, jurisdictional lines and fiscal boundaries are persistent realities, considering this country's anachronistic atomistic jurisdictional and tax structures, city-suburb antagonisms, and attachments to home rule, all in face of metropolitan and regional economies and lifestyles and the digitization of knowledge. Architect and urban historian Witold Rybczynski, likening the contemporary American city to the open cities and towns of the ancient world, comments, "The physical distinction between the city and its surrounding territory—that is, between central cities and suburbs—is blurred; the legal definition of the city remains, but the reality of metropolitan life has become mobile and decentralized."[75]

Public libraries, voluntary and open, can be frequented but not necessarily fully used by anyone. This is a problem that regionalists like Joeckel discussed in the 1930s, but it has been exacerbated by the economic and demographic growth of the late twentieth century. Given the prevalent American metropolitan milieu, many people might well be closer to a library outside than inside their city or town or county or state line and willing to drive to any library, near or far, that might have what they want, whether their taxes support it or whether they have any representation on its board. But in a world where jurisdictional lines still exist, where financial support is based on them, and where levels of such support are unequal or derive from different sources, how much free assistance—uncompensated or minimally compensated lending of materials or extensive information service or help with computers or use of the Internet—will any one community be willing to offer? This can be an acute question when disparities between adjacent communities are wide: equal access is a professional ideal, but inequity in library resources and funding is a fact. In some states or regions pragmatic solutions have been devised, such as issuing universal or reciprocal library cards or creating electronic information networks to help bridge gaps. Some arrangements involve reimbursement for net lending to nonresidents but do not necessarily cover the full costs. Fees for nonresident use or restrictions on such use, imposed by boards or local officials and not necessarily favored by librarians, are still to be found, and some libraries are restricting access to the Internet, their online catalogs, or their online information query systems to local library card holders or residents.

Part of the sometime tension between central city libraries and surrounding independent libraries (which in some places no doubt mirrors traditional city-suburb friction) derives from basic institutional differences. Individual suburban libraries, many of them heavily used, tend not to have very large collections and to focus on popular materials. County systems, some comprising millions of physical volumes but representing many fewer separate titles, may have important special collections but often not the central all-around collections and the many specialist librarians that city libraries, some of them not heavily used any more, may have. Conversely, residents of a central city may find it more convenient to frequent a nearby suburban library, which may have a more up-to-date popular collection and a more attractive building in nicer surroundings than the city's library branches.

A number of older central city libraries contain the most substantial fully public collections and information resources in their region. This is true to a degree, for example, of the Seattle Public Library, which has a reciprocal free-use arrangement with the surrounding King County Library. The county system, with its larger revenues, more service units, and a larger population area than Seattle's, has been attempting to strengthen its collections by retaining and replacing more items and acquiring more current materials in depth—that is, more individual titles and fewer copies. Its new Bellevue Regional Library is especially strong in business and government materials.

It is hard, however, for any recently developed library to duplicate the retrospective collections built up in older institutions over many years, in some as much as a century or more. Nor would it be particularly wise, as much of that material is not frequently called for and would not in any case be readily available on the market. This means, though, that unless special arrangements are made among particular libraries or by the state, people from outside the city may be using expensive collections—both new and old—and calling on reference services that they as taxpayers do not pay for. For example, in New Jersey, Newark Public Library's central library attracts approximately a quarter of its users from outside the city, which is surrounded by suburbs with their own public libraries. Some of the latter are quite good but not comparable to the historically strong collection in Newark, which has had a low tax base and few sources of private contributions. A New Jersey State Library technology plan for the state's libraries, announced in 1996, declares that "special needs of urban libraries will be addressed," but in its first articulation the plan did not spell this out.[76] Some states handle inequities in resources through regional systems that subsidize access to large central libraries or special collections, but the picture is variegated. And when there has been recognition by a state of the problem in regard to a particular library, tensions may crop up when money is tight. Boston Public Library, because of its status as the major public research collection in New England, receives special state funding, but that is not always appreciated by other public libraries in Massachusetts.

As far as current information sources are concerned (and some older ones as well), fast-moving technology may somewhat relieve problems of inequitable holdings among libraries as more and more materials go digital and are not site specific. But questions of cost and eligibility will not go away, and the American Library Association stances on fee versus free access do not really address this issue. Who will pay for what in a world in which library and information resources will be available through tele-communications, which theoretically has no boundaries? Libraries' funding base is so far still essentially local and geographical; information sources today can transcend geography. A number of libraries already have World Wide Web sites, and the proportion of American public libraries reporting to the 1996 NCLIS survey some kind of Internet connection had risen in 1996 to 44.6 percent, up from 20.9 percent in 1994. Although there were regional disparities in overall figures, nearly every public library with a legal population area of a hundred thousand or more had an Internet connection. The 1997 follow-up study showed that 72.3 percent of all public libraries surveyed (all sizes) were connected to the Internet, a considerable increase over 1996 but with higher figures for denser population areas and for urban as compared with rural libraries. Internet access was offered in 1997 directly to the public at 60.4 percent of all libraries, compared with 27.8 percent the year before. It was predicted that both connectivity and public access to the Internet would rise to the point where by 1998 almost the entire United States population would have such access in a library, again with the exceptions in rural areas.[77]

So far few public libraries levy charges for their public-access Internet services. But provision of these services is not expense free, and libraries reporting no connectivity to the Internet in the 1996 NCLIS survey, more often the smaller ones, identified cost factors as barriers to such connectivity. This is a situation that was found in the 1997 survey as well and one that the discounts for telecommunications and Internet access under the 1996 Telecommunications Act, along with state programs, were intended to help remedy. If as expected, in the near term a good deal of use of multimedia computers and help with that use will take place in public libraries or through connections with public libraries, there is the matter of eligibility for such services, if they are funded mainly by local jurisdictions. Furthermore, when libraries, receive, as many now do, e-mail queries from all over the world and their holdings are displayed on the Internet and therefore open to interlibrary loan or transmission through the mails, photocopy, or fax request, they must consider who bears the cost. What are libraries' professional and fiscal responsibilities to such remote users, and will there be a scale of service priorities? Generally, public libraries restrict unlimited loan of their books and other "physical" materials to eligible users; if they mount document texts or databases online and make them freely accessible, almost anyone anywhere can view them, download them, or print them out, at no charge. The scale of such use is potentially much greater than that of noncardholders who physically visit the library and see materials on site. One wonders whether local boards of trustees or government officials will question this "free" service. And, depending on future copyright laws and decisions, national and international, there may be in the future additional costs, in the form of license or other fees involving the use of intellectual property in digital form. These issues go beyond those of local institutional divisions and turf wars, and their implications are just beginning to be felt and debated.

The dichotomy between the public library as a geography-based institution with primarily local funding and much of its current information base increasingly in cyberspace emerged as a major theme of an interdisciplinary conference on "The Transformation of the Public Library: Access to Digital Information in a Networked World," held in late 1995 at the Library of Congress and sponsored by the library and five prominent library and information organizations, plus Harvard's John F. Kennedy School of Government. The problems were not resolved or fully explored in a one-day discussion. The nonlibrarian speakers heralded a new world of ubiquitous bits and bytes and a new economics, not yet in place, to pay for it. The librarians spoke more of their economic and political realities, their own evolving electronic offerings, and the need for collaborative action with other organizations. There seemed to be a general assumption, even among the computer types, that the book, a convenient, efficient artifact, would not disappear, that the library as institution would continue to exist, and that it retains important social functions as a community gathering place and symbol of democratic culture as well as navigator in an immense, ever-evolving, inchoate cyberspace. This was also the consensus of the "Summit of World Library Leaders," the meeting of chief executives of major world libraries convened at the New York Public Library in April 1996 (at which William Bowen spoke) to discuss "Global Library Strategies for the 21st Century." A point implied at both conferences was the value of public libraries as agencies serving the public interest in the dissemination and preservation of information and knowledge as opposed to serving private interests and market values.

Another dichotomy, one rarely discussed openly but not unimportant, was raised in a report issued in November 1996 by the Benton Foundation and financed by the Kellogg Foundation, *Buildings, Books, and Bytes: Libraries and Communities in the Digital Age.* The report, which has been widely discussed in the library community, essentially summarized and commented on three sources of information—the results of a national public opinion sample survey, the views of leaders of eighteen recipients of Kellogg Foundation Human Resources for Information Systems Management grants, and a single focus group of eleven white male and female library users, residents of one affluent Washington, DC, suburb. The grantees included information-related organizations, four library and information schools, the Urban Libraries Council, the American Library Association, and two atypical libraries, the Library of Congress and the New York Public Library. The report endorsed the vision promulgated by the "library leaders" (that is, the grantees): the public library as a cyberspace yet real space, traditional yet innovative information agency. In their written vision statements the "leaders" strongly favored the library's role as an "information safety net" for "information have-nots" (read the poor and foreign born). Private phone interviews with the "leaders," however, turned up reservations that an excessive or exclusive focus on that role might marginalize the library and vitiate its political support among the middle class (and, one might say, by implication categorize it as a welfare or social-service organization and thereby threaten its government funding in an antiwelfare climate). How representative or deep these reservations are is not clear. We ourselves can say, possibly at the risk of naiveté, that our visits to libraries, discussions with many librarians, and perusal of their programs, publications, and Web sites indicate continued commitment, however difficult and even problematic, in the field to broad democratic service.

3

The National Perspective: The Federal Role in Library Development

In the popular view the public library is perceived as a ubiquitous feature of the local landscape, but for almost a century leaders of the library profession have shown considerable interest in making their presence known on the national scene. The stimulation of what they themselves have called "the federal role" has been a frequent topic of discussion not only at library conferences but also in the library press. In fact, so much attention has been given to the issue that some observers might say that the leadership of the profession as well as that of the American Library Association has been not merely concerned with the federal role but instead has been obsessed by it. In referring to a federal role, librarians do not necessarily include such governmental benefits as the exemption of libraries from taxation. What they mean is the direct intervention of the federal government in local institutional support. An early precursor of this idea was the endorsement by the Council of the American Library Association (ALA) in 1919 and again in 1921 of a congressional bill, which, although not enacted, would have created a federal Department of Education and made available funds to decrease illiteracy among school children and to extend public library services in support of education. The real momentum behind the rhetoric of a "federal role" in support of the nation's public libraries occurred, however, when the ALA published its first national plan for libraries in 1935. Acknowledging that some ten thousand libraries of all types were then operational in the United States, the plan's drafters found little coordination among them. What was needed was a "proposed library system," fostering greater cooperation among libraries dedicated to the support of research and scholarship and a greater scrutiny of the inequities of tax support, especially for those libraries serving the general public and the public schools. Explicit in the plan was a call for federal aid as an essential component in compensating for tax inequities among the states.

Throughout this chapter there are many references to the American Library Association, which has served and continues to serve as the principal policy actor eliciting federal support for libraries. It would be misleading, however, to leave the impression that the Association is a bureaucratic integer, the employees of which are to be credited with the creation of national policies toward libraries. The ALA is a membership organization, and its important committees, such as the Committee on Legislation or the Intellectual Freedom Committee, have from their inception been primarily composed of practicing librarians or library school educators. Both the Council of the Association (a legislative body drawn from its membership) and also its Executive Board (a smaller group including the ALA officers and eight Councilors) oversee the Association's policies, often generated by its committees, and exert responsibility for the adoption of resolutions and position papers on matters relevant to the profession. This is not to say that the staff of the Association's Chicago headquarters and particularly the lobbyists in its Washington office have not been influential in the pursuit of library goals or in the fashioning of governmental policy positions. Indeed, they have, but their efforts must be understood within a more inclusive framework, embracing, over time, the ideas and conceptualizations of many hundreds of librarians who serve on the various committees and bodies that comprise the ALA. In this sense, the references made here to the Association are intended not to suggest that it is a monolith but rather to delineate its role as a focal point for professional concerns that often fluctuate to meet the dictates of changing situations and changing times. In this regard, what follows represents the thinking of the library profession concerning the role of federal aid that the Association's staff often articulates but does not necessarily initiate.

Throughout the 1930s, a number of reports and documents enunciating the need for federal library aid were published. Conservatives in the library community expressed alarm, however, that the receipt of federal tax support would be tantamount to the acceptance of government control. A petition ominously entitled, "Do You Want Federal Supervision?" sent chills of apprehension among librarians fearing federal interference in the selection of books and other materials, and in 1935 one-fifth of the personal membership of the American Library Association appealed to its Council to rescind its previous year's endorsement of federal aid for public libraries. Nonetheless, the largess of the coffers of the alphabet relief agencies, brought into being during Franklin Roosevelt's administration, was sufficient enough to influence the leadership of the library profession, and it moved slowly but inexorably to endorse some form of federal aid for the nation's public libraries. The 1930s was a particularly apt time for the library profession to institute a campaign for federal aid. In that decade, the national government assumed a major share of responsibility for public welfare, entered the housing field, and supported public works of many kinds at local levels of government. Political scientists and academicians were then beginning to write of a "new federalism" that represented a sharing of responsibility between the nation and its states and localities rather than a division of responsibility, the so-called dual federalism between nation and state that had prevailed in earlier periods of American history.[1]

A concise statement of the need for federal intervention in the local conduct of libraries, *Library Service*, was issued in 1938 as a separately published staff study for President Roosevelt's Advisory Committee on Education. Written by Carleton Joeckel, the 107-page report assessed current trends in the support of the major types of libraries in the United States—academic, school, and public. Specific recommendations were made for strengthening their services and collections, in part through a program of federal grants in aid. Particular focus was given to the public library, characterized by Joeckel as "the most distinctive American contribution to the world pattern of library development." Although conceding the high standard of public library service evident in states with well-supported municipal libraries, Joeckel demonstrated the gross inequity afforded people living in parts of the country where no public libraries existed or those resident in areas where the services provided were of inferior quality. Among the numerous disparities in the provision of public library services among the various states, he noted that public library expenditures per capita ranged from $1.08 in Massachusetts to $.02 in Arkansas and Mississippi and that per capita circulation of library materials ranged from 9.14 in California to .36 in Mississippi. Pointing to the total absence of public libraries in areas of the nation serving 40 million rural people, a number representing 74 percent of the total rural population of 54 million, Joeckel found that "the problem of providing complete public library service is essentially a rural problem."[2]

Joeckel, who served during this period as the principal architect of the ALA's drive toward the establishment of a federal role, did not limit his concerns only to rural America. Instead, he laid out a broad list of desiderata, encompassing the establishment of regional centers for library service in a general program of coordination of library resources on a regional and national scale, the assurance of a nationwide minimum of library service through federal grants to public and school libraries and those in the system of public higher education, and the provision of federal support for library buildings in support of American public education. Joeckel's memorandum was written at a time when national socioeconomic planning was reaching an apogee. Indeed, the issuance in 1935 of the first national plan for libraries was a direct result of the national ferment for the concept of a planned society.

National Socioeconomic Planning

The complex origins of the national movement toward socioeconomic planning stem in part from earlier reforms of the Progressive Era. City planning, exemplified in 1909 by Daniel Burnham's successful plan for Chicago, became increasingly professionalized, producing its own journals and sponsoring national conferences devoted to the topic. Academic recognition of city planning as a specialized field of study came in 1929 when Harvard University established a School of City Planning, the same year in which the first volume of the *Regional Plan of New York and Its Environs* was published. The rationalization of industry, with its emphasis on research and development, brought about by the work of Pennsylvania engineer Frederick W. Taylor, also had its effect on the public sector, and a new cadre of city managers—professional administrators appointed to their offices in contrast to mayors who were elected—was recruited to manage municipal governments. Although the city management form of government was instituted in 1908, it did not attract national attention until Dayton, Ohio, voted for the practice in 1914; by 1930, some four hundred municipalities were to adopt it. Also accelerating the movement toward national planning was the furtherance of surveys of governmental services, based on the empirical research of social scientists and increasingly buttressed by statistical data. The proliferation of these social surveys is evidenced by the extensive bibliography of almost three thousand surveys—in such fields as child welfare, the aged, education, delinquency, and health care—published by the Russell Sage Foundation in 1930. Also linking the social scientists and the government was the creation of research bureaus devoted to issues of public administration. The first of these to be housed in a municipal government was the New York Bureau of Municipal Research, established in 1906; some three years later the Municipal Research Bureau at the University of Wisconsin became the first to be formed in an American university.

Although causal relations among these rather disparate events are not easily demonstrated, they nonetheless served in the aggregate as harbingers of the socioeconomic planning ethos, linking the previous distinctive spheres of industry and government through the clearly articulated concerns of both public- and private-sector managers to achieve a greater sense of direction in the conduct of national and civic affairs. The chaos attendant on the Great Depression only intensified the need for national planning, and a locus for this activity was found in the federal government when President Roosevelt created the National Resources Planning Board. From 1933 to 1943, this board, under four distinctive titles, existed as the planning and research arm of the federal government. Largely through Joeckel's efforts, members of the planning board staff became interested in the public library movement and granted funds to underwrite the first major set of public library standards, *Post-War Standards for Public Libraries*, issued by the ALA in 1943 but with the name of the National Resources Planning Board prominently displayed on the document itself. Based on exemplary library service in American communities, the standards were qualitative or quantitative measures for evaluating the adequacy and efficiency of public libraries. Included were standards specifying appropriate numbers of library personnel, the recommended size and scope of the book collection, and costs for the building of library facilities.

Joeckel's approach toward the development of a systemic plan for total library service, characteristic of the trend toward rational planning generic to the period, was less enthusiastically received by other members of the ALA leadership. Influenced by the efforts of Carl H. Milam, the Association's powerful executive secretary, an incremental approach in the shaping of the national policy agenda was substituted that relied heavily on the achievement of one specific objective—a federal subvention to establish public libraries in rural America. In 1946, a modest program to achieve this goal, the Public Library Service Demonstration Bill, was introduced in both houses of Congress. Revised in 1951 and renamed the Library Services Act, the legislation finally achieved enough votes to secure congressional passage in 1956 and was signed into law somewhat reluctantly by President Eisenhower on June 19 of that year. The Republican administration was leery, then as now, of adding to the number of grant-in-aid programs to assist in matters better left to the concerns of state and local governments. The legislation initially subsidized public library services in localities having less than ten thousand inhabitants, and the federal funds were administered by the state library agency, which either was located in various offices of state government, including in a number of cases the state department of education, or was independently established as a board or commission, usually appointed by the governor. In some states, the state library agency emerged from the state legislative reference library, while in others it was an outgrowth of a political entity that originated in 1890 in Massachusetts, the first state to form a library commission designed to further the cause of public libraries beyond the municipality.

The Library Services Act was authorized for a five-year period beginning with fiscal year 1957, and President Eisenhower's message concerning the bill made it clear that at the close of this period the program would be continued by local and state efforts but not by the federal government. The enactment was a classic example of a categorical grant, which allows funds to be expended only for a specific and sometimes narrowly defined purpose. Appropriations under such a program are often based on a formula, which in the case of the Library Services Act was based on the size of the rural population in each state compared to the rural population of the nation as a whole. In addition, a basic allotment of $40,000 was made to each state in an effort to ensure at least a modicum of federal aid in sparsely populated states. (See table 2 for the legislative chronology of the federal public library enactments, 1956 to 1997.)

Table 2
Federal Aid for Public Libraries: Legislative Chronology, 1956 to 1997

Date	Legislative Event
6-19-56	P.L. 84-597. Library Services Act (LSA). Provided federal aid for public library services solely in rural areas.
8-1-56	P.L. 84-896. Added Guam to the list of Territories.
8-31-60	P.L. 86-679. LSA reauthorized for five years.
9-25-62	P.L. 87-688. Added American Samoa.
2-11-64	P.L. 88-269. Abolished rural restriction and made urban areas eligible. Added Title II, Construction. Program extended to the District of Columbia. Enactment now cited as Library Services and Construction Act (LSCA).
7-19-66	P.L. 89-511. Library Services and Construction Act Amendments of 1966. Reauthorized LSCA for five years. Added Title III, Interlibrary Cooperation; Title IVA, State Institutional Library Services; and Title IVB, Library Services to the Physically Handicapped. Added the Trust Territory of the Pacific Islands.
11-24-67	P.L. 90-154. Technical amendments. Permitted acquisition of existing buildings for public library use as eligible expenditure under Title II.
12-30-70	P.L. 91-600. Library Services and Construction Act Amendments of 1970. Reauthorized LSCA for five years. Consolidated Titles I, IVA,and IVB. Emphasized services to low-income families, provided for strengthening state library administrative agencies and metropolitan libraries that served as regional or national resources. Removed the matching requirement for Title III.
5-3-73	P.L. 93-29. Older Americans Comprehensive Services Amendments of 1973. Added a new LSCA Title IV, Older Readers Services, which was never funded.
10-19-73	P.L. 93-133. National Foundation on the Arts and the Humanities Amendments of 1973. Amended LSCA by redefining the term *public library* to include research libraries meeting certain criteria.
8-21-74	P.L. 93-380. Education Amendments of 1974. Amended LSCA by adding program priority for service to areas of high concentrations of persons with limited English-speaking ability.
10-7-77	P.L. 95-123. Library Services and Construction Act Amendments of 1977. Reauthorized LSCA for five years. Added emphasis on strengthening major urban resource libraries.
8-13-81	P.L. 97-35. Omnibus Budget Reconciliation Act of 1981. Reauthorized LSCA, Titles I and III, through fiscal year 1984.
3-24-83	P.L. 98-8. Emergency Jobs Appropriations Act. Made available $50 million for public library construction.

10-17-84   P.L. 98-480. Library Services and Construction Act Amendments of 1984. Reauthorized LSCA for five years. Added three new titles— Title IV, Library Services for Indian Tribes; Title V, Foreign Language Materials Acquisition; and Title VI, Library Literacy Programs. Added Northern Mariana Islands.

11-22-85   P.L. 99-159. National Science, Engineering, and Mathematics Authorization Act of 1986. Amended LSCA, Title III.

10-31-88   P.L. 100-569. Reauthorized LSCA, Titles V and VI through fiscal year 1989.

3-15-90   P.L. 101-254. Library Services and Construction Act Amendments of 1990. LSCA reauthorized for five years. Increased emphasis on technology within the framework of Titles I, II, and III. Created a new Title VII for evaluation of LSCA and a new Title VIII, Library Learning Center Program.

7-25-91   P.L. 102-73. Changed title of the Trust Territory of the Pacific Islands to the Republic of Palau.

10-20-94   P.L. 103-382. Improving America's Schools Act. Reauthorized LSCA for one year.

9-30-96   P.L. 104-208. Omnibus Consolidated Appropriations Act, 1997. Title VII, Section 101(e), Museum and Library Services Act of 1996. Amended the Museum Services Act and other acts to establish an Institute of Museum and Library Services, consisting of an Office of Museum Services and an Office of Library Services, and to provide for federal grants to states for library programs and to museums for improving their service. Subtitle B of the Museum and Library Services Act is cited as the Library Services and Technology Act.

12-1-97   P.L. 105-128. Museum and Library Services Technical and Conforming Amendments of 1997.

Sources: Office of Educational Research and Improvement, U.S. Department of Education; various issues of the *ALA Washington Newsletter; United States Code Annotated,* 1997 Popular Name Table (Library Services and Construction Act; Library Services and Technology Act).

During the twenty-year trajectory that occurred between the ideation of the rural aid program in the 1930s and its actual enactment, the whole course of American demographics had begun to show major change. The one-third of the population living during the 1930s in rural and farm communities who were unserved by a local public library was gradually diminishing as large numbers of families moved closer to urban areas, where there was greater proximity to public libraries under municipal auspices. As a consequence, the first major amendments to the legislation, enacted in 1964, abolished the rural restriction and permitted each state library agency to expend funds throughout its state. The basic federal floor allocating the sum of $40,000 to each state, regardless of population size, was increased to $100,000, and, in addition, a separate title was added for public library construction, a major innovation since the Carnegie building program had ceased in 1917. In endorsing the continuance of a federal role, at least one senator perceived the new dimensions of the information age:

We are living in a complex and rapidly changing age. It is an age built upon the creation, the collection, and the rapid dissemination of accurate information. At the very heart of this communications chain stands the American free public library which collects and makes available books and other materials to all who have need of them. . . . On every single issue of major importance, our citizens turn to their public library. If they are to make intelligent choices and decisions in their daily lives, they must be provided with information which is pertinent, dependable, and up to date.[3]

The Library Services and Construction Act

Political scientists would classify the 1964 enactment, entitled the Library Services and Construction Act (LSCA), as "distributive legislation," defined as legislation that subsidizes services or goods believed to be of benefit to society as a whole. Examples of distributive legislation include the allowance of deductions for home mortgages and property taxes, grants for scientific research in universities, and grants to localities for the construction of such facilities as airports or hospitals.

In 1965, the year following the successful passage of the LSCA, three additional distributive legislative programs affecting library service were enacted. Title II of the Higher Education Act (HEA) allocated funds for the purchase of books for collegiate and university libraries, and Title II of the Elementary and Secondary Education Act (ESEA) made available funds for books and audiovisual materials to be used in the libraries of elementary and secondary schools. Spearheaded by public health officials in the Johnson administration, the third enactment was the Medical Library Assistance Act, which subsidized certain activities of the nation's medical library community in an effort to accelerate the dissemination of biomedical information. The addition of a library title to both the HEA and the ESEA was predominantly the work of the ALA, which endorsed the medical library program but did not originate it. Though Democratic leadership in the White House, including that of both President Kennedy and President Johnson, favored library legislation, the erosion of fiscal support became noticeable toward the close of Johnson's administration, when the escalating costs of the war in Vietnam coupled with increases in uncontrollable expenditures, such as those for Social Security, caused a significant reduction in administration requests for federal library aid.

With the advent of President Nixon's administration, the tide turned against the continuation of categorical-aid programs, such as the Library Services and Construction Act. Nixon had run on a plank espousing revenue sharing, which in contrast to categorical aid would redirect substantive amounts of federal tax dollars to assist state and local governments in pursuing priorities largely of their own devising. Godfather of this type of general purpose grant was economist Walter Heller, chair of the President's Council of Economic Advisers from 1961 to 1964, who attempted to define the new phenomenon:

A whole family of synonyms has been spawned by various observers to identify this form of assistance. Unrestricted, unencumbered, unconditional, general-assistance, untied, no-strings, and block grants are among the candidates for the christening if this blessed fiscal event should one day occur. My own choice is "revenue sharing."[4]

With the passage of the State and Local Fiscal Assistance Act in 1971, revenue sharing, extolled by one Republican Congressman as the "great Republican alternative to the Great Planned Society," was introduced to the nation. Nixon, of course, had no intention of launching a major revenue-sharing initiative while at the same time continuing all of the many categorical-aid programs then in existence, and in January 1973 the administration announced that its request for federal support for all types of libraries, academic, school, and public, would be zero in the fiscal year 1974 budget. The only library program to escape this threatened extinction was that supporting medical libraries, which had resulted, as has been noted, from measures recommended by federal public health officials and not solely from the American Library Association's lobbying efforts.

Consternation is the best way to describe the library community when the news of this budget cut was made known. Many state library agencies employed personnel who, although state employees, were paid entirely out of federal funds, and these positions would have to be transferred to state budgets or layoffs would ensue. Adding to the dilemma, the public library program had no particular following in the national house of education, then located in the Department of Health, Education, and Welfare. Whereas the programs assisting libraries in the nation's schools (ESEA Title II) and those in higher education (HEA Title II) were seen, at least in some ways, as supportive of the educative role of their respective institutions, the public library was perceived by many government bureaucrats as lying outside the educational mainstream, useful no doubt in some ways affecting reading and literacy, but tertiary to the Office of Education's primary concern, elementary and secondary schooling.

In hoping to target funds for special groups, such as the poor, the handicapped, racial and ethnic minorities, and other special-interest groups with higher priorities on the educationist's agenda, officials of the Office of Education put forth little effort to save the interests of the public library constituency. Consequently, the Nixon administration's budget request was accepted without challenge at the highest levels of the educational bureaucracy. The congressional leadership, however, which had sponsored the program as a bipartisan effort from its inception, took exception to the administration's recommendations for either no funding or very limited funding, and during the Nixon-Ford years Congress disregarded them by providing some funds for the public library program.

Although various amendments were added to the basic legislation throughout the LSCA's history, its primary thrust has been in three major categories. Title I of the law allowed almost unlimited latitude to the states to expend funds for services, consultancies, grants to local public libraries, books and materials, and indeed almost anything that could be construed under the rubric of public library service. Title II, the construction title, provided funding for new library buildings as well as the costs incurred in remodeling older ones. In the case of both Titles I and II, matching funds were required from the states. Title III, added in the 1966 amendments, was Interlibrary Cooperation, designed to encourage the sharing of resources not only through public library cooperatives but also with those that included libraries of other types, such as a university collection having reciprocal arrangements with a local public library or a school library linked to a public library. From 1970, Title III required no matching funds from the states. Although other titles, mandating such initiatives as services to the handicapped or programs promoting literacy, were added to the enactment, Titles I, II, and III received the bulk of the annual appropriation. From 1957, the first year in which funds were allocated, through 1997, appropriations for the Library Services Act and for all titles of its successor, the Library Services and Construction Act, totaled $2,995,278,500.

Interestingly, it was the Republican administrations of Presidents Nixon and Ford that first attempted to shift the emphasis of the Library Services and Construction Act from that of a distributive grant-in-aid program to that of a redistributive one. Redistributive legislation goes beyond the parameters of distributive legislation in that it seeks to reallocate wealth, property, rights, and resources among socioeconomic classes or ethnic or racial groups. The graduated income tax in which the more affluent pay a higher percentage of their income in taxes, the food stamp program, and affirmative action requirements affecting employment or school admission are all examples of legislation intended to redress some imbalance in the social and economic order. Whereas Democratic administrations had furthered federal support for public libraries under the rubric of the general welfare, the Nixon and Ford administrations proposed legislation to single out the poor and the underserved as the principal beneficiaries of the public library law. The Library Partnership Act, initiated during Nixon's presidency, would have supported grants to demonstrate innovative library services solely for the benefit of the economically disadvantaged, the institutionalized, and the physically challenged. Funding for this legislation was also recommended in the fiscal year 1976 budget of the Ford administration, but the Library Partnership Act was never enacted.

Fiscal Federalism and Public Libraries

The debate as to whether categorical aid or revenue sharing was the most appropriate vehicle to allocate federal dollars to state and local governments came to a head in 1976 as Congress considered the renewal of general revenue sharing. Signed by the President in October 1976, the renewal legislation included a significant mandate for the U.S. Advisory Commission on Intergovernmental Relations (ACIR) to undertake a thorough examination of the future of federalism, using the word *federalism* as synonymous with the phrase, *intergovernmental relations*, which signifies the political, administrative, and fiscal processes by which higher units of government share revenues and other resources with lower governmental units. Specifically, the study was intended to reveal the degree of federal involvement in the affairs of state and local governments and to determine the effectiveness of federal revenues. During the next four years, the ACIR wrestled with the problem, producing in the end an eleven-volume series of which seven volumes were case studies analyzing the dimensions of the federal role in addressing welfare, unemployment, elementary and secondary education, higher education, environmental protection, fire protection, and libraries.

Noting that federal library appropriations amounted to only $6 million in 1960, the ACIR report on libraries compared this figure to the $250 million library appropriation "spread to every portion of the nation and every type of jurisdiction" that was being made in 1980. Full credit for this dramatic increase was given by the ACIR to the American Library Association: "In the play 'Libraries Get Federal Aid,' the name at the top of the marquee should be the American Library Association. That is, the chief credit or the blame (depending on your point of view) for the establishment of a federal role in libraries lies with ALA."[5] In contrasting the influence of various policy actors in the seven cases undertaken for the study, the ACIR found that the most vivid instance of special-interest group initiative or entrepreneurship was that of the American Library Association, which excelled at classic coalition building. Identified by the ACIR as allies in the ALA's cause were other more specialized library associations, the education lobby, the farm organizations that had supported the Library Services Act for rural libraries, and the urban groups that contributed to the passage in 1977 of amendments to the Library Services and Construction Act that earmarked public libraries in major urban areas. In assessing ALA's role as instigator of federal legislation, the ACIR added this prescient comment:

In the years to come, when thoughtful historians reflect upon the last two decades, they will undoubtedly note the rise of special interests as one of the most significant variables in governmental and societal development. Surely these interests have had a profound impact upon the shape of policy and the institutional responses of government. Yet, the opposite causal pattern—the effect of policy and institutions upon the strength and proliferation of special interests—may prove to be even more notable, for while in the inception and development of some programs there has been a clear interest group role, in the birth and maturation of most newer special interests there has been a prior governmental policy or program.[6]

This assessment is particularly true of the American Library Association, which created and sustained a federal role in libraries through many congressional sessions and, since 1956, nine presidential administrations, five of which were either indifferent or diametrically opposed to its goals. Equally true, however, is the ACIR's prediction that in areas of newer special interests a prior governmental policy often already exists, forcing many interest groups to respond to ongoing federal priorities rather than to instigate them. Such is the case in the current delineation of the national information infrastructure, so far a somewhat imprecisely defined aggregate of governmental, industrial, commercial, and educational interests of which libraries and librarians are but a part. The positioning of the library profession in that infrastructure will be more fully discussed in chapter 4. It should be noted here, however, that librarians are staking out new claims for a continuing federal subvention based in part on their computer-based informational services rather than on their formerly perceived needs for books and buildings.

Although the ACIR concluded its work with the observation that the current network of intergovernmental relations had become dangerously overloaded and that any continuance of the tendency to "intergovernmentalize practically all domestic questions" should be firmly resisted, Congress continued to support the LSCA. Amendments to the law, extending the program for another five years, were signed by President Reagan in 1984, and President Bush signed the LSCA amendments of 1990. Both presidents, however, indicated their lack of enthusiasm for the continuation of the program by requesting either no funds or very limited funds to implement it. Not since the Nixon administration had a President proposed a zero budget for all library programs, but in its fiscal year 1983 budget the Reagan administration had recommended the elimination of all library programs, which either "have achieved their objectives or which are more appropriately the responsibilities of States, local governments, or private institutions."[7] In an additional action, the Reagan administration refused to release a portion of the federal funds for public libraries that had already been appropriated for expenditure in the fiscal year 1982 budget, an impoundment deemed illegal by the General Accounting Office and eventually revoked by the Reagan administration after ten states instituted a lawsuit in federal court for the release of the funds.

In a reprise of earlier Republican policies, both Reagan and Bush sought congressional endorsement of an administration-sponsored bill, the Library Services Improvement Act. Yet another example of redistributive legislation, the bill singled out people who were economically disadvantaged and people who had disabilities as the only beneficiaries of library aid. Like the Library Partnership Act of 1974, sponsored by the Nixon and Ford administrations, this latter-day measure was never seriously debated in Congress and was never enacted. The library profession, by this time inured to the animus of Republican administrations toward library legislation, looked to Congress and not to the executive branch for the continuance of any federal presence in the support of libraries.

Initially, the public library legislation addressed the issue of disparity among Americans owing to their geographic location, hence its emphasis on the lack of public libraries in rural America. Over time, new constituencies, new premises, and new requirements were identified, and by 1990, the Department of Education was tracking information for the Library Services and Construction Act in almost twenty legislated categories. Among the individual and institutional priorities identified were those who were economically disadvantaged, the elderly, people with disabilities, persons with limited proficiency in the English language, libraries serving major urban areas, community information referral centers, cooperative library networks, and several others. Somewhat overburdened by this proliferation of goals, the public library legislation began to resemble a worthy but rather creaky seagoing vessel encrusted with barnacles. The time seemed ripe to reconsider the dimensions and purpose of the Library Services and Construction Act.

In 1994 Senator Claiborne Pell (Democrat, Rhode Island) included a simple one-year extension of the law as an amendment to the reauthorization of the Elementary and Secondary Education Act. Then chair of the Education, Arts, and Humanities Subcommittee of the Senate Labor and Human Resources Committee, Pell began to plan for the process of reauthorizing the public library program by holding hearings in the spring of

1995. His agenda was put on hold, however, as senators from the new Republican majority assumed their seats after the November 8 elections in 1994. The chair of the Senate subcommittee was assumed by Senator James M. Jeffords (Republican, Vermont), while Senator Pell became its ranking minority member. The Washington sea change brought with it a number of proposals calling for substantial reductions in federal programs as a way to accommodate tax cuts. An advisory issued by the ALA Washington Office in January of 1995 warned librarians that all federal library programs were at risk:

In short, the entire federal role in support of libraries and information services could be severely damaged or wiped out in a rush to cut and eliminate government programs and services to downsize government. In a new "devolution" movement, some federal roles could be shifted to the states. However, governors have already expressed concern that they do not have the resources, nor are they likely to receive the resources from the federal level, to take on all these roles.[8]

The Library Services and Technology Act

In order to keep alive the federal presence in support of public libraries, task forces representing the American Library Association, the Urban Libraries Council, an organization representing the larger metropolitan libraries, and the Chief Officers of the State Library Agencies identified two major goals that they believed worthy of federal support—the improvement of information access through technology and the educational empowerment of those who still live outside the mainstream of quality library service. House and Senate versions of a successor bill to the LSCA, incorporating much of the work of the task forces, emerged in the 104th Congress, and a compromise version was enacted toward its close. The new legislation, now named the Library Services and Technology Act (LSTA), specifies two distinctive categories for the $150 million program that was to be authorized for fiscal year 1997 and continued by "such sums" as are needed for each of the years ending in 2002: (1) the establishment of electronic linkages among libraries, library consortia, career centers, and other service providers; and (2) the targeting of library and information services to those who have difficulty in using a library and to underserved urban and rural communities, including children from families living below the poverty line. In addition, the legislation, at the instigation of both Senators

Jeffords and Pell, transfers the administration of federal aid to public libraries from its historic locus, the Department of Education, to a newly created Institute of Museum and Library Services. At the same time, the legislation requires that the Department of Education initially receive the appropriated funds and then transfer them to the Institute. Through this maneuver, the Senate and House appropriations subcommittees dealing with labor, health and human services, and education will oversee LSTA appropriations.

The Institute is comprised of two entities—an Office of Museum Services and an Office of Library Services, the latter being responsible for approving state plans that will afford access to information by all people through "[s]tate, regional, national, and international electronic networks."[9] Funds for library programs under the LSTA are allocated as follows: grants to the state agencies (91.5 percent); national leadership competitive grants and contracts (4 percent), services for Indian tribes (1 1/2 percent), and an allowance for federal level administration of the program (capped at 3 percent). The 4 percent set aside for the national leadership program funds competitive grants for the education and training of personnel in library and information science, for research and demonstration projects in the areas of computer and communications technology and the preservation and digitization of library resources, and for model programs demonstrating cooperative activities between libraries and museums. The legislation authorizes the U.S. National Commission on Libraries and Information Science to serve in an advisory capacity to the Institute in the selection of the museum and library discretionary grants. Participation in the selection of the grantees of these funds represents a new responsibility for the National Commission, one that links it directly to the annual federal appropriation process supporting public libraries. The programmatic emphasis of this 4 percent set-aside continues at least some of the thrust of Title II of the Higher Education Act, which in addition to its subvention for academic libraries also allocated funds specifically for research and training in library and information science. Under the new legislation, Title II of the Higher Education Act is repealed. During its end-of-session negotiations, congressional leaders incorporated the Library Services and Technology Act in the massive omnibus appropriations bill for fiscal year 1997. On September 30, 1996, the Senate passed the bill with its thousands of pages, and President Clinton signed it the same day, thus clearing the decks for the fiscal year beginning on October 1.

Public Libraries in the National House of Education

One of the more interesting aspects of the legislation involves the transfer of the federal administration of the LSTA from the Department of Education to the newly created Office of Library Services in the Institute of Museum and Library Services, which is also a new federal entity. At the outset, the U.S. Bureau of Education, established in 1867 under the aegis of the Department of Interior, proved a not inhospitable locus for library interests. Indeed, the comprehensive compendium known as *Public Libraries in the United States of America*, compiled by the Bureau's staff and issued in the nation's centennial year, remains even today the most complete picture of nineteenth-century American librarianship. Also in 1876, the Commissioner of Education underwrote the cost of mailing notices to prospective attendees of a librarians' convention, held that year in Philadelphia, at which the American Library Association was founded. In 1893, the Commissioner of Education and his staff aided the work of the American Library Association by providing space in the U.S. Government Building at the Chicago World's Fair for an exhibit of a model book collection suitable for a small-town library. Although published by the ALA, the catalog of the five thousand books that were displayed was printed at government expense. In 1938, a separate library division was established in the Office of Education, primarily charged with the collection of library statistics, the provision of technical assistance, and the fostering of cooperation between libraries and public schools.

After the passage in 1956 of the Library Services Act, the staff of this division were redirected to duties concerned with grants management, and with the creation in 1965 of the National Center for Education Statistics, the library division's initial primacy as the collector of library statistics was displaced. Having an even greater impact on the library division, however, was the passage in 1965 of major legislation designed to remedy some of the educational deficiencies of economically disadvantaged students enrolled in elementary and secondary schools, as well as those in higher education. Of necessity, the Office of Education devoted more and more of its energies to the administration of new and expanded programs for formal schooling, with the result that the library legislation was pushed further and further on to the back burner of the Office's interests. Consequently, the role of libraries in the educative process was either underestimated or overlooked. In *A Nation at Risk*, the widely publicized report of the National Commission on Excellence in Education, published in 1983, the contribution of libraries to education was so slighted that a special committee was formed by the American Library Association to address the issue of "libraries and the learning society." As a result of the librarians' endeavor, a subsequent publication, *Alliance for Excellence: Librarians Respond to A Nation at Risk*, was issued by the Department of Education in the summer of 1984 with an introduction by Secretary of Education Terrell H. Bell. Its contents, based on a series of seminars sponsored with federal support throughout the country, emphasized the role of libraries in lifelong learning, but to many librarians the publication of this second document exemplified the old axiom "too little, too late."

In more recent years, after the election of a Democratic president, the Department of Education has been more receptive to the role of libraries, and Secretary of Education Richard Riley has been particularly sensitive in testifying to the need for telecommunications access in both libraries and schools. Although the Department proposed no continuation of the Library Services and Construction Act after its scheduled expiration in 1996, its lack of action should be attributed to the fact that the Department, given Republican demands for its abolition, was itself in jeopardy. The possible dissolution of the Department influenced the Senate to take action to find another locus for the administration of the library legislation. The Institute of Museum and Library Services, the Department's successor in administering the library programs, is an independent agency, defined as an administrative entity not included in the Executive Office of the President or in any executive department comprised in the Cabinet. Among the best known of such units is the Smithsonian Institution.

The new locus for library activity has both advantages and disadvantages. Having left a Cabinet-level department with several thousand employees, the library unit brought with it approximately fourteen staff positions to administer a program for library support initially authorized at $150 million. Its partner in the new enterprise, the Office of Museum

Services administered fiscal year 1997 grants in the amount of $22 million to improve museum services.[10] In terms of staff size and appropriation amounts, the new agency is on a par with some of the small independent agencies, such as the Appalachian Regional Commission, the Corporation for Public Broadcasting, and the National Foundation of the Arts and the Humanities, but not with the large independent agencies, such as the Environmental Protection Agency or the General Services Administration. On the positive side, library concerns may be better served by having a higher visibility in an agency where their programmatic funds are dominant and where they are not overshadowed by the far greater emphasis afforded the nation's schools. In effect, the Library Services and Technology Act, now Title IIB of the Museum and Library Services Act of 1996, is a federal block grant that embraces constituents from all types of libraries and gives considerable latitude to the states in entertaining proposals for innovative projects that will address the need for both advanced technology and improvement of library services to the underserved and the poor. Unlike the categorical-aid programs formerly meted out to distinctive recipients, such as the school, academic, and public libraries, a block grant, such as the LSTA, is designed to address a variety of activities involving libraries of differing types within a broad functional area of library service.

The demise of the Library Services and Construction Act ends forty years of federal support primarily designed to assist public libraries, since under the Library Services and Technology Act, other claimants to the federal purse, such as collegiate, school, or research libraries, can and probably will be recipients of federal funds appropriated to the states for the purposes of the new legislation. Although considerable benefits have accrued from LSCA funds over the years, one that is less apparent has been the development of an increased statewide responsibility for public library support.

State Support for Local Public Libraries

Writing in 1938, Carleton Joeckel commented that "a general appraisal of the record of the States in library service must conclude that they are the weakest link in the chain of library development," and he added that the proportion of expenditures for library purposes to total state expenditures had declined steadily since 1915, although the amount of the appropriations themselves had increased.[11] Three years earlier, in his treatise on public library governance, Joeckel had already commented on the extremely modest encouragement to local libraries by state governments, with only ten states making any direct contribution to the localities, a subsidy, with some few exceptions, that was limited to $100 to each library. By the time that the Library Services Act was nearing congressional passage in 1956, the picture had changed somewhat. During fiscal year 1955 to 1956, twenty-two states awarded cash grants to local libraries, and in addition Alabama expended funds for books to be locally distributed. The latest available figures for fiscal year 1994, however, reveal a far more sizable state subvention, with only three states, South Dakota, Vermont, and Wyoming, distributing less than $200,000 to local public libraries or library systems and consortia. The total for state aid (exclusive of Hawaii, which supports public libraries almost entirely from state funds) to local libraries in fiscal year 1994 amounted to almost $485 million, almost doubling the appropriations for all titles of the Library Services and Construction Act, which amounted that year to $249 million.[12]

Although considerably improved since the initial enactment of the federal legislation, the percentage of funding for local public libraries derived from state revenues is still nowhere comparable to the states' share of expenditures for local public schools. The outcome of several important court cases dealing with the disparity in local property taxes for public schooling precipitated a movement toward fiscal educational reform during the Nixon administration. Prominent among these cases was *Serrano v. Priest*,[13] a suit initiated in 1968 by John Anthony Serrano, who had moved from a poor, largely Chicano neighborhood in East Los Angeles to Whittier, California, a more affluent school district that would better accommodate the educational requirements of his two sons. The immediate issue was the effect of inequitable local property taxes on school expenditure, but the case entailed far broader constitutional implications in that children enrolled in poorer school districts were conceivably being denied their rights under the equal protection clause of the Fourteenth Amendment. In 1971, the California Supreme Court decided in favor of Serrano, holding that the wealth of the school district should not be a criterion affecting the level of spending for a child's education.

Similar court cases were litigated throughout the country, and in 1972 the U.S. Supreme Court announced that it would review the appeal in the class action suit of *Rodriguez v. San Antonio Independent School District*,[14] a case that was similar to *Serrano* but that had been adjudicated in a federal rather than state court, a factor influencing the Supreme Court's acceptance of this particular case. The claims of the original plaintiffs, Rodriguez and other Mexican-American parents of children enrolled in an urban school district in San Antonio, Texas, had been supported by the federal district court, which further ruled that the method used by Texas to finance local education was unconstitutional. Representatives of the Texas educational establishment appealed this ruling, and in 1973, in a five-to-four decision the Supreme Court, in *San Antonio v. Rodriguez*,[15] found in favor of the school district appellants, holding that education was not among the rights afforded explicit protection under the Constitution. Notwithstanding its opinion that the inequity in local school expenditure was not a matter for redress by the federal government, the Court made it abundantly clear that its action was not to be construed as inhibiting the actions of state legislatures, all of which could institute reforms leading to a more equitable funding pattern among school districts.

The *Serrano* and *Rodriguez* cases gave ample support to a vigorous reexamination by state governments of their role in support of local schooling with the result that many states legislated new mechanisms to absorb more of the local financial burden. In 1975, within two years of the *Rodriguez* decision, state governments provided from their own revenue sources 43.6 percent of public school expenditure, with local governments contributing 48.6 percent and the federal government 7.8 percent. In a study undertaken for the Urban Libraries Council, questionnaires submitted to the state library agencies revealed the percentage distribution of library expenditures for the three levels of government during the same year. With forty-one states responding, the study found that local government contributed 82 percent, state government 13 percent, and the federal government 5 percent, thus demonstrating a wide disparity between state expenditures for schools and libraries in 1975.[16] Writing in 1979, Alec Ladenson, a former director of the Chicago Public Library and an attorney with special expertise in the field of state library legislation and expenditures, commented: "The issues raised in *Rodriguez* and *Serrano* have important implications for public library service. . . . Since public libraries are deemed to be part of the educational system of the state, the state is responsible for insuring that the quality of library service, made available to each citizen, is on an equal basis throughout the state. The only practical way of eliminating the disparities in the amount of revenue available for public library service within the various local governmental units is to inject large doses of state aid for purposes of equalization."[17]

His optimistic tone is not reflected in the current situation, in which the states contributed in 1994 only 12.3 percent of total public library revenues, while state support in 1993 for the public elementary and secondary schools amounted to 42 percent of total public school revenues.[18] Because of the fiscal insignificance of public library expenditures in the total financing of state and local services, it was probably impossible for public libraries to have achieved a percentage parity with the public schools in the matter of educational funding during the mid-1970s. Nonetheless, it is regrettable that public libraries were largely unaffected by the movement toward fiscal educational reform, with the result that they are, in many instances, still primarily supported by revenues derived from property taxes. The outcome of the property tax revolt in over thirty states, typified by California's Proposition 13 in 1978 and by Massachusetts's Proposition 2 1/2 in 1980, only underscored the vulnerability of local libraries to the vagaries of local property tax assessments.

Since the 1930s, various schemes have been put forth in an attempt to determine an equitable distribution of library support among the local, state, and national levels of government. Recommendations have been made for a federal share of 75 to 90 percent, an expanded state share of 75 to 90 percent, or, perhaps more realistically, a balanced intergovernmental funding system with an allocation of 20 percent to the federal government, 50 percent to the states, and 30 percent to the localities.[19] Given the current political climate of governmental downsizing, the implementation of any one of these recommendations would seem to have little likelihood today.

In 1989, in preparation for the second White House Conference on Libraries and Information Services, the Public Library Association of ALA sponsored a symposium devoted to the "federal roles in support of public libraries." In advance of this event comments were solicited from the field, and these covered a wide variety of suggestions, not all of them very original. One respondent, however, suggested a somewhat unique rationale for federal support. Anticipating that more and more information would be delivered to remote locations with the result that municipal or county funding authorities would be less inclined to support local library service, since the impact of the service would not directly affect their constituents, he urged federal support in the development of regional patterns of library service and emphasized the need for a research and development capability comparable to that enjoyed by librarians in a university environment. The position paper resulting from the symposium, "Public Library Services for a Diverse People," dealt with federal aid in more general terms, emphasizing the information needs of a culturally pluralistic and ethnically diverse population. Acknowledging that the primary support of public libraries was still locally derived, the drafters of the document nonetheless urged a partnership of the federal government and the states to ensure that "Americans have access to a full range of information and knowledge resources in the century ahead."[20] This document, along with many others, was forwarded to the White House conference delegates, but its impact would be difficult to ascertain and certainly its approach was not consonant with the fiscal restraints urged by the Bush administration.

LSCA as an Instrument of Public Policy

If one phrase could be used to summarize the greatest benefits of the Library Services and Construction Act, it might be "cambium layer," that is, federal aid often permitting public libraries to experiment with newer services and, increasingly, as developments in information retrieval became more intrusive, with the newer technologies. Writing in 1996, Don Sager observed:

The provision of federal funds through the Library Service[s] and Construction Act (LSCA) allowed public libraries to develop computerized applications, purchase essential equipment, modify buildings to accommodate the hardware, establish cooperative agreements essential for the support of computer-based resource sharing, and train the personnel essential for maintenance and operation. While federal funds were always a relatively small portion of public library funding, they often played a critical role in the research and development of computerized applications. . . . Indeed, if the last half century was a golden age for public library service, I believe it was primarily due to the prudent application of a relatively small amount of federal funds by enlightened local, state and federal officials willing to test new programs, services, and applications.[21]

As a library insider, Sager, a former director of a number of public libraries, including that of Milwaukee and Chicago, perceives the role of federal aid as a change agent. But for some observers outside the library profession, the Library Services and Construction Act does not appear to have had high visibility as an instrument of public policy. Although recognizing that "access to information has historically been addressed by public libraries, not by telecommunications carriers," the director of the Information Infrastructure Program at Harvard University, Brian Kahin, further comments: "Public libraries are subsidized on the order of $83,000,000/year through Library Programs in the Department of Education, but this funding has not been used as [a] policy tool. Although digital information in a networked environment flows instantly across the nation and the world, the library remains a creature of local policy."[22]

Kahin's remarks may have been true of the early years of the LSCA when much of the federal aid was spent on bookmobiles, a somewhat imperfect mechanism but one capable of quickly distributing books to areas of the states unserved by public libraries. The evidence of more recent years, however, attests to the use of federal funds for policy initiatives having national implications. Contributing to this change were two factors: the first factor was the role taken by some states in developing larger units of service and in emphasizing resource sharing among libraries. Reflecting this development, a new Title III directed to "interlibrary cooperation" was added to the Library Services and Construction Act in 1966. The interlibrary cooperation title proved to be a broad mantra encouraging all of the states to use federal monies for many cooperative activities, including the development of library consortia not only among public libraries in various locations but also between public libraries and those operated under other jurisdictions, such as school or collegiate libraries or the special libraries in research or industrial organizations. As these networks emerged, public library users were afforded an infinitely larger pool of accessible materials, and the considerable disparities between libraries of different size and resource strength were greatly reduced. Certainly, one outcome of federal support for these cooperatives was a greater sharing of the nation's intellectual wealth. At the same time, these networks proved fertile ground for the second factor affecting national library policy, the application of computer technologies to library operations. In many cases, these two factors became intertwined as online catalogs were developed, allowing readers in one community to learn about the library holdings in another. Our present Internet accessibility to the library catalogs of many major public libraries has in many cases resulted from the original investment of federal seed money into the computerization of library activities.

Over ten years ago, literary critic Hugh Kenner wrote that

every new technology, when it applies for admission to a citadel of the intellect, has invariably received its first welcome from the librarian. . . . Nearly a century ago, libraries were the first buildings to be getting incandescent electric lights; a half-century ago they were among the first buildings to be air-conditioned. When copying machines escaped from corporate offices, the first place where they became accessible to the public was the library. . . . And it is libraries, in this decade, that are welcoming the computer.[23]

Librarians applied computers to their work relatively early. Harbingers of the computer and communications revolution were apparent in the 1960s, a decade in which all of the following developments occurred. MARC (the machine-readable cataloging data for materials acquired by the Library of Congress) was made available for the use of libraries across the country, obviating the need in many cases for each institution to generate its own cataloging data. The National Library of Medicine computerized its major indices to the biomedical literature. And OCLC (originally the acronym for the Ohio College Library Center, now the OCLC Online Computer Library Center) was incorporated, the first of the bibliographic utilities or networks employing telecommunications to facilitate online cataloging and interlibrary loan for their member libraries.

Almost all of these advances were achieved through federal aid, either through direct subsidy, as in the case of the federally supported libraries, or through the award of federal grants. Exemplifying this trend was the development of RLIN (the Research Libraries Information Network), the second of the major bibliographic utilities but one characterized by its linkage of the nation's larger research and academic libraries. During its gestation period at Stanford University this project was greatly supported by research funds administered by the U.S. Department of Education. In company with WLN (the Western Library Network), headquartered in the State of Washington, RLIN and OCLC comprise the three major bibliographic utilities in the United States. Now containing literally millions of electronically encoded entries, these utilities allow users to determine the exact location of a given item, thus facilitating transactions of interlibrary loan by reducing the former tedious delays between borrowing and lending libraries.

At the outset, libraries, both academic and public, tended to use the new technologies for internal operations, such as their catalogs, the circulation records of their borrowers, and the acquisition of materials. With the development of the personal computer and the use of modems to achieve connectivity to the Internet, libraries have gone well beyond the automation of their own activities and are now serving as public access points, embracing a whole host of informational services, including the creation of their own Web pages with linkages to many sources of information. The ubiquity of the computer is apparent in almost all library concerns. Access to electronic information dominates the pages of the many library and information science journals, not only in the articles themselves but in the countless advertisements promoting the products of library vendors. It is evident at all library conferences whether locally or nationally sponsored and has become a decisive factor informing the training and education of prospective employees. Finally, it is the subject of countless related issues, involving ethics, economics, user confidentiality, security of records, and many others. All of this might superficially appear to be a response to technological innovation, but throughout this period of ever-accelerating computer use a simultaneous development has occurred, which invested information with the properties similar to those of a natural resource. Rather than being construed as an intellectual property, generated by those who are enabled to receive copyright protection for their ideations, information now has become analogous to such environmental resources as oil and water, which require conservation, recycling, and protection. More and more the socioeconomic world has recognized the value of information, and it increasingly regards information as a commodity.

The Economics of Knowledge and Information

Formerly the province of educators and philosophers, the words *information* and *knowledge* became identified with the concerns of sociologists and economists as the postwar economy shifted from manufacturing to service-based jobs employing persons working in the so-called knowledge industries. During the mid-1950s, the knowledge industries accounted for one-quarter of the gross national product, and they grew to one-third by the mid-1960s and one-half by the late 1970s. Peter Drucker credits himself for the coinage of the phrase "knowledge worker," which appeared in his book *The Landmarks of Tomorrow*, published in 1959. That same year, Princeton economist Fritz Machlup gave the first of five lectures devoted to the economics of knowledge. Considerably enlarged and enhanced, these lectures became the basis of his seminal 1962 work, *The Production and Distribution of Knowledge in the United States*, the first major analysis of the knowledge-producing industries and occupations. Building on Machlup's work, Marc Uri Porot analyzed the new informational workforce, including producers and salespersons of information machines (such as photocopiers and computers), accountants, educators, secretaries, lawyers, and, of course, librarians, library aides, and archivists. The salaries of this latter group represented less than 3 percent in the aggregate compensation paid to all information workers in 1967.[24] Knowledge and technology were defined by Harvard sociologist Daniel Bell as the central structural components of the postindustrial society. Their transforming role not only in the American economy but also in that of the world was the burden of his 1973 book, *The Coming of Post-Industrial Society*. These benchmark works represent only a fraction of the burgeoning literature devoted to public policy issues that have been affected by the growth and increasing specialization of knowledge and the rise of a technically oriented workforce.

The knowledge explosion, compounded by the increased availability of all kinds of documents through new techniques for inexpensive copying and electronic storage and retrieval, caused major rifts between the librarians and publishers. On the one side, the library profession promulgated the public's interest in obtaining full access to information while, on the other, the publishing industry focused more and more on the constitutionally protected right of copyright proprietors. To the industry, the meaning of *fair use*, originally and often painfully associated with the laborious task of hand copying long excerpts from copyrighted works, a process that by its very nature tended to establish limits on the amount copied, was now being circumvented by the deposit of a few coins in a copying machine. Although bills to revise the basic Copyright Law of 1909 had been circulated in Congress during the early 1960s, the major enactment revising the earlier legislation was not passed until 1976. So complicated were questions relating to the newer technologies of document reproduction and storage that a National Commission on New Technological Uses of Copyrighted Works (CONTU) was authorized in 1974 to examine matters relating to databases, interlibrary loans, and computer software. Several recommendations made by CONTU resulted in agreements between the librarians and the publishers, such as the permissible amounts of copying for interlibrary loan, but a number of issues remained unresolved. Observed one commentator: "Dealing with copyright is like aiming at a moving target. Technology continues to introduce new ways to select, store, search, display, transfer and disseminate information. Copyright is affected by such developments, which occur faster than we can keep up with them legislatively."[25]

However useful CONTU was to easing some of the dichotomies between the copyright proprietors and the librarians, it was but one of an almost unprecedented number of federal study commissions dealing with the information agenda that flourished during the 1970s. Their titles are indicative of the wide range of activities then being scrutinized: the National Commission on Libraries and Information Science (1970), the Commission on Federal Paperwork (1974), the National Commission on Electronic Fund Transfer (1974), the Privacy Protection Study Commission (1974), the National Study Commission on Records and Documents of Federal Officials (1975), and the Domestic Council Committee on the Right of Privacy (1974), which in its 1976 report to the President called for the creation of an Office of Information Policy in the Executive Office of the President. This latter document, in countering the proliferation of so many disparate bodies addressing various aspects of the information agenda, set forth the need for an overarching national information policy:

Although the term "information policy" can have different connotations, the various perspectives which are brought to it are all part of a common family of interdependent and intersecting interests. It is this larger context and the expectation that information policy issues will become more pressing in the future which compel a national information policy. The interrelationships which exist between and among information communications, information technology, information economics, information privacy, information systems, information confidentiality, information science, information networks, and information management have signalled the need for a broader, more comprehensive approach to the problem.[26]

Although an Office of Information Policy as a central locus for federal policies dealing with the information agenda was not created in the White House, a greatly expanded Office of Management and Budget (OMB) emerged as a surrogate candidate for that role. In an earlier effort to control excessive paperwork, the Federal Reports Act of 1942 had ceded responsibility to the Bureau of the Budget (later renamed the Office of Management and Budget) to determine whether the information requested of private citizens, governmental entities, or businesses by federal agencies was absolutely necessary for the proper performance of their respective duties. For a number of reasons, including the advent of automated data processing, which in many ways contributed to the generation of more information, the 1942 enactment proved inadequate in controlling the burgeoning information requirements of the federal government, and during President Ford's administration the Commission on Federal Paperwork was created to examine the problem anew. Estimating that more than $100 billion was being expended annually on the federal paperwork burden, the Commission examined a broad range of issues, among them the assurance of data confidentiality, the management and control of information activities, the interrelationship between state and local governments and the federal government in the collection of information, and the burden of cost both to the government as well as to the data providers.

After generating thirty-six separate monographs and submitting over seven hundred recommendations, the Commission, in its final report, called for the creation of a Department of Administration to be established with Cabinet-level status. This new agency would be empowered to undertake not only the organization of federal programs for a more effective delivery of services to government claimants without the undue burden of unnecessary paperwork but also the coordination of various ongoing programs related to information, such as the Bureau of the Census and the National Archives and Records Service. One member of the Commission, Elmer B. Staats, comptroller general of the United States, took exception to this proposal, recommending instead that an augmented Office of Management and Budget be charged with responsibilities "for all aspects of statistical collection, analysis, dissemination, and paperwork management." Perhaps in deference to his objection, the Commission's final report indicated that, in lieu of creating a new Cabinet-level agency, the Office of Management and Budget could be given broad responsibility for the organization and coordination of federal information activities.[27] And it was this latter directive that became a cornerstone of the Paperwork Reduction Act of 1980, enacted in the final days of the Carter administration.

OMB and the Office of Information and Regulatory Affairs

Authorized within OMB was a new Office of Information and Regulatory Affairs (OIRA) with responsibility for the conduct of federal statistics, records management, automated data processing, telecommunications, and other functions that would be contained within the definition of "information resources management." In brief, "OIRA's most sweeping statutory mandate was to develop comprehensive information policies for the entire Federal government."[28] Given its charge as the planning and budgeting arm of the executive branch, it is not surprising that circulars issued by OMB dealing with federal information resources should emphasize cost effectiveness and efficiency. Among these advisories was OMB Circular A-130, "Management of Federal Information Resources," which was issued late in 1985 and created a firestorm within the American library community. Although acknowledging that "the free flow of information from the government to its citizens and vice versa is essential to a democratic society," the Circular qualified this statement by noting that the dissemination of government information products and services should be carried out "in the manner most cost effective for the government, including placing maximum feasible reliance on the private sector."[29] In her analysis of this new policy, sociologist Nancy Andes noted: "The federal government's general principles of information management entailed in this policy emphasize the commodity value of public information. . . . The implications of the commodification of government information come dangerously close to censorship of potentially unprofitable or embarrassing items. Through these policies the administration demonstrates an acceptance of a philosophy that the government and private sector should make a profit, regardless of the intrinsic or social value of information."[30]

Rising to fever pitch during President Reagan's administration, the privatization and commodification of government information resulted in the demise of one out of every four of the government's sixteen thousand publications. In response to this major retrenchment effort and the growing mood of national conservatism, a host of new interest groups came into being, charged with some aspect of the protection of the public's right to know. Among these newly minted not-for-profit organizations were OMB Watch, Computer Professionals for Social Responsibility, the National Security Archive, and the Taxpayer Assets Project. The American Library Association, founded in the nineteenth century and traditionally associated with older means of communication, such as the book, began to promote the concept that librarians were the first information professionals and that their work was vital to the development of the information age. In fact, the ALA Washington Office initiated a semiannual newsletter, *Less Access to Less Information By and About the U.S. Government.* This ongoing chronology, documenting efforts to restrict and privatize government information, was begun in 1981 when President Reagan placed a moratorium on the production and procurement of new government publications and the OMB issued a model plan to implement presidential policy with the somewhat ominous title, "Elimination of Wasteful Spending on Government Publications, Pamphlets, and Audiovisual Products."

The issuance of this chronology is but one instance of the changing role and increasing responsibilities of the ALA Washington Office. Founded in 1945, primarily to promote public library legislation, the Office now embraces the concerns of academic and school libraries, as well as public libraries, the federal libraries, and those libraries designated to serve as depositories for federal documents. In addition, it testifies before Congress on many other issues relating to information and information technology, including copyright, intellectual property, encryption devices, and privacy. On the occasion of its fiftieth anniversary in 1995, it added to its charge the creation of a new Office for Information Technology Policy, designed to further position the ALA's role in the information age. Throughout its first half century, the ALA Washington Office has employed extremely skilled lobbyists to advance library interests, the majority of whom were recruited from positions in public libraries. Without the ALA Washington Office, there would have been no federal subventions to aid public, school, or academic libraries. The two White House Conferences on Libraries and Information Services, the first held in 1979 and the second in 1991, would not have taken place. Legislated in 1970 as a consequence of ALA's backing, the U.S. National Commission on Libraries and Information Science would not now exist, and the passage of the Library Services and Technology Act in 1996 would not have occurred. Yet, at the same time, it must be admitted that the original public library emphasis of the ALA Washington Office has been, of necessity, curtailed, as new and quite legitimate claimants to its attention have arisen. The special interests of the larger research libraries in the country are served by the Association of Research Libraries (ARL), which, although working closely with ALA in the formulation of positions on federal issues, maintains its own Washington-based headquarters and staff. Whether public library interests should be coalesced in a distinctive Washington-based organization, similar to the ARL, remains an unanswered question but one that may have to be addressed in the years to come.

That there is a federal presence in the support of libraries, other than those that are part of the federal government itself, is indisputably the result of the activities of the ALA Washington Office. Among other highlights of its fifty-year career have been the specific mention of libraries in President Kennedy's special message to Congress on education in 1963 and President Johnson's acknowledgment of libraries in his State of the Union message in 1964 (in both cases, a first for libraries). The office has engendered the continued loyal support of a cadre of concerned senators and representatives, who literally kept the legislative program alive during periods of executive branch animus and budgetary retrenchment, and it has certainly earned the recognition of countless librarians and library users that the federal legislation has indeed made a significant contribution to the conduct of the nation's public libraries.

On the other hand, the lobbying effort has been and continues to be faced with a number of difficulties. Although it is true that congressional leaders of both major parties and in both houses rescued the public library program from the onslaughts of indifferent Republican administrations, that rescue effort has not been without cost. Significant growth in a federal program is difficult to achieve when the administration recommends a bottom line of zero, and grant amounts in successive years of the LSCA sometimes merely duplicated the previous year's appropriation instead of enhancing it. In 1970 to 1971, the federal share of public library expenditures derived from governmental sources was 7.4 percent, slightly less than the federal share that year of 8 percent for the public schools. In 1994, the federal share in total public library expenditures is 1.1 percent.[31] In analyzing the declining federal role, Libraries for the Future, an advocacy group based in New York City, gave as an example the fiscal year 1992 appropriation for LSCA Titles I, II, and III of approximately $118 million, which when adjusted for inflation, amounted to only $71.7 million in 1980 dollars, an amount only slightly more than the $67.5 million actually appropriated in 1980. Library use from 1980 to 1992, however, had increased 48 percent.[32]

Of even greater difficulty to the lobbying effort, perhaps, than the effect of inflation is the matter of identifying the public library constituency. Users of public libraries do not take tests, register for courses, or indicate on registration forms their age, sex, income, religious affiliation, educational level, or ethnicity. Historian Daniel J. Boorstin once aptly characterized the alumni of public libraries as "anonymous, invisible, and unenlisted," and given the almost totally voluntary nature of public library usage it is hard to counter his descriptors. The kinds of aggregate statistics assembled by schools and colleges, so pertinent to the preparation of congressional testimony, elude the library profession, leaving the ALA Washington Office dependent on anecdotal accounts and largely input-oriented statistics, which simply cannot quantify the impact of public library service on members of the public. Government officials have sometimes criticized the ALA for what they would call its "soft data" approach, but without the information on student performance available to the schools and institutions of higher education, any other approach seems unlikely. Nonetheless, through good times and bad, the ALA Washington Office and the members of its Committee on Legislation have achieved a considerable record of success as advocates of the library cause. Today the Association faces a new challenge in projecting its influence into the development of the national information infrastructure, which was initiated without the lobbying efforts of librarians since at least 1800, when members of the Congress in legislating a library for their own use established the Library of Congress.

4

The National Perspective: The National Information Infrastructure

Having examined the part played by federal legislation in the direct support of public libraries, we shift our focus and concentrate instead on initiatives, both positive and negative, dealing with information that have been stimulated by the federal government. Here the library profession is perceived not solely as a proponent of special-interest legislation but also as a reactor to federally induced stimuli.

Some twenty years ago Joseph Becker, a founding father of the then-emerging discipline of information science, addressed the dimensions of national information policy, defining information as "the messages of human experience." He noted that there were two perspectives from which an information message could be viewed—"first, from the point of view of its content, and second, from the point of view of its processing and transfer":

The intellectual essence of an information message is content. Process, on the other hand, refers to the means we use to produce, publish, communicate, organize, store, retrieve, and otherwise transfer information messages. It is useful to draw the distinction between content and process because . . . separate national policies are required for each.[1]

Librarians historically have been concerned with informational content, which until recently was encapsulated in artifactual form, whether book, pamphlet, journal, or even reel of film. The process by which that content was packaged, however—involving not only the original act of authorship but also those activities dealing with publishing and distribution—was of tertiary concern to the librarian's decision to acquire the particular item. Matters such as the readability of the print or the durability of a book's binding were taken into account, but the paramount concern was the intellectual value of the item to the collection and its contribution to that collection's users. What is making the profession's present discontinuous with its past is the realization that information is now both content and process. The demarcation between the two, manifest in a book-dominated collection, is no longer obvious, since the electronic message, unlike the book, is volatile, having no protocol for determining its reliability or authority and no assurance of its preservation. The distinction, however, between process and content in the shaping of national information policy is useful in understanding the librarians' perception of that policy and their role in its evolution.

The National Information Infrastructure

Although no one would have referred to it as such, a national information infrastructure under the auspices of the federal government has existed in the United States since the Constitution provided protection to holders of copyrights and patents and the Bill of Rights sanctioned the freedom of speech and the press. During the nineteenth century, other information-related enactments involved the founding in 1800 of the Library of Congress and the establishment in 1813 of a depository program for libraries in each of the states to receive congressional literature, later extended in 1857 to also include the receipt of executive branch documents. The Government Printing Office (GPO) was created in 1860, and the passage of the Printing Act of 1895 provided in the GPO a locus for the office of the Superintendent of Public Documents, previously housed in the Department of the Interior. The National Archives was chartered in 1934, a long-overdue measure for a nation that was being recognized as a world power. But it was during the aftermath of World War II and the initiation of the Cold War that certain policy directives, in part induced by major technological development, were implemented that substantively altered the course of the national information infrastructure. Some aspects of this change had a direct effect on the library community; three of these are discussed here.

The first federal policy directive that influenced the library community was shaped by events beginning in 1947, the year of the passage of the National Security Act, which established both the National Security Council and the Central Intelligence Agency. In that year, President Truman issued an executive order requiring a surveillance activity entitled the Federal Employees Loyalty Program. Some state governments subsequently enacted laws providing that government employees subscribe to loyalty oaths, and public librarians soon found themselves caught up in the nationwide frenzy occasioned by the extreme anticommunist tactics of the period. The second policy directive affecting libraries was the postwar recognition that computer technology might aid in the bibliographic control of the burgeoning scientific and technical literature often subsidized by federal research dollars. And the third policy directive significant for libraries was research commissioned by the Department of Defense to prevent the collapse of the nation's communications infrastructure in the event of a nuclear war. This research led to the creation of ARPAnet (the network of the Advanced Research Projects Agency). In 1969 this network connected three computers in California and one in Utah and was known only to a handful of government researchers and scientists. This modest network was the precursor of the present Internet. These three developments, concomitants of the Cold War years, are not necessarily causally related, but taken together they have helped librarians reframe the objectives of the information professions.

Reprisals brought against public libraries and individual librarians during the 1950s were part of the legacy of governmental intimidation induced by McCarthyism. Vulnerable to attack and sometimes dismissed were library employees who refused to sign loyalty oaths or who resisted the demands of vigilante groups to label allegedly pro-Communist materials. Librarians urged action through their national association to adopt in 1950 a resolution condemning loyalty oaths and in 1951 a statement that materials labeling was a violation of the Library Bill of Rights. In 1953, the U.S. Department of State directed its overseas libraries to discard books about Communism or those purportedly written by Communists. A small group of representatives from the American Library Association and the American Book Publishers Council, meeting in the spring of that year, sought ways to resist this latest threat to American civil liberties. Still in print and now available on the Internet is the Freedom to Read Statement that emanated from that meeting and was subsequently endorsed by the national library and publishing associations.[2] Concerns expressed by both the librarians and the publishers over the purges of the overseas libraries finally prompted a response from President Eisenhower, who in a speech on June 14, 1953, at Dartmouth College enjoined his audience: "Don't join the book burners." In a subsequent letter, read that year to the membership attending the ALA conference in Los Angeles, Eisenhower further commented: "we must in these times be intelligently alert not only to the fantastic cunning of Communist conspiracy—but also to the grave dangers in meeting fanaticism with ignorance. . . . The libraries of America are and must ever remain the homes of free, inquiring minds."[3]

With the censure of Senator McCarthy in 1954, the worst excesses of governmental intimidation appeared to be over, but a new threat to civil liberties emerged in the 1960s relating to the privacy rights of library users. Although not mentioned in the Constitution, the right to privacy became increasingly recognized as a civil libertarian issue late in the nineteenth century, when the tapping of telephone and telegraph wires or the use of cameras to take unsolicited photographs made it possible to circumvent individual privacy. At the outset, wiretapping and similar devices were largely restricted to law enforcement agencies for the detection of criminals. But as information technology became more sophisticated, banks, businesses, credit agencies, hospitals, insurance firms, and government departments were enabled to collect and store machine-readable records about individuals that could be subsequently used in ways those individuals could perceive to be harmful to them. Evidence of the mounting concern over the protection of personal privacy are the forty-seven separate sets of congressional hearings and reports on privacy-related matters issued from 1965 to 1974, the year in which Congress passed the nation's first Privacy Act.[4] This law was intended to be a companion piece to the 1966 Freedom of Information Act, which requires that federal agencies make available information about their operations in response to legitimate inquiry. In contrast, the Privacy Act prevents the federal government from disclosing information inimical to the rights of an individual.

In 1970, a series of troublesome incidents involving the protection of reader privacy occurred in a number of public libraries. In the spring of that year, Internal Revenue Service (IRS) agents of the U.S. Treasury Department requested permission of the Milwaukee Public Library to examine circulation files of materials dealing with explosives. The use of these records was part of an investigative technique to assist the Treasury

Department in quelling bombings. Initially, an official of the library refused, but after the federal agents received an opinion from the city attorney's office that library files were public records, the library complied. Public libraries in Atlanta, Cleveland, and Richmond (California) also reported similar inquiries by IRS agents. A statement urging libraries to maintain the confidentiality of their records was issued by the ALA. In defending the library profession, Senator Sam J. Ervin, Jr. (Democrat, North Carolina), later to become the principal architect of the Privacy Act, wrote to the Treasury Department: "Throughout history, official surveillance of the reading habits of citizens has been a litmus test of tyranny."[5] The following year, the American Library Association adopted its "Policy on Confidentiality of Library Records," which advised the profession not to surrender circulation records unless due process procedures, such as the issuance of a subpoena, had been invoked.[6]

This instance was not the last in which federal agents pursued surveillance activities in libraries. In 1987 agents of the Federal Bureau of Investigation (FBI) approached the staff of a Columbia University departmental library, seeking information about foreign nationals who were allegedly exploiting library resources for the use of Soviet intelligence. The Columbia foray and similar approaches to other academic and public libraries, including a large public library in Florida and two in New York City, were part of what the FBI called the Library Awareness Program. In testimony before the Senate Judiciary Committee in 1988, FBI director William Sessions presented a report charging that agents of the Soviet intelligence services had been manipulating American technical libraries for subversive purposes since 1962.[7] Although representatives of the national media, professional societies, higher education, and several members of Congress were visibly outraged over the FBI's investigations, some members of the National Commission on Libraries and Information Science took a different stance. In a closed session, held early in 1988 during the ALA midwinter meeting, the Commission met with the FBI's deputy assistant director of operations for foreign intelligence. A transcript of this session obtained through the Freedom of Information Act revealed the sympathetic view of some Commissioners to the FBI's position, which showed little understanding of the intellectual freedom aspects of these incidents or of the privacy rights of the nation's library users.[8] As we later show, the Commission's posture during this period alienated many members of the ALA, which had extensively lobbied for the Commission's establishment as an independent agency of the federal government in 1970. In regard to the confidentiality of library circulation records, it should be noted that the majority of states have now adopted legislation protecting such records from unwarranted surveillance.

Another fallout from World War II and the ensuing Cold War was the burgeoning nature of scientific and technical information (STI), produced in many cases by the infusion of federal funds into research carried out by universities, industrial laboratories, and the government itself. The dissemination of STI has been a constant throughout the history of federal information activities, resulting in the establishment over time of many government libraries and information centers. But the bibliographic control of this literature through the potential of mechanization was a postwar development. Some observers believe that an early recognition of this phenomenon is the essay by Vannevar Bush on "memex," published in the July 1945 issue of the *Atlantic Monthly*. But of equal import is the government report written by Bush that same year, entitled *Science: The Endless Frontier*. As director of the Office of Scientific Research and Development, Bush had coordinated the work of some six thousand American scientists during the war years. At its close, in examining the endless and expansive frontiers of science, he anticipated that the scientific energy that had been dramatically harnessed to the war effort would be converted to peacetime uses and to the increase of knowledge. One important aspect of that task was the distribution and dissemination of research findings to the scientific and technological communities.

Already existing in the United States was a de facto system of information exchange, including the nation's federal, state, local, research, and academic libraries, plus any number of information centers and libraries catering to the needs of industrial researchers, professional societies, and privately operated research and development corporations. Although communications among this aggregate of organizations concerning loans of materials and their acquisition did exist, there was no single identifiable locus for centrally locating and finding relevant documents. In at least one effort to coordinate the dissemination of some of the vast literature devoted to science and technology, Congress mandated a clearinghouse for unclassified scientific and technological documents in 1950. Renamed the National Technical Information Service (NTIS) in 1970, this clearinghouse functions as a central point in the United States for the public distribution and sale of government-funded research and development reports and other analyses produced by federal agencies, their contractors, and their grantees. Vigorous efforts during the Reagan administration to privatize the NTIS proved unsuccessful, and it still exists as a self-supporting federal agency.

Further mobilizing the scientific and technological communities was the Soviets' launching of Sputnik in 1957, which accelerated competition between the United States and the Soviet Union for dominance in outer space. The following year, during which the National Aeronautics and Space Administration was established, the President's Science Advisory Committee published its findings in a report entitled *Improving the Availability of Scientific and Technical Information in the United States*, sometimes called the Baker report after the name of its chair, William O. Baker of the Bell Telephone Laboratories. The Baker report was one among many documents issued in the late 1950s and 1960s that dealt with the identification and control of scientific literature, often through the application of automation. In 1962 the Federal Council for Science and Technology, itself established by executive order in 1959, created a Committee on Information, which later adopted the name Committee on Scientific and Technical Information (COSATI). To determine the state of the "present de facto national system" for the dissemination of the STI literature, COSATI soon launched an intensive examination of fifteen major plans prepared by scientists and computer analysts for the establishment of a national document-handling system for science and technology.[9] All this activity was emblematic of the increasing awareness of the potential of digital computers in the storage, retrieval, and transmission of information. A new discipline, that of information science, was emerging, which not only analyzed the properties of information and the nature of its users but also assumed the importance of information in and of itself.

In 1965, the American Library Association formed a new division devoted to information science and automation (now the Library and

Information Technology Association). In 1966, the pilot project inaugurating the use of the MARC (machine-readable cataloging) format for the cataloging data of the Library of Congress was begun, and a year later, the American Documentation Institute, founded in 1937, changed its name to the American Society for Information Science. The training and education of these new professionals became a concern of American higher education, resulting in a variety of approaches. Some library schools, situated as graduate professional schools within universities, instituted courses dealing with information science and computer applications to library operations. Among the earliest of these new programs was the one initiated at the library school of Western Reserve University, which in anticipation of the trend toward automated document retrieval had established in 1955 a Center for Documentation and Communication Research. Engineering schools, including the Georgia Institute of Technology and Lehigh University, inaugurated curricula for the training of information scientists, while various university departments, such as linguistics and psychology, also undertook instruction in this area.

It would be misleading to leave the impression that the federal government was unique in influencing the course of this new discipline. Certainly, academicians representing many disciplines, bibliographic specialists including documentalists and librarians, and industrial researchers contributed to its development, but there is no doubt that the federal government acted as a catalyst in shaping the information science agenda. The research of its own personnel, the grants that it made available for study and demonstration, and the body of documents that it generated were all contributing factors to the recognition of this new discipline. One of the unfortunate and perhaps unforeseen results of these activities was the furtherance of a distinction between the work of librarians and information scientists, the latter afforded greater recognition because their work was identified with "science," not books. The recent closing of many library schools in American universities and the trend among those that remain to substitute in their titles the word *information* in place of *library* is but one consequence of this development. Faced with a stereotypical depiction of their work and often undervalued, public librarians uneasily and somewhat warily watched the rise of this new and better-paid information profession.

The Internet

Finally, the national information infrastructure was and is being shaped by what is now called the Internet. Begun as a federally supported initiative designed to provide means of communication if enemy attacks wiped out the conventional telephone system, the Defense Department's Advanced Research Projects Agency (ARPA) developed a new kind of computer network during the late 1960s. Its innovative aspect was its packet-switching capability, which split data into tiny packets, each of which could take a distinctive route to its destination. Packet switching allowed a network to resist large-scale attack, even a nuclear one, since a network outage in one location could be bypassed without disruption to the network as a whole. As an afterthought, ARPAnet researchers also found a way to send messages over the network from one research site to another; electronic mail or e-mail, as it became known, turned the network into a new means of communication. By 1971, there were twenty-three hosts on the ARPAnet; two years later it became international, with connections to England and Norway. Also in 1973, the federal government launched a research program to develop communications protocols allowing networked computers to communicate with one other. The TCP/IP protocols (Transmission Control Protocol/Internet Protocol) resulting from this endeavor became the lingua franca of networked computers. The process by which these protocols were used to integrate distinctive networks was called the Internetting project, and the system of networks emerging from this research became known as the Internet. The Internet, then, is not a single entity but a collection of computer networks using common technical protocols enabling computers to communicate and share services, initially throughout the nation and today throughout the world.

Having created the Internet, federal funds for a number of years sustained it. During the 1980s, the National Science Foundation (NSF) took the lead in funding research into network deployment and use. In 1986, the NSFnet backbone program was launched connecting various universities and other research institutions to NSF-supported supercomputer centers. As a result, regional networks came into being with responsibility for specific geographic areas of the country. The NSF's funding arrangements eventually gave rise to a multitiered hierarchial network structure: a local area network (LAN) that serves a specific campus or research installation and is largely a matter of local investment is connected to a metropolitan or regional network, which in turn is connected to a very-high-speed wide-area backbone network. NSF's contribution aided the regional and backbone services. Subsequent developments in recent years have altered the pattern of NSF support. In 1992, plans to phase out the federal support of NSFnet were announced, and three years later, the community-level service was turned over to private-sector Internet service providers. The NSF has continued, however, to aid the Internet's transition to that of a privately operated network.

Although other factors could, of course, be cited, the three phenomena described here, all byproducts of federal policy, changed the dimensions of the information age and the librarians' perception of it. Increased governmental surveillance over the conduct of the nation's libraries and the habits of their users, augmented in recent years by the ease with which electronic records can be analyzed, has made librarians wary of a federal presence beyond their control. Whereas formerly, especially during the Depression years, many library leaders had looked to the federal government as the primary equalizer of educational opportunity, the excesses of the witchhunts in the 1950s and the misuse of presidential power during the Watergate scandals of the 1970s left the profession with a sense of ambivalence about the federal government's role in library affairs, even though librarians did want and did accept federal aid for their libraries. At the same time, librarians could not help recognizing that the federal government's scientific and technical research agenda, its significant contribution to the new discipline of information science, and its fostering of the Internet were all developments that could only have been achieved within a national policy framework. Hoping to be beneficiaries of the great potential inherent in the computer and telecommunications revolution, subsidized initially by the federal government, public librarians nonetheless continue to espouse local control, with no federal interference, over library governance and practice. Their ambivalence about the federal presence in their activities has a direct bearing, as is shown later, on their reaction to the Telecommunications Act of 1996: on the one hand, the American Library Association, representing some fifty-six thousand members, sued the federal government over the issue of Internet censorship mandated by Title V of the enactment; on the other, the ALA, on behalf of those same members, lobbied vigorously for the discounted rates to facilitate public library access to the Internet mandated by the universal service provisions of the same legislation. To most librarians there was no dichotomy in their position, for the censorship requirements of the law dealt primarily with information as content, while the connectivity issue related more specifically to information as process.

The dramatic developments in electronic computing and networking elicited congressional interest, and one senator in particular emerged as a spokesperson for the potential benefits of a nationwide telecommunications infrastructure. Senator Albert Gore, Jr. (Democrat, Tennessee) introduced the National High-Performance Computer Technology Act of 1988 in the fall of that year. Title II was originally entitled the National Research Computer Network, but in 1989, when the bill was reintroduced, this title was renamed the National Research and Education Network (NREN). Urging that the federal government be a catalyst for the development of the NREN, Senator Gore commented: "Libraries, rural schools, minority institutions, and vocational education programs will have access to the same national resources—data bases, supercomputers, accelerators—as more affluent and better known institutions."[10] Originally, the National Research Computer Network was intended to link supercomputer centers and to accommodate the enormous amounts of data produced by high-performance computer projects, but influenced by the advice of educators and government officials, Gore expanded its role to include schools, libraries, and other institutions. In an opinion piece in the *Washington Post*, Gore wrote: "If we had the information superhighways we need, a school child could plug into the Library of Congress every afternoon, jumping from one subject to another, according to the curiosity of the moment."[11] Increasingly, the phrase *information superhighway* became linked to Gore's support of and identification with telecommunications networking. Gore's father, the senior Albert Gore, also a United States senator, had championed the federal interstate highway system during the 1950s; the younger Gore's reference to information superhighways can be seen as an extension of his father's interest in advancing American transportation. The phrase is neither accurate nor felicitous, for implicit in it is the principle of agreed-upon "rules of the road," which was certainly not characteristic of the often chaotic aspects of the emerging global networking environment. Notwithstanding, the phrase caught on and remains the popular form of reference to the national information infrastructure.

The higher education community and that of academic and research librarianship were quick to appreciate the value of the NREN, which inspired the creation in 1990 of the Coalition for Networked Information, through the joint action of the Association of Research Libraries and two of the nation's leading higher education technology organizations, CAUSE and EDUCOM (which merged in 1998 as EDUCAUSE). The Coalition's mission is the promotion of networked information resources to advance scholarship and intellectual productivity. Also in 1990, under the aegis of ALA's Library and Information Technology Association, the library community sponsored a major program devoted to the NREN's potential which one thousand people attended. With some few exceptions, however, public librarians appeared less visible in response to the proposed national educational network than their academic library colleagues. In part, their reaction was conditioned by the fact that, unlike university libraries that relied on their institutional affiliations to provide access to supercomputing technology, thus facilitating the inclusion of machine-readable library catalogs on the Internet, public libraries, as free-standing agencies, would be expected to bear the full cost of electronic linkages to make access to the NREN feasible.

Late in 1991, President Bush signed the High-Performance Computing Act, establishing the National Research and Education Network and providing for the development of high-performance computing and communications technologies. For the past several years, this legislation has supported longitudinal research in the development of high-performance computing and communications technologies and their application to the so-called Grand Challenges of engineering and science, including weather forecasting, climate prediction, the improvement of environmental quality, and the building of energy-efficient automobiles and airplanes. An additional focus, the development of information technologies, was added in 1994. But in light of the emerging power of the Internet and the dramatic increase in the number of its users, the concept of the NREN was largely subsumed under the broader rubric promulgated by the Clinton administration that called for the creation of the National Information Infrastructure.

Having caught the attention of the mass media, the concept of a data superhighway, especially one that would stimulate the nation's economy and would be more accessible to many Americans who were not necessarily concerned with or involved in pure research, became an important component of presidential candidate Clinton's economic policy. Soon after his election in 1992, the President-elect sponsored a seminar on the economy at which a spirited exchange took place between Robert E. Allen, chair and chief executive officer of AT&T, and Vice President-elect Gore. Allen espoused the role of the private communication and computer companies in the building of the network, while Gore held firmly to his view that the federal government should take the lead in fashioning it and leave its ultimate operation to the private sector. Fearing that if there were no governmental involvement, libraries, schools, hospitals, and other public-sector institutions would find it difficult to afford access to the network, advocates for these public service organizations supported Gore's position.[12] As Carol Henderson of the ALA Washington Office remarked: "There is the danger of the public interest being lost here. . . . We see libraries as the public institution available everywhere that could be the safety net for those who can't afford such access."[13]

With many of the technological and economic issues still unresolved, the Clinton administration in the fall of 1993 nonetheless issued an "agenda for action," calling for the "construction of an advanced National Information Infrastructure (NII), a seamless web of communications networks, computers, databases, and consumer electronics that will put vast amounts of information at users' fingertips."[14] And in his State of the Union address in January 1994, the President stated a further objective: "we must also work with the private sector to connect every classroom, every clinic, every library, every hospital in America into a national information super highway [sic] by the year 2000."[15]

Governing the infrastructure are nine principles, including the protection of privacy and intellectual property rights and the extension of the "universal service" concept, implicit in the 1934 Communications Act, to ensure that information resources will be available to all at affordable prices. The first of the nine principles was the promotion of private-sector investment in the NII, a significant departure from Vice President Gore's original premise that the federal government should take the lead in establishing the infrastructure. Even though the locus of federal authority dealing with the NII is diffused among some twenty locations, two distinctive new entities were established to launch the information agenda—the Information Infrastructure Task Force (IITF), an interagency committee of leading federal administrators, and the Advisory Council on the National Information Infrastructure, a group of lay experts, representing stakeholders in the NII from both the public and private sectors.

Still ongoing in its operations, the first of these two bodies, the Task Force, comprises over forty representatives of the federal agencies most concerned with information policy. Chaired by the Secretary of Commerce, it has organized its work within the framework of four broadly conceived areas—a telecommunications policy committee dealing with universal service and network reliability; an information policy committee concerned with intellectual property, privacy, and the electronic dissemination of government information; a committee on applications and technology including health, education, and libraries; and a forum devoted to national security issues that cuts across the activities of the committees and the various working groups subsumed under them.

In contrast to the Task Force, the Advisory Council was composed of over thirty members intended to represent the American public. That a majority of the total membership was drawn from business and industry owed much to Clinton's philosophy of reliance on the private sector for the development of the data highway, but the imbalance in the Council's membership exposed the President to criticism for his seeming neglect of many organizations serving the public. Less than half of the membership represented in effect the "all other" aspects of American life—state and local government, the not-for-profit sector, labor groups, and education. One teacher was selected from the Arlington (Virginia) County public schools, and the dean of the School of Library and Information Science at the University of Pittsburgh, Toni Carbo Bearman, presumably represented the interests of the library and information science communities as well as those of higher education, since no other academic official was appointed. Completing its work early in 1996, the Advisory Council submitted its report, *A Nation of Opportunity: Realizing the Promise of the Information Superhighway,* to the President at a White House meeting on February 13. Also issued by the Council was a second document, *KickStart Initiative,* a compendium of exemplary community-based projects, most of them federally supported, designed to promote Internet access through schools, libraries, museums, and community networks. Indeed, the Council envisioned the role of these institutions as platforms for networking entire communities.[16]

The Advisory Council's work, important as it was in highlighting the public service aspects of the information highway, was almost totally eclipsed in the mass media by the successful congressional passage on February 1 of the Telecommunications Act of 1996, the first comprehensive rewrite of the Communications Act of 1934. President Clinton signed the legislation on February 8 in a dramatic ceremony at the Library of Congress. Designed to deregulate the telecommunications industry, the legislation is based on the premise that customers and users will get cheaper and better service if local telephone companies, long-distance carriers, and cable television providers are allowed to infiltrate each other's markets. Thus, telephone companies could offer video services, such as movies on demand, while cable companies could supply local telephone service, reducing the monopolistic control of the so-called Baby Bells, the regional Bell operating companies. Even though considerable promise was held out for consumer savings, the passage of the bill also provoked some pessimistic comments: "In reality, no one, not even the shrewdest and most powerful media moguls, knows exactly what to expect next. . . . At its simplest, the bill's core purpose is to unleash a 'digital free-for-all.' " Given the complexities of the legislation, however, "it will actually spawn a mountain of new regulations and lucrative fees for lawyers."[17]

The unleashing of this alleged digital free-for-all to create greater competition and lower rates for consumers certainly did not occur in 1996. On the eve of the first anniversary of the Telecommunications Act, sponsors of a symposium devoted to its evaluation enumerated the painful record of the past year:

The development of robust competition in local telecommunications has been stymied by court challenges; local telephone companies have retreated from their promises to build advanced video systems; cable television operators are reexamining their strategies in telecommunications; an explosion of mergers, acquisitions, and corporate alliances has substantially increased the concentration of ownership and control in media industries, especially broadcasting; jobs are being eliminated; telephone and cable television prices are rising; and the debate about a competitive, two-wire "information superhighway" to the home seems an increasingly remote dream.[18]

The comment of Gene Kimmelman, the codirector of Consumers Union in Washington, was more succinct but equally germane: "If we're supposed to be on the road to new services and declining rates, we're off to a horrible start."[19]

Although competitive activity within the telecommunications industry was almost nonexistent in 1996, the value of mergers in the industry accounted for one-sixth of the total domestic merger transactions during the year. Mergers and acquisitions in which one telecommunications company seeks a linkage with a partner are expected to promote a more advantageous edge for industry components as they invade each other's markets. In 1996, the five largest mergers in the telecommunications industry involved transactions valued at $83.89 billion. For almost $23 billion, the largest of these mergers links two Baby Bell companies, Bell Atlantic and NYNEX. Having passed muster with the U.S. Department of Justice, the merger was approved by the FCC in August 1997. Even greater competition in the telephone business during 1997 was anticipated by industry analysts, but even they were taken aback in the late spring of that year by the premature disclosure in the *Wall Street Journal* that the AT&T Corporation might merge with SBC Communications, Inc. Itself the result of the union of two former Baby Bell companies, Southwestern Bell and Pacific Telesis, SBC Communications controls one-third of the local phone lines in the country, while AT&T, although beset by competition from Sprint and MCI Communications, is still the nation's top long-distance provider. Had it occurred, the merged AT&T and SBC cartel would have resulted in the largest corporate combination in history, creating, in the words of industry analysts, the "behemoth" of mergers.[20] Rebutting the whole rationale behind this consolidation, FCC chair Reed Hundt commented: "Congress, in my view, intended these companies to be in separate war rooms, planning strategies directed at each other's markets. Congress did not intend AT&T and the Bells to be in each other's board rooms discussing combinations."[21] For many complex reasons, the creation of this behemoth seems to have died aborning, but the very fact that it was anticipated raises serious questions over the possible revival in the late 1990s of the Bell telephone monopoly—the old "Ma Bell"—even though landmark federal court rulings dismantled it in 1984. In any case, the discussion of an AT&T and SBC alliance, widely aired in the media, only contributed to further reservations about the feasibility of a thriving free-market telecommunications industry that the Telecommunications Act of 1996 was meant to create. Observed Gene Kimmelman: "The fact that this deal fell apart does not change the fundamental dynamic of massive consolidation in telecommunications rather than head-to-head competition."[22] As the year 1997 ended, another proposed merger was announced between Worldcom Inc. and MCI Communications Corporation, thus bringing to nearly $100 billion the total value of the mergers in the telecommunications industry since the Telecommunications Act was signed in 1996. The merger mania in the industry continued unabated into 1998.

Notwithstanding the lack of commercial and industrial entrants into the competitive price wars, anticipated by proponents of the Telecommunications Act, two of the law's provisions were of immediate concern to a number of organizations and institutions, including libraries. The first, dealing with the content of materials disseminated by computer networks, was the Act's inclusion of the provisions of the Communications Decency Act, the first attempt to regulate speech on the Internet, and the second was the legislative mandate dealing with the process by which "access to advanced telecommunications and information services" would be enhanced for the nation's schools, health-care facilities, and libraries.

The Communications Decency Act

The Communications Decency Act (CDA), filed as an amendment to the Communications Act of 1934, was introduced by its chief architect, Senator James Exon (Democrat, Nebraska), and Slade Gorton (Republican, Washington) on February 1, 1995. In an effort to outlaw the use of computer and telephone lines in transmitting salacious material, the measure proposed the imposition of a substantial fine and a possible two-year jail sentence on those who used a "telecommunications facility" to transmit "indecent" material to persons under the age of eighteen. Further penalized was the transmission of material deemed "patently offensive." Provisions of the U.S. Code (47 U.S.C. sec. 223) prohibit obscene or harassing telephone calls, and in effect the Exon measure extended the antiharassment, indecency, and antiobscenity restrictions placed on telephone calls to "interactive computer services" and an entire range of "telecommunications devices." In referring to the legislation, Senator Exon cited the need to prevent computer networks from turning into a "red light district" and to create an "information superhighway as safe as possible for kids to travel." In March, the Senate Commerce Committee voted to attach the CDA as an amendment to the omnibus telecommunications reform bill, S. 652, then pending in the Senate. Swiftly moving to defeat Exon's initiative, Senator Patrick J. Leahy (Democrat, Vermont) introduced a countermeasure, commissioning the Department of Justice to determine the necessity, if any, of adopting new legislation. Leahy's bill received support from only fifteen of his colleagues, thirteen Democrats and two Republicans. On June 14, while brandishing a bright blue binder labeled "Caution," Senator Exon invited the Senate to examine the binder's contents, salacious pictures taken during that week from the Internet. Following these theatrics, the Senate voted 84 to 16 to attach the Communications Decency Act to S. 652.

The "Internet porn panic," as one commentator described it, reached its apogee in late June when the July 3 issue of *Time* magazine was released with the cover story entitled "On a Screen Near You: Cyberporn." A number of photographs, including that of a nude male clutching a computer and seated on a keyboard, embellished the story. Relying heavily on research conducted by Marty Rimm while he was a Carnegie Mellon undergraduate, *Time*'s reporter cited Rimm's grimmest and most misleading statistic that 83.5 percent of the images on the Usenet were pornographic. The 83.5 percent figure, however, was derived from a limited examination of postings to only seventeen of some thirty-two Usenet groups that typically carry image files. Usenet actually comprises thousands of newsgroups, the majority of which are text based and do not include pictures. Although Rimm's research was almost immediately discredited for its inaccurate statements and spurious conclusions, the *Time* feature lent considerable publicity to alleged pornographic traffic over computer networks, and the 83.5 percent figure was bandied about on the floors of Congress. Undertaking his own campaign in this regard, Senator Charles E. Grassley (Republican, Iowa), introduced on June 7 a bill for the Protection of Children from Computer Pornography, sponsoring later that summer what he termed "the first-ever Congressional hearing on the topic of pornography in cyberspace." In December, a House-Senate conference committee urged the enactment of tougher regulations prohibiting the transmission of indecent material over computer networks, and the way was paved to incorporating the decency amendment into the final version of the telecommunications bill. On February 1, 1996, the House voted 414 to 16 and the Senate voted 91 to 5 to pass the Telecommunications Act, including as Title V the Communications Decency Act. No congressional hearings were ever held on the CDA.

The introduction of the Communications Decency Act had prompted many organizations, viewing the legislation as "new age Comstockery," to flood the Internet with analyses of its provisions and the text of petitions that could be sent electronically to members of Congress urging the CDA's defeat. Several anticensorship organizations worked with congressional leaders to draft legislation that would allow content-filtering technologies to be used in controlling the Internet, thus eliminating Senator Exon's approach, which made the producers or distributors of questionable material criminally liable. Although this attempt failed, industry efforts to filter Internet content, rather than criminalize electronic speech, coalesced in the Platform for Internet Content Selection, or PICS, a consortium formed a few months after the Exon amendment was introduced. Among its corporate members are Microsoft, IBM, Apple Computer, Netscape Communications, AT&T, America Online, and Compuserve. The acronym PICS is also used in reference to the technical protocols, established by members of the PICS consortium, that permit labels to be attached to Internet content, facilitating the blockage of certain sites, such as those dealing with violence or anarchy, hate or racist groups, pornography, or drugs. Rating systems, such as SafeSurf, Net Shepherd, and RSACi (Recreational Software Advisory Council), all employ PICS protocols.

Both the ALA Washington Office and the ALA's Office for Intellectual Freedom had vigilantly watched the progress of the Exon amendment, holding that it infringed on First Amendment rights and urging Association members to communicate to Congress their dismay over its possible passage. On February 8, 1996, the day that the Telecommunications Act was signed by President Clinton, the American Civil Liberties Union, in consort with nineteen other organizational and personal users of online computer networks, petitioned the U.S. District Court for the Eastern District of Pennsylvania, located in Philadelphia, for a temporary restraining order to forestall the enforcement of the provisions of the CDA regarding "indecency." Some two weeks later, on February 26, the American Library Association became a lead plaintiff in a second lawsuit challenging the enactment. The Association, along with the Center for Democracy and Technology and America Online, coordinated the work of a newly formed Citizens Internet Empowerment Coalition (CIEC), which included over twenty representatives of libraries, booksellers, book publishers, newspaper editors, commercial online service providers, and a number of nonprofit groups. In part, the CIEC suit challenged the Communications Decency Act on the grounds that it would subject librarians and the commercial online service providers to criminal prosecution for posting allegedly indecent materials even though these same materials would be legally protected in other media, such as print or broadcast:

Examples of "indecency" could include passages from John Updike or Erica Jong novels, certain rock lyrics, and Dr. Ruth Westheimer's sexual advice column. Under the CDA, it would be criminal to "knowingly" publish such material on the Internet unless children were affirmatively denied access to it. It's as if the manager of a Barnes & Noble bookstore could be sent to jail simply because children were able to wander the store's aisles and search for the racy passages in a Judith Krantz or Harold Robbins novel.[23]

In both suits, the defendant was the U.S. Department of Justice, represented by Attorney General Janet Reno.

On February 15, Judge Ronald L. Buckwalter granted a limited temporary restraining order, preventing the Justice Department from prosecuting online transmitters of so-called indecent material until the constitutionality of the indecency provision could be resolved. That same day a panel of three federal jurists, including Judge Buckwalter, was convened to hear arguments in the case. In a subsequent action, the ACLU and CIEC lawsuits were consolidated to ensure the presentation of a united front to the judicial panel. During the hearings held in the spring of 1996, Robert Croneberger, director of the Carnegie Library of Pittsburgh, testified that the library had many titles of books and compact discs in its online catalog, containing words that some communities might consider indecent. Cited as one example was the book *The Ice Opinion: Who Gives a Fuck?*, which was written by Ice-T and read by many young people and which discusses race relations in inner cities.

On June 12, in a 175-page decision, the panel found that provisions of the CDA failed the judicial test of strict scrutiny and was unconstitutionally overbroad. All three judges wrote individual opinions supporting their joint decision to enjoin the Department of Justice from pursuing, or even investigating, potential violators of the ban against the transmission of indecent material. In his separate opinion, Stewart Dalzell, a member of the three-judge panel, noted that the control of the mass media was increasingly being concentrated into the hands of the few: competing newspapers in major cities had been eliminated, and television and radio stations were now operated by the same interests that control the local newspaper. In contrast, the Internet was achieving "the most participatory marketplace of mass speech that this country—and indeed the world—has ever seen." In concurring with the plaintiffs' findings that there were "democratizing" effects of Internet communication, allowing individual citizens of limited means to speak to a worldwide audience on issues of concern to them, Judge Dalzell stated that "the Internet deserves the broadest possible protection from government-imposed, content-based regulation":

True it is that many find some of the speech on the Internet to be offensive, and amid the din of cyberspace many hear discordant voices that they regard as indecent. The absence of governmental regulation of Internet content has unquestionably produced a kind of chaos, but as one of the plaintiffs' experts put it with such resonance at the hearing: What achieved success was the very chaos that the Internet is. The strength of the Internet is that chaos. Just as the strength of the Internet is chaos, so the strength of our liberty depends upon the chaos and cacophony of the unfettered speech the first Amendment protects. For these reasons, I without hesitation hold that the CDA is unconstitutional on its face.[24]

The Family Research Council, one of a number of conservative groups supporting the CDA, castigated the decision as "arrogant." Commented its director of legal studies: "What else should we expect from an ACLU-hand-picked judge than a sweeping, radical decision allowing adults to knowingly send and display pornography to minors on the Internet?"[25] On the other hand, civil libertarians were jubilant. "We are ecstatic," said Judith F. Krug, director of the ALA's Office for Intellectual Freedom. "Librarians can continue to provide ideas to the public regardless of the format, without concern about fines or jail terms. This is a victory for anyone who uses public libraries."[26] The victory, however, was rather short lived, since the Justice Department's appeal to the Supreme Court for reversal of the panel's decision resulted in the high court's acceptance of the case in December 1996.

The concern of conservative groups regarding access for minors to interactive media had already been aired in the amicus curiae brief introduced in support of government regulation during the hearings held by the three-judge panel. The brief consolidated the views of five organizations, including the Family Research Council, the National Law Center for Children and Families, the "Enough Is Enough!" Campaign (a grass-roots effort to eliminate cyberporn from computer networks), the National Coalition for the Protection of Children and Families, and Morality in Media. In arguing that the CDA should be narrowly interpreted to prohibit only "hard-core" pornography, the brief labeled ridiculous any suggestion that library personnel would be in any way jeopardized by an implementation of the CDA:

The ALA's assertion that they would have to spend 100,000 dollars to hire people to read every book to find any pornography in the library is absurd. Numerous indexing and categorizing resources are available which help identify pornographic content available via the Internet or in "adult" bookstores. It would be very surprising to find any of this hard-core pornography in a public library. Certainly, listing a library's card catalogue on the Internet would not be patently offensive. Therefore, libraries have no burden imposed by the CDA.[27]

Nonetheless, libraries do have a burden. Unlike home terminals where parents can employ filtering techniques preventing their children from viewing questionable sites on the Internet devoted to sexuality or other objectionable topics, library terminals can be equally available to both children and adults. Concerned that its terminals were being used for the viewing of pornography, a Florida library system installed a software program on the machines that would enable viewers to block sites in any one of twenty-eight broad categories. The library, however, did not allow adults or even minors with parental permission to switch off the software program while using the terminals. The ACLU, considering litigation against the library, expressed at the time (1997) no objection to screening mechanisms as long as access by adults was not restricted. What the ACLU, perhaps, did not perceive is that children walking past a library terminal are often inadvertently exposed to images screened by an adult user. The situation is totally different from the previous experience of libraries in the use of a printed medium in which it was and still is practically impossible for a child to see what an adult is reading. As June Garcia, director of the San Antonio Public Library, put it: "To a certain extent, if you have a book or a magazine, you're afforded a greater degree of privacy just because of the placement of the item, whether it's a book on guns or abortion or poetry."[28] The development of special polarizing screens making the display of material visible only to the person sitting at the computer may be one way to obviate this problem, but many library patrons find them irksome and remove them.

Another complication facing libraries is how far these commercial software ventures go in monitoring network sites. Critics of CyberSitter, a filter privately produced in Santa Barbara, for example, note that there is no real way of knowing what sites have been proscribed. Although advertising that it avoids sites dealing with illegality, bigotry, racism, drugs, or pornography, CyberSitter also, unknown to its subscribers, filtered out sites devoted to feminism, such as the Web site for the National Organization for Women. In commenting on this particular case, the *Washington Post* editorialized: "it will be a while before a Better Business Bureau arises to give cyber-dwellers anything resembling truth in labeling."[29] Some library observers believe that the use of filtering sites in public libraries, however undesirable, will be inevitable; others consider the restriction of patron access to electronic information an infringement of intellectual freedom. Obviously, the boards and administrators of individual public libraries will set their own policies, but the Association's actions to override the federal Communications Decency Act, as well as its undertaking litigation in January 1997 to overturn a New York State statute, similarly banning the electronic transmission of indecent material to minors, have reinforced the animus regarding the Association among conservative groups. At a national conference of ALA's Public Library Association, Karen Jo Gounaud, founder of the movement for Family Friendly Libraries, raised the issue of ALA's leadership:

Finally, consider one last time the children. The ALA leadership recently declared that it believes in protecting electronic information from ANY limitations, REGARDLESS OF CONTENT OR THE AGE OF THE USER. Many of you are parents yourself [sic]. Do you REALLY believe that our freedoms in America are seriously compromised if a thoughtful library board, in response to local concerns, decided on a policy preventing your 10 or 15-year-old child from clicking on the free library Internet to see women raped or children molested for the sexual pleasure of sick adults?[30]

Since the location of sex-oriented sites on the Internet is not easily discovered and many require payment by credit card or other identification, the situation may not be as grave as Gounaud suggests, but her concerns have been conjoined with those of other citizen activists hoping to suppress children's access to unsuitable materials on library terminals.

The Association's foray into the constitutionality of electronic transmission, evidenced in part by the depositions of librarians made during the Philadelphia hearings, represents a significant departure for the profession in dealing with issues of intellectual freedom. In the past, the censorship of allegedly obscene books, such as James Joyce's *Ulysses* or Henry Miller's *The Tropic of Cancer*, both of which were liberated from proscription by the decisions of federal jurists, primarily involved, for libraries at least, the author's right to speak and the public's right to know. For librarians, the issue was solely the protection of intellectual content, having little to do with the publishing or packaging of that content. Although it is quite true that judicial review of films and broadcasts has occurred many times, public libraries have until recently collected educational films and documentaries, not those currently being shown in theaters, and they do not circulate radios or television sets. Even though many public libraries are now purchasing video cassettes of commercially produced entertainment films, these have already been vetted in the marketplace and pose little censorship threat to a public library distributor. As a result, Supreme Court rulings in such precedent-setting cases as *Jenkins v. Georgia*, 418 U.S. 153 (1974), involving the film *Carnal Knowledge*, and *Federal Communications Commission v. Pacifica*, 438 U.S. 726 (1978), involving the "dirty words" radio broadcast by comedian George Carlin, have had little direct effect on public library practice.

But in the case of allegedly obscene or indecent materials on the Internet, not only are librarians coping with the protection of intellectual content, but they are also dealing with the process by which that content is disseminated. Unlike books, broadcast, and film, an interactive computer network is an entirely new medium, controlled by no one entity and restricted by no spatial consideration. This new medium is making available an enormous spectrum of information, education, and entertainment resources, and the potential of enlarging that spectrum seems limitless. At the same time, it is being used for the issuance of hate speech, racist and gender-based jokes, salacious images, and spurious information of many kinds. Librarians, accustomed to judging books and journals in part based on the authority and stature of their authors and publishers, are now dealing with a medium in which the best determinant of value seems to lie almost wholly in the eyes of the beholder. For that reason libraries place notices on their Web sites or their terminals that they cannot be held responsible for Internet content or for children's access to it, leaving site surfers to their own devices. At the same time, the dilution of the entire range of networked resources to the level of whatever may be acceptable for children—a dilution that is inherent in the provisions of the Communications Decency Act—seemed to many librarians an unwarranted and rather drastic course that had to be resisted to protect the principles of intellectual freedom. Conservative activists, however, have identified themselves as protectors of young people, and during the early months of 1997 national attention was accorded efforts by pressure groups and local officials to control access to the Internet in local libraries. The mayor of Boston instigated a movement to place filtering technology on all city-owned terminals, including those of the Boston Public Library; the borough president of Staten Island in New York City threatened the suspension of public funds until the allegedly pornographic sites on branch library terminals were abandoned; and a local paper in Brooklyn took up the cause with a front-page headline, "Kids Can Get Porn for Free at Library," and a cartoon showing one boy admonishing another not to buy from a kiosk of "adult" material because it was "kid stuff. Let's use the Library's Internet."[31] The article and the illustration were particularly offensive to the library's administration because no complaint, either verbal or written, had been received from any borough resident. These incidents and others elsewhere in the country were highlighted in a series of special online MSNBC reports devoted to the controversy over access by minors to the Internet, issued in the spring of 1997.[32]

However much some local officials deplored the increased availability of unfettered Internet access, federal courts in two jurisdictions, one in New York State and the other in Georgia, handed down decisions on June 20, 1997, overturning state enactments attempting to regulate the Internet. In the New York case, *American Library Association v. Pataki*,[33] the Association had been the lead plaintiff, and its officials expressed considerable gratification at the outcome of both cases, since they set a precedent for other states: "These decisions tell legislatures to think twice before attempting to regulate the Internet," an ALA news release proclaimed.[34] More to the point, however, these cases appeared to be a hopeful augury of the impending Supreme Court action.

As many observers had expected, on June 26, 1997, the Supreme Court in the essentially unanimous decision in *Reno v. ACLU* found two key provisions of the Communications Decency Act unconstitutional. The first of these, known as the "indecent transmission" provision, would penalize anyone who transmits any "obscene or indecent" communication to recipients, knowing that such recipients are under eighteen years of age, and the second, the "patently offensive display" provision, would prohibit the transmission to persons under eighteen years of age of any communication that describes or depicts "in terms patently offensive as measured by contemporary community standards, sexual or excretory activities or organs, regardless of whether the user of such service . . . initiated the communication."

Although Justice Sandra Day O'Connor and Chief Justice William Rehnquist jointly submitted both a concurring opinion and a dissenting opinion, the majority of the Justices were in accord with the findings. In rendering the opinion of the Court, Justice John Paul Stevens noted that the breadth of the statute's coverage, including not only commercial speech but also that of nonprofit entities and individuals, was wholly without precedent, further commenting that the language used in the statute was both ambiguous and imprecise:

The general, undefined terms "indecent" and "patently offensive" cover large amounts of nonpornographic material with serious educational or other value. Moreover, the "community standards" criterion as applied to the Internet means that any communication available to a nation-wide audience will be judged by the standards of the community most likely to be offended by the message. The regulated subject matter includes any of the seven "dirty words" used in the Pacifica monologue. . . . It may also extend to discussions about prison rape or safe sexual practices, artistic images that include nude subjects, and arguably the card catalogue of the Carnegie Library.[35]

Concluding that "governmental regulation of the content of speech is more likely to interfere with the free exchange of ideas than to encourage it," the Court reaffirmed the principles of the First Amendment: "The interest in encouraging freedom of expression in a democratic society outweighs any theoretical but unproven benefit of censorship." The Court's decision made two strong points. First, the Internet was accorded the same constitutional protection as the medium of print, which in effect gives it the highest judicial protection, since traditionally the Court has been more restrictive in dealing with the content of film or broadcast media. Second, although the Court recognized the government's interest in protecting children from harmful materials, this interest cannot be held to justify an unnecessarily broad suppression of speech addressed to adults: "[t]he level of discourse reaching a mailbox simply cannot be limited to that which would be suitable for a sandbox."

News of the opinion, which was available on the Internet within an hour of the Court's decision, reached many members of the library profession while they were attending the ALA's annual conference in San Francisco. An ALA-sponsored victory rally had already been anticipated, with Bruce Ennis, the attorney arguing the appellants' case before the Supreme Court, and the Association's intellectual freedom spokesperson, Judith F. Krug, scheduled to speak. On the East Coast, at a live cybercast news conference, ACLU executive director Ira Glasser hailed the ruling as an unprecedented breakthrough in determining the future of free speech into the next century: "Everyone knew the CDA was unconstitutional, but Congress passed the law and the President signed it. Today's historical decision affirms what we knew all along: cyberspace must be free."[36]

Other respondents were not quite so celebratory. President Clinton immediately issued a somewhat cryptic statement regarding the Court's decision: "We will study its opinion closely," he commented, adding that his administration "remains firmly committed to the provisions—both in the CDA and elsewhere in the criminal code—that prohibit the transmission of obscenity over the Internet and via other media." As a parent himself, the President sympathized with parental concerns that children are "accessing inappropriate material." He then announced that he would convene industry leaders and members of groups representing parents, educators, and librarians to develop a solution for the Internet that would be comparable to the use of the v-chip in restricting material on television. "With the right technology and rating systems," Clinton concluded, "we can help ensure that our children don't end up in the red light districts of cyberspace."[37] One is left to wonder whether the President's reference to "the red light districts" was just a turn of speech or a more purposeful echo of Senator Exon's warning that his bill would prevent the information superhighway from turning into a "red light district." Subsequently, on July 1, President Clinton presented "A Framework for Global Electronic Commerce," the work of an interagency task force to guide policy development and outline the administration's positions on a number of issues affecting the global information infrastructure (GII). Among the policy issues included in the "Framework" was the sensitive area of content control, and here the substance of the President's press statement was reiterated. In its efforts to shield parents and their children from inappropriate or offensive materials, "the Administration . . . supports industry self-regulation, adoption of competing ratings systems, and development of easy-to-use technical solutions (e.g., filtering technologies and age verification systems) to assist in screening information online."[38]

The decision in the CDA case is certainly a reaffirmation of First Amendment protections, and, in terms of the ALA's role as litigant, it can be viewed as a further step in the liberal agenda that many of its members espouse. But in a very practical sense, the Court's opinion did little to resolve the issue of library filtering or to curtail citizen protest over the possible damage incurred by minors in encountering inappropriate material on a public library terminal. Filtering technology in children's rooms, employed already in some libraries, may seem to some people to address the use of the Internet by younger children, but middle-school and high school students, the majority of them minors, need the more advanced materials available to them only in the adult sections of public libraries where terminals are not usually filtered. Neither the decision of the three-judge panel nor that of the Supreme Court really addresses this issue. The reliance of some of the federal jurists on the potential of market mechanisms to protect children at home and under the scrutiny of their parents simply does not cover the use of interactive media in an institution freely open to the public of all ages.

Notwithstanding the somewhat mixed picture affecting public library use of filters, the American Library Association strongly affirmed its liberal stance on July 2, 1997, when the ALA Council at its annual conference recommended and passed a policy statement, affirming that the use of filtering software by libraries blocks access to constitutionally protected speech and abridges the Library Bill of Rights. Two weeks later, on July

16, the controversy over Internet filtering was further heightened when at a White House meeting called by President Clinton and Vice President Gore to discuss strategies for making the Internet "family friendly," industry leaders vied with one another to promote the use of blocking, filtering, and labeling technology. Subsequently civil libertarians expressed their view that these same technologies were becoming tools, in the ACLU's phrase, to "torch free speech on the Internet." A White House press release put forth the administration's position to enforce vigorously federal prohibitions against child pornography and obscenity over the Internet and to stem its use by pedophiles in enticing children to engage in sexual activity. The President also directed key federal agencies to develop policies for labeling executive branch Web sites. Briefly mentioned in this news release was the ALA's national campaign, "Librarian's Guide to Cyberspace for Parents and Kids," which included a listing of "50+ Great Sites" recommended for preschool and elementary school children that was mounted on the ALA Web site where it would be continuously updated and expanded.

Stunned by the tenor of this White House meeting and its "unabashed enthusiasm for technological fixes that will make it easier to block or render invisible controversial speech," the ACLU issued its own manifesto, "Fahrenheit 451.2: Is Cyberspace Burning?"; it documents the threat to civil liberties in the indiscriminate use of filtering technology.[39] By the close of 1997, two schools of thought had emerged: those who believed that the Internet industry would, like motion pictures and television, employ some form of self-regulation and those who held that such regulation would proscribe speech that is constitutionally protected.

Affordable Telecommunications Rates for Libraries and Schools

In contrast to the profession's concern over the decency provisions of the CDA, which primarily pertained to the role of information as content, the other provision of the Telecommunications Act of 1996 that had long-range implications for libraries dealt specifically with equity issues in the distribution of information through electronic technology. Here the main emphasis is the process by which information is disseminated, rather than its content, although, of course, the process facilitates the dissemination of the content. When the major revision of the Communications Act of

1934 was being deliberated in the Commerce Committee of the Senate, Senator Olympia J. Snowe (Republican, Maine), backed by Senator John D. (Jay) Rockefeller IV (Democrat, West Virginia), introduced language to provide affordable telecommunications rates to schools, libraries, and rural health-care facilities. Precedent for this action was the long-held tradition of the principle of universal service, implicit in the 1934 legislation that "all the people of the United States" would be afforded "a rapid, efficient, Nation-wide, and world-wide wire and radio communication service with adequate facilities at reasonable charges."[40] In effect, affordable access to POTS (plain old telephone service) would be expanded to include the provision of advanced telecommunications services to certain key entities, assuring their constituents access to the information superhighway.

Earlier versions of this proposal had extended eligibility also to zoos, museums, and aquariums, but Senator Snowe deleted them in favor of institutions deemed the most essential. Subsequently endorsed by the two Nebraska senators, both Democrats, Robert Kerrey and James Exon, this measure is known as either the Snowe-Rockefeller amendment or the Snowe-Rockefeller-Kerrey-Exon amendment (SRKE). The passage of the amendment through the full Senate was stormy, with Republican Senator from Arizona John McCain (now chair of the Senate Commerce, Science, and Transportation Committee) opposing it on the grounds that no allowance was made for income differentials among the beneficiaries. Consequently, the amendment could prove to be an ongoing entitlement for wealthy schools, libraries, and hospitals. Its proponents, said McCain, also discriminated against many groups of equally worthy stature, such as the Salvation Army and the Veterans of Foreign Wars. Facetiously, Senator McCain suggested that he himself might propose amendments guaranteeing eligibility for the library of the generously endowed J. Paul Getty Museum. Language sensitive to some of Senator McCain's concerns, however, was agreed to by the amendment's sponsors, and on June 15, 1995, it was passed in the Senate by a vote of 98 to 1.

Although the House version of the telecommunications legislation went to the House-Senate conference committee with no provision for the school and library program similar to that adopted by the Senate, the SRKE amendment was retained in the conference report published on January

15, 1996. And in the final version of the bill, enacted on February 1, the school/library discount provisions were included as Section 254(h) of the legislation. Mandated in the new law was the establishment of a Federal-State Joint Board on Universal Service, charged with the task of recommending to the FCC the means of implementing the provisions dealing with all of the universal service policies in the new enactment, including those making basic phone service available to all Americans. Appointed to the Joint Board were three commissioners from the Federal Communications Commission, four state utilities commissioners, and one consumer advocate. Reed Hundt, chair of the FCC, served as the Board's chair.

As part of his reelection strategy in late 1996, President Clinton forcefully urged the FCC to "give every elementary, middle and high school and library in the country the lowest possible E-rate [educational rate], free basic service to the Internet. For more sophisticated services, like teleconferencing, the FCC should require discounted rates, with the deepest discounts going to the poorest schools and areas."[41] In tandem with the Commerce Department, the Departments of Agriculture and Education proposed the Clinton plan in a filing to the Joint Board in the fall of 1996. Several Bell companies were less than ecstatic at the idea of an E-rate. Frank Bumper, NYNEX vice president for federal regulatory planning, said NYNEX believed free anything was a bad idea: "Someone is going to have to pay for it. This money is going to be raised from other consumers."[42]

Throughout a lengthy and complicated process, the ALA Washington Office had been constant not only in pressing the need for the inclusion of Senator Snowe's amendment in the Telecommunications Act but also in submitting the detailed documentation required by the Joint Board and the FCC. The ALA filed submissions in its own right and also in the spring of 1996 joined a consortium, the Education and Libraries Networks Coalition (EdLiNC), comprised of more than thirty national organizations representing public and private schools and libraries, to further the equity principle in telecommunications services. In addition, the Association solicited some thirty thousand signatures submitted on Equity Petition forms that were subsequently presented to representatives of the Joint Board or the FCC at ceremonies held in San Francisco, Tallahassee, and Washington, DC.

After eight months of work and the receipt of more than twenty-seven thousand pages of filings submitted by over five hundred individuals and private- and public-sector organizations, the Joint Board voted on their recommendations to the FCC on November 7, 1996, releasing their findings the following day. Disregarding the administration's proposal that schools and libraries be given free access to the Internet, the Joint Board nonetheless came up with a generous package, capping total expenditures for the discounted rates supporting schools and libraries at $2.25 billion per year but also allowing any funds not disbursed in a given year to be carried forward. Discounts ranging from 20 to 90 percent were proposed for all telecommunications services, internal connections, and access to the Internet, with the largest discounts reserved for rural and insular schools and libraries and those situated in either high-cost areas or areas having a high incidence of low-income residents.

Discounts on internal connections, including inside wiring, routers, hubs, wireless LANs and others, were also recommended, although spokespersons from the telecommunications carriers, such as BellSouth, Sprint, and MCI, had opposed the use of discounts to cover inside wiring. Representative Jack Fields, then chair of the House Telecommunications and Finance Subcommittee, believed that the federal universal service fund was intended by Congress to support subsidies for services only, not for plant and equipment. The Joint Board disregarded this distinction, determining that disadvantaged schools and libraries would not be able to take advantage of below-cost rates for telecommunications services if they could not finance internal connectivity.

FCC chair Reed Hundt committed himself on several occasions to full support of the proposed recommendations. Speaking as "a former teacher, the son of a teacher, the brother of a librarian, and the father of three students," Hundt described November 7, 1996, as "a date that will long stand out in the history of American education" because the notion that every child is entitled to the same quality of education was given concrete form by the Joint Board's recommendation. Horace Mann and John Dewey and other great teachers, he said, owed the Joint Board an "A for appreciation."[43] But there was no "A for appreciation" forthcoming from some of the common carriers, which were expected to ante up the $2.25 billion universal service fund for schools and libraries. A representative of the Consumer Federation of America noted that the Baby Bells, with the exception of NYNEX, had proposed a less ambitious program for schools and libraries than that advanced by the Joint Board. Anticipating that the costs of the fund would eventually be transferred to the consumer, a BellSouth spokesperson said: "Frankly, we're a little concerned about the size of this universal-service fund: $2.25 billion is a lot of money." And a vice president for the Competitive Telecommunications Association pessimistically predicted that the universal service provisions being considered by the FCC would end in litigation: "whoever loses is going to take it to court."[44] In a gesture of good will toward the new provisions, however, officials of AT&T, Bell Atlantic, and NYNEX filed a proposal with the FCC in April 1997 stating their intent to fully fund the recommendation for discounted rates affecting schools and libraries and to ensure the availability of basic telephone service for residents in high-cost rural areas and for those in economic need.

On May 7, 1997, the FCC voted unanimously on the final rulings to implement universal service, establishing a fund of $4.6 billion to include such essential services as voice-grade access to the public telephone network; touch-tone service; access to emergency numbers, including 911; access to operator services and directory assistance; and the expansion of services to low-income consumers through the Lifeline and Link Up programs currently sponsored by the FCC. Consistent with the recommendations of the Joint Board, the FCC also made provision for health-care providers in rural areas to receive support from the universal service fund, not to exceed an annual cap of $400 million. Regarding the discounted rates for schools and libraries, the FCC closely followed the recommendations of the Joint Board. The highest discounts in a range of 20 to 90 percent were to be granted to schools and libraries with a high incidence of disadvantaged clients or those located in high-cost areas. Economic disadvantage was to be determined by the number of students eligible for the national free and reduced-cost school lunch program. Libraries were to use the measure of school lunch eligibility for the school district in which they are located or the nearest district. Participating libraries were those defined in the Library Services and Technology Act, those operating as nonprofit organizations, and those whose budgets are separate from an institution of learning, such as a college or university. This latter criterion effectively precluded the libraries of colleges or universities from receiving discounted rates. In an effort, however, to facilitate cooperation among academic libraries, public libraries, and other types of institutional partners, such as community networks, the FCC encouraged the establishment of consortia but allowed the allocation of discounts only to those members of a consortium that are specified in the legislation—namely, schools, libraries, and health-care providers.

Initially, the administration of the program was scheduled to begin on July 1, 1997, with distribution of the funds to commence on January 1, 1998. This somewhat optimistic time table had to be readjusted, however, as the complexities of managing the various aspects of the universal service provisions came more clearly into focus. In September 1997, shortly before his resignation, FCC chair Hundt announced the establishment of three boards charged with the implementation of the provisions—the Universal Service Administrative Company, the Rural Health Care Corporation, and the Schools and Libraries Corporation. Elected as chair of the Schools and Libraries Corporation was Kathleen (K.G.) Ouye, city librarian of the San Mateo (California) Public Library. Deeply involved in telecommunications issues in California, Ouye had chaired that state's Task Force on Telecommunications Infrastructure for schools and libraries and had also served on the Governor's Council on Information Technology.

A potential interruption to the schedule for administering universal service funds had surfaced on June 18, 1997, when, as was anticipated by industry commentators and the library leadership, one of the telecommunications carriers brought a lawsuit in federal court alleging that the discounted rates for schools and libraries represented a new tax. SBC Communications, Inc., the company that failed to merge with AT&T, filed its suit in the Eighth Circuit Court of Appeals in St. Louis. Disappointed but not surprised, officials of the American Library Association believed it was possible to encourage the court not to let the suit delay implementation of the discounted rates. Pointing to the fact that the new provisions do not include funding for training and equipment, as claimed in the SBC suit, Mary R. Somerville, director of the Miami-Dade Public Library and 1996 to 1997 president of the ALA, commented: "It is extremely disappointing to see a company such as SBC, which owns Southwestern Bell and Pacific Telesis—and has huge profits—oppose these library and school rates. . . . Rather than fight over what amounts to pennies for a company like SBC, we would welcome the opportunity to work with SBC to ensure that every American has access to electronic information."[45] In a subsequent action on August 15, 1997, the BellSouth Corporation, the telephone company for most of the nation's southeastern region, mounted a second legal challenge to the universal service provisions. The case was filed in the Eleventh Circuit Court in Atlanta.

New Complexities

By the end of the summer of 1997, the library profession could look back on what appeared at the time to be two very successful encounters, the first with congressional leaders and the second with the highest court in the land. In May of that year, the FCC had voted unanimously to accept the final rulings of the Joint Board to implement the universal service program for schools and libraries, and in June, the Supreme Court had issued its decision to overturn two major provisions of the Communications Decency Act. By the close of the year, however, the librarians began to sense that their victories were only Pyrrhic as new challenges, both to the availability of the universal service funds and to the unfettered use of the Internet, began to appear. Among the first harbingers of these challenges was a letter, written in November, to the newly appointed FCC chair, William E. Kennard, by Senator Conrad Burns (Republican, Montana), chair of the Senate Communications Subcommittee, in which he expressed his "serious concerns . . . regarding the reasonableness and efficiency of the FCC's plans for implementing the Universal Service provisions of the 1996 Act."[46] That same day, an amendment to the fiscal year 1998 appropriations bill for the Departments of Commerce, Justice, and State required the FCC to review the implementation of the universal service provisions and submit a report to Congress by April 10, 1998. Also in November, Senator Ted Stevens (Republican, Alaska) asked the General Accounting Office (GAO) to report on the legitimacy of the FCC's actions in creating the Schools and Libraries Corporation and the Rural Health Care Corporation, since it was his contention that the creation of such entities was solely the responsibility of Congress.

The issuance of the GAO's report in February 1998 confirmed Senator Stevens's charge that the FCC had exceeded its authority in the creation of the new corporations. And as a result of this finding, three senators, all members of the Commerce Committee, called into question the mechanisms by which the FCC intended to implement the funds for schools and libraries, now popularly referred to as the "E-rate." Joining Senators Stevens and Burns in their criticism of the FCC was the Commerce Committee's chair, John McCain, who said, "I fully support the goal of bringing advanced telecommunications services to schools and libraries, but as I have stated in the past, I don't believe that multimillion-dollar bureaucracies are necessary in order to accomplish this goal."[47]

Exacerbating the situation of senatorial uncertainty about the implementation of the FCC's rulings was the unrest among executives of the nation's leading long-distance phone companies, who voiced their complaints over the projected expenses of the now augmented universal service fund to members of Congress. Increasingly, editorial commentators and news analysts indicated that the E-rate program was in for a tough fight. Reacting to rumors of pending congressional legislation to cut the program or derail it, Vice President Gore reaffirmed his belief in the value of wired schools and libraries in a speech made late in February: "There are those who would pick the money from the pockets of our poorest schools. I would like to say to them loudly and clearly: Your efforts to block the e-rate is an effort to ration information and ration education and it would darken the future of some of our brightest students. We will not let you do it."[48] Also expressing concern over the threat to the E-rate program, EdLiNC, the educational coalition of which the ALA is a member, sent a lengthy letter to FCC chair Kennard in March 1998, asking for his renewed commitment to the viability of the program. Having already been apprised of the FCC's decision made in December 1997 to reduce the amount of the common carriers' contributions during the first six months of 1998 from $1 billion to $625 million, with the funding level for the remainder of the year to be determined, the EdLiNC coalition feared a further lowering of the funds for schools and libraries:

A restructuring of this program midstream or an eleventh-hour lowering of the funding cap will do irreparable harm to communities all across the nation that have undertaken significant, long-term financial obligations in anticipation of this program. Either outcome would not only upset the legitimate expectations of all applicants and leave them "holding the bag," but will work particular harm on the low-income rural and inner-city communities that the program was designed to benefit most.[49]

Notwithstanding the support of the Clinton administration and the rash of letters sent to the FCC by concerned educational organizations, the agency was further bombarded when two members of the House, prominent in the drafting of telecommunications legislation, Representatives John D. Dingell (Democrat, Michigan) and Thomas J. Bliley, Jr. (Republican, Virginia), chair of the House Commerce Committee, joined Senator McCain and Senator Ernest F. Hollings (Democrat, South Carolina), a former chair of the Senate Commerce Committee, in forwarding a letter to Kennard urging the FCC to suspend any further collection of funds for the E-rate program, calling it a "spectacular failure" and "a raw deal to consumers." The letter further added that it was "too late for the [FCC] to rescue itself merely by tinkering with a fundamentally flawed and legally suspect program."[50] The strong tone of the letter was in part stimulated by announcements made by AT&T, MCI, and other carriers that they planned to impose a surcharge on the bills of residential customers and to inform them that the fee was in support of access to the Internet for schools and libraries. Although the E-rate had been proposed by members of the Senate and adopted by both congressional houses, opponents of the program erroneously and indeed unfairly called this proposed levy the "Gore tax," in recognition of the Vice President's long-standing support of a wired society.

On June 12, 1998, a beleaguered FCC capitulated to congressional pressure, announcing significant changes in the administration of the E-rate. Although the FCC had received 32,000 applications from the nation's schools and libraries for about $2 billion in funds, commissioners of the FCC voted three to two to shrink the monetary pool to $1.275 billion for the first year of funding, a 40 percent cut in the amount anticipated. The FCC announced that the loss of funds would not result in an across-the-board cut in all the services the program was intended to cover, and it further specified that eligible applicants would receive their funding requests for at least two items: telecommunications services and Internet access. The remaining funds, approximately $521 million, would be used to cover the cost of wiring rooms and buildings. Twice that amount had been requested by the applicants for such projects. Since the FCC decided that this money should be directed to the poorest schools and libraries first, some schools and libraries will be unable to pay for wiring their facilities.[51]

Other actions taken by the FCC in response to congressional requests included a proposed merger of the corporation dealing with schools and libraries and the corporation for rural health care into the Universal Service Administrative Company, which would serve as the single entity responsible for administering the funding for schools, libraries, and the rural health care providers by January 1, 1999. The FCC also changed the E-rate's initial funding period from twelve to eighteen months in order to allow the next funding cycle, beginning on July 1, 1999, to coincide with the operation of school-year calendars. Total funding through July 1, 1999, will be $1.9 billion.

In elucidating his version of the often hard-fought political debate over the E-rate, Representative Bliley made this comment, "The FCC blew it. Thanks to that agency and Vice President Gore, the American people, including less-fortunate Americans, are stuck with higher phone rates."[52] On the other side of the aisle, Representative Major Owens (Democrat, New York), a former librarian, appealed to the parents of children to take action against the telecommunications giants: "You have a telephone. Call AT&T now! Call your Congressman! . . . The Grinch will not steal the E-rate from the kids of America!"[53] In any case, nearly half of the E-rate subsidy was at this writing seemingly wrested from the hands of the Grinch, and only time will tell if the wiring of schools and libraries will continue to be supported from the coffers of the universal service fund.

The second major complication affecting the use of the universal service funds involved the resurgence of the Communications Decency Act in new guises. In November 1997 Senator Dan Coats (Republican, Indiana), a cosponsor of the CDA, introduced a bill to prohibit commercial distribution on the World Wide Web of material harmful to minors. In effect, the bill would require commercial distributors of adult material to make it available only to holders of credit cards or personal identification numbers. Referred to the Senate Committee on Commerce, the bill was reported favorably on March 12, 1998.[54] Of far graver import was the proposed Internet School Filtering Act, introduced in February 1998, by Senator McCain and various cosponsors. This bill would prohibit the receipt of universal service funds by any elementary or secondary school unless its administrator certified to the FCC that the school had installed on its computers filtering software capable of blocking material deemed inappropriate for minors. The bill also would prohibit a public library from receiving such funds unless it too certified that it employed filters on one or more of its computers. The determination of what was deemed "inappropriate" was left up to local officials, without interference from the federal government.[55] Although McCain's bill was approved by the Senate Commerce Committee in March, the reaction of its members was mixed. Republican as well as Democratic senators anticipated that compromise language would have to be employed before the full Senate considered the legislation. A *New York Times* editorial described the McCain initiative as "legislation that would harm free speech in the name of protecting children."[56]

As expected, civil libertarians were quick to assail this new threat to intellectual freedom, which posed the question: do children have any First Amendment rights? Conversely, conservative groups were encouraged to believe that the potential damage to young people inherent in the new technologies might be avoided. Further support for their position came from Vice President Gore, who issued a statement on March 23 calling for federal legislation to mandate the adoption of local policies regarding Internet access for minors. Since the Vice President's statement was construed by many people as endorsing McCain's bill, a White House spokesperson clarified his position: "We do not support the McCain bill. . . . The legislation [Clinton and Gore] would support would not require blocking, it would just require that schools and libraries put a plan in place regarding their students and patrons accessing inappropriate material." If a school or library wanted to allow open access to all online material, even including that deemed "inappropriate," then the decision would be made by the school and community, the spokesperson added.[57]

Because it linked the provision of discounted rates for libraries with a mandate for filtering, the McCain bill presented a special challenge to librarians. As we have shown, the library profession held two distinct positions regarding the Telecommunications Act. On one hand, it protested with considerable vigor the provisions of Title V of the enactment, the Communications Decency Act, as an abridgement of the full freedom of expression; on the other, it worked with equal vigor to support the discounted telecommunications rates that would enable libraries to take advantage of the information revolution. That there was no dichotomy in the profession's position was owing to its perception that the issues inherent in the CDA were related to intellectual content, while the library discounts affording telecommunications access were a concomitant of modern processes of information dissemination, no different in principle than the process of printing from type on paper. By making the receipt of the universal service funds dependent on the acceptance of some form of Internet filtering, the McCain bill conjoined content and process in a way that few librarians could have anticipated.

Actions to regulate the Internet were not limited to the Senate. A companion bill to Senator McCain's measure was introduced in the House of Representatives on February 11 by Representative Bob Franks (Republican, New Jersey). Entitled the "Safe Schools Internet Act of 1998," it was subsequently affixed to a House appropriations bill. Adding to this increasing number of initiatives proposing computer filtering was the "Child Protection Act of 1998," introduced in June by Representative Ernest Istook (Republican, Oklahoma). His measure exceeded the scope of the McCain and Franks bills by requring that all public schools and libraries using federal funds to purchase a computer install software designed "to prevent minors from obtaining access to any obscene information using that computer." The bill mandates that the software must be operational whenever federally funded computers are used by minors, but makes provisions for an adult designated by the school or library to aid students in accessing nonobscene Web sites inadvertently blocked by a software filter. Even though Istook allowed that the Internet is a "great educational resource," he also noted that it is "overflowing with pictures and material that shouldn't be available to our kids. . . . Unless we use special software, this pornography can pop up on the screen even when a child is not looking for it. And we also want to remove the temptation, so kids won't be trying to find it. When our tax money is used to provide Internet access, it must also protect our children from obscenity."[58] Attached to the appropriations bill for Labor, Health and Human Services, and Education, the Istook amendment was approved by the House appropriations subcommittee on June 23 without a hearing.

In the Senate matters came to a head in midsummer when in a three-day period, July 21 to July 23, four measures affecting the Internet that dealt with privacy and free-speech issues were added to a Senate appropriations bill, in all but one case without debate. Senator Coats's bill was attached to the fiscal year 1999 $33 billion spending plan for the Departments of

Commerce, State, and Justice, while Senator McCain's bill was offered as an amendment to the Coats measure. Two additional measures were also passed, the first giving the FBI access to the customer records of Internet service providers during investigations of pedophilia with no requirement for an order from a court or grand jury, and the second banning gambling on the Internet because Internet gambling is "accessible by minors." This last measure was the only one to be debated on the floor.

Although Ron Weich, legislative consultant to the ACLU, defined the entire process as "sloppy legislating," Mark Buse, policy director for the Commerce Committee, defended the procedure. Noting that Senator McCain had tried unsuccessfully to schedule his bill for floor debate, Buse added, "There were certain Democrats fronting for the ACLU who would not allow us to bring the bill up for debate. We had no choice but to offer it as an amendment." Although the protection of children is the ostensible reason for this rash of legislation, the long-term implications for the preservation of free speech and individual privacy are, in the opinion of many civil liberties advocates, serious indeed. As Ron Weich observed, the Congress, dealing with a complex new phenomenon, "has not begun to consider the important constitutional and practical considerations of these bills."[59]

Some congressional leaders, however, have tried to show judicious restraint in the projected policing of the Internet. During March 1998 when both the Coats and McCain bills were being considered by members of the Senate Commerce Committee, Senator Burns, chair of the Senate Communications Subcommittee, announced that he would introduce legislative language requiring schools and libraries to certify that they have instituted appropriate Internet use policies before receiving the E-rate discounts. The distinction between his proposal and those of his Senate colleagues may appear subtle, but his alternative approach would have left the responsibility for determining Internet use policies in the hands of local school and library boards, and there would have been no federal requirement to install filtering software. On March 12, when the Senate Commerce Committee approved the McCain bill, there was consensus among the senators that modifications in the language of the bill would be made to accommodate the Burns alternative and an additional recommendation made by Senator John B. Breaux (Democrat, Louisiana) that called for flexible or customized filtering to permit access for adults. Although the official announcement from the Senate Commerce Committee reported that the McCain bill was passed without modification, proponents of the Burns alternative were confident that it would be considered before the bill was submitted to the full Senate.

By attaching their measures to the appropriations bill on July 21, when they were adopted by voice vote as "amendments," Senators McCain and Coats effectively blocked Senator Burns from offering his alternative Internet Use Policy to the McCain proposal. In summarizing these congressional actions in the July 22 edition of the ALA *Washington Office Newsline*, the editors commented:

In the past few weeks both Sens. McCain and Coats made efforts to bring their bills to the floor. Because of the controversial nature of the bills and the pre-recess schedule, unanimous consent was needed but neither Senator was successful. By attaching both measures to the appropriations bill, the two Senators bypassed the process of getting unanimous consent. They also avoided any serious debate on the merits of their legislation, repeating the pattern similar to the Communications Decency Act—passing suspect legislation without full consideration of the constitutional questions.[60]

At this writing it is not possible to project the future course of these recently passed measures, but if Congress ultimately enacts them civil libertarian organizations will no doubt seek redress in the courts. Senator Burns, perhaps unhappy at the outcome of his own endeavors, introduced on July 23 an entirely new bill, in which a portion of the federal excise tax on telephone bills would be used to fund the E-rate discounts, thus entirely eliminating the universal service fund for schools and libraries. Administration of the new program would be transferred from the FCC to the National Telecommunications and Information Administration of the Department of Commerce. A comparable bill was also introduced in the House.

Anticipating that the thrust of congressional efforts to protect children from using the Internet indiscriminately would continue, the ALA Office for Intellectual Freedom moved ahead to draft "Guidelines and Considerations for Developing a Public Library Internet Use Policy," a document designed to answer specific policy questions from an intellectual freedom perspective. Intended to aid local public libraries in initiating policy statements, had they not already done so, the guidelines reinforce the principle that "libraries are *the* information source in our society. They link individuals with the knowledge, information, literature, and other resources people seek. It is never libraries' role to keep individuals from what other people have to say." Reaffirming its stance against the use of filtering or blocking technologies, the ALA, through its Intellectual Freedom Committee, recommended several courses for local libraries: the adoption of a written Internet use policy; the communication of that policy to library users, including parents; the sponsorship of programs to educate library users, again including parents and children, in the use of the Internet; and the recommendation of appropriate sites for children and youth, particularly the two Web sites the ALA maintains for children and young adults. The guidelines were presented to the ALA Council in June 1998, and their text was made available on the ALA Web site.[61]

Also in June, the ACLU issued a special report providing an in-depth look at "why mandatory blocking software is both inappropriate and unconstitutional in libraries." Although the ACLU conceded that such software can be useful in the hands of parents, it held that in the hands of government, and such governmentally supported agencies as the public library, "blocking software is nothing more than censorship in a box." The report continues:

Censorship, like poison gas, can be highly effective when the wind is blowing the right way. But the wind has a way of shifting, and sooner or later, it blows back upon the user. Whether it comes in a box or is accessed online, in the hands of the government, blocking software is toxic to a democratic society.[62]

Again, only time will tell if these directives prove useful to the library profession, but in all probability it is safe to say that the totality of concerns—including White House disquiet over the need to protect children, congressional scrutiny in this regard, the increasing incidence of local lawsuits dealing with the use or nonuse of filtering by public libraries, and the ever-augmenting list of state statutes restricting Internet access to minors— does not portend a quick or easy solution to the issues faced by public libraries in affording Internet access to children and youth.

The *Mc*Web Site

The amount of attention given by the professional press to both the Association's foray into the constitutionality of the CDA as well as the federal provisions for school and library telecommunications access is almost overwhelming. But many of these sometimes breathless day-to-day accounts of imminent victory or defeat for the library cause often lack a sense of detachment—a long look at what the Internet has become and what will happen to it as it becomes increasingly dependent on the marketplace. In a sense, both President Clinton and Vice President Gore still cling to their vision of the Internet as a global encyclopedia offering children and adults alike electronic access to the Library of Congress and other great institutions in the empyrean of knowledge. But in the opinion of *New Republic* contributor Brian Hecht, the Clinton Internet policy is "actually rooted in an anachronism, drawing upon ideas long outdated." During the years of Clinton's administration, the Internet, "once a text-only medium for the dissemination of no-frills information . . . has morphed into the World Wide Web, which can deliver graphics, sound and movies straight to your home computer." Vanity home pages, marketing gimmicks, and trashy infomercials now glut the vehicle, which was once heralded as the world's most powerful library card.[63] Sociologist Ritzer might be tempted to add yet another entry to his list of areas influenced by American fast-food giant, McDonald's: the *Mc*Web site.

When the decision was made to encourage private-sector dominance in the production and maintenance of the data superhighway, it was inevitable that its original emphasis on cutting-edge research and the advancement of new knowledge would become less prominent. In our egalitarian society, perhaps this should not be a matter of regret, but it does make for strange Internet bedfellows, with *Hustler* magazine occupying a Web site similar to those of the U.S. Congress, Harvard University, and the Vatican. The battle pitched here is not one between conceptualizations of high and popular culture but rather one between a medium having great educational potential and one that is increasingly being dominated by commercial and entertainment interests. This is not to say that the nation's librarians and teachers should not have pressed on with their campaign for discounted rates, but the possibility should be considered that unless great guidance and discretion are used with this new tool, the result may be, as commentator Hecht suggests, a "net loss" not only for the Internet but for many of the nation's self-learners and its children.

Instigated by the federal government, the so-called Next Generation Internet (NGI) Initiative may provide a solution to the overcommercialization of the Internet. An advisory committee devoted to high-performance computing and the NGI has been named by President Clinton, with two members representing the library community: Ching-Chih Chen, an authority on the uses of advanced communications technology, who teaches at the Graduate School of Library and Information Science, Simmons College, and Sherrilynne S. Fuller, director of the health sciences libraries and information center at the University of Washington. The Next Generation Internet Initiative incorporates and builds on a project known as Internet2, which connects over one hundred universities and research installations to the very high-speed Backbone Network Service (vBNS), supported by the National Science Foundation. Designed to develop leading-edge applications, such as teleimmersion, digital libraries, and virtual laboratories, Internet 2 allows researchers to make use of powerful super-computers at remote locations to perform complex calculations that would be difficult to execute over conventional telecommunications networks. The vBNS, the link among the Internet2 institutions, can transmit as many as 611 million bits per second. Eventually, it will be capable of transmitting 2.4 billion bits per second. By comparison, the average modem in a home personal computer transmits 28,000 bits per second.[64] How public libraries will be affected by this new development is not known. In commenting on an NGI concept paper promulgated by the Clinton administration, the ALA Washington Office warily remarked: "Since technology flowing from the NGI program is intended to be eventually adopted by a larger user community, more thought is needed towards areas such as libraries, education, museums, historical societies, the cultural community, and health."[65]

In any case, the ALA's presence on the national scene has not been without immediate effect: on various fronts the Association has moved vigorously to exert pressure on both the judicial and legislative branches of government in pursuit of its goals. In both the suit against the Communications Decency Act and also in the campaign to implement the discounted rates, the Association displayed considerable political know-how and interest-group competence. In both cases, the ALA also linked itself with partners of equal, if not surpassing, strength on the national scene, participating in a process that communications professor William J. Drake terms the NII "public interest coalition." The mobilization of noncommercial stakeholders, generated over the social and equity issues affecting the information infrastructure, is a phenomenon, Drake observes, that has received little attention in the mainstream press. This lack of attention, he comments, "is ironic in an era when pundits are decrying the breakdown of civil society's collective institutions and community groups."[66]

The existence of the NII public-interest coalition was demonstrated in part by the creation in 1993 of an informal consortium devoted to telecommunications issues. Members of some forty groups, including the ALA, organized the Telecommunications Policy Roundtable (TPR) and in September of that year issued a statement of "public interest principles." Included were the right of affordable access to the NII, freedom to communicate, protection of privacy, and encouragement of broad discussion and debate over the development and regulation of the NII.[67] This statement was subsequently circulated to a forum of fifteen national library and information associations (including the ALA and five of its subdivisions), which adopted their own "principles for the development of the National Information Infrastructure."[68] The library principles did not deviate in any marked degree from those promulgated by the Telecommunications Policy Roundtable, but they were more specific about intellectual freedom and property issues and those ensuring interoperability of audio, video, and data communications devices.

The principles were predicated on the following assumptions: libraries will play several key roles in the evolution of the national infrastructure— as both providers and consumers of information, as public access points to the information infrastructure, and as responsible agents for the protection of the public interest in access to information. Certainly, one could hardly take issue with the need for any of these roles, except to note that neither the ALA nor the library community is the sole instrument for their implementation. Various affirmations of the uniqueness of the library as the public on-ramp to the information highway are often stated in the library literature and, even allowing for pride of place, they do raise a number of real questions.

Community Networks and Information Kiosks

New entities, already on the horizon and viable, are asserting their own roles as participants in the information infrastructure. One of the most prominent is the community or civic network, specifically mentioned by

President Clinton in his executive order of September 15, 1993, which created the Advisory Council on the National Information Infrastructure. Civic networks or community networks (the terms are often used interchangeably) emerged from early electronic innovations, such as computer bulletin boards and electronic cottages pioneered in the late 1970s and early 1980s. The first Free-Net in the United States was dedicated in Cleveland in 1986, and in 1989 the National Public Telecomputing Network (NPTN) was founded to serve as an information hub of the emerging movement. Although NPTN went bankrupt in September 1996, a similar umbrella organization, the Association for Community Networking, was incorporated in Colorado to address the challenges of assisting thousands of local communities to develop online technology. Although the exact number of these networks is difficult to ascertain, observers estimate that there are several hundred in the United States and abroad.

As defined by Doug Schuler of Computer Professionals for Social Responsibility, "a community network is a computer-based electronic network that provides a wide range of community-based information and services to people in a community for little or no cost."[69] A more imaginative analogy likens these networks to the town halls or the commons of early New England, where people gathered to exchange views and share information. Typically, the screens of these electronic networks display a menu listing local events and activities. A list of community organizations—under such broad rubrics as education, recreation, government, employment, health, and social service—is also provided, each one of which can then be tapped by the viewer for more in-depth information. Community networks have been founded by local and state governments (Santa Monica PEN and Hawaii FYI); through public and private partnerships among academic institutions, local communities, and business interests (Blacksburg Electronic Village, supported by the Town of Blacksburg, Virginia, Virginia Polytechnic Institute, and Bell Atlantic Southwest); and through the collaboration of users and members who are assessed fees (the Whole Earth Electronic Link, or WELL, San Francisco).

Mushrooming in the United States, the civic networks are the subject of an expanding literature and the focus of both the Center for Civic Networking, headquartered in Cambridge, Massachusetts, with a Washington, DC, office, and the Morino Institute, a Virginia-based educational organization established in 1994 to advance the use of public-access networks. In addition, messages of their movers and shakers are distributed by an active listserv, the "Communet: Community and Civic Network Discussion List."[70] Of particular value to the emerging movement has been the contribution of the Telecommunications and Information Infrastructure Assistance Program (TIAAP) of the Department of Commerce, which administers grants to encourage a broad range of organizations to develop advanced systems connecting them to the information superhighway. In 1994, the first year of the program's operation, the category of grant proposals receiving the largest amount of funding from the Commerce Department was civic networking, with a total of over $7 million granted to twenty-four civic networking projects. This pattern was repeated in 1995 with $8.4 million awarded to civic networking and in 1996 with $4.6 million again given to civic networks.[71] The 1997 program made available $5.4 million for a category entitled Communitywide Networking, a figure slightly less than the highest-ranked category, Education, Culture, and Lifelong Learning. (Readers should be mindful that the categories of TIIAP grant awards vary slightly from year to year, thus making exact comparisons in the allocation of funds difficult to assess.) Another source of funding for this new phenomenon was the Civic Networking Initiative (CivNet), sponsored by the Corporation for Public Broadcasting, which created partnerships between public broadcasters and local organizations in supporting a community network. Apple Computer, Inc. also created partnerships between civic networking and libraries through its Apple Library of Tomorrow program, which was discontinued in the fall of 1997 as a result of corporate downsizing. Among its institutional beneficiaries were the Flint (Michigan) Public Library, which took a leading role in spearheading the Flint Community Networking Initiative, and the Boulder (Colorado) Community Network in which the Boulder Public Library also played an important part.

Public libraries have sometimes been integral to the formation of these networks, and some have benefitted from TIIAP support, particularly Charlotte's Web, which although now independent was brought about in part by the efforts of the public library in Charlotte and Mecklenburg County, and the Three Rivers Free-Net, situated in the public library of Pittsburgh. Public librarians or library school faculty influenced the creation of a number of networks, including the Buffalo Free-Net, Prairienet in Urbana-Champaign, ORION in Springfield, Missouri, and the Seattle Community Network. The School of Information at the University of Michigan has been particularly active in addressing the interrelationship between the public library and the civic network, maintaining on its Web site a listing of collaborative efforts between the two agencies.[72] But for those civic networks in which there is no public library involvement, their emphasis on local events and activities and their capacity to link themselves to other sources of information, including the Internet, could lead perhaps to an encroachment on or even a displacement of the public library's information and referral (I and R) services, which some librarians believe were among the precursors of community networking.[73]

Nonlibrarian exponents of the new medium sense, however, that the networks represent the next phase in a continuum of community information delivery that in the past included the public library:

There is a sense of inevitability to the development of community computing. Simply stated, we find ourselves unable to imagine a 21st century in which we do not have community computer systems, just as this century had the public library. Moreover, we believe that the community computer, as a resource, will have at least as much impact on the next century as the public library has had on ours.[74]

In pursuing this analogy, the statement's author reflects that the rise in literacy rates initially promoted the establishment of the public library, whereas today the increasing sophistication of computer "literacy" is stimulating demand for public-access computerized systems. One wonders whether the author of these remarks believed that the two organizations were inimical. Although some observers predict and even espouse an eventual merger between the public library and the civic network, others criticize the networks for fostering the growth of highly discrete and specialized enclaves that are the very opposite of a communitarian exchange. In a paper prepared for the Kettering Foundation that is sympathetic to the aims of civic networking, Scott London nonetheless defines some of the dangers inherent in cyberspace communities: "Virtual communities are, more often than not, pseudocommunities. They lack many of the essential features of real communities, such as face-to-face conversation, the unplanned encounter—the chance meetings between people that promote a sense of neighborliness and familiarity—and, perhaps most important, the confrontation with people whose lifestyles and values differ from yours."[75] Even more pessimistic is the view expressed by the director of a library that operates a community network: "How do we reconcile the quest for civilized discussion via the Internet when so many discussion forums turn out to be a cacophonous blend of ego, questionable facts, and flame fests of absolutely no use to us? . . . If this is what 'community networking' promises for the future, then its demise is assured."[76]

So diverse are the viewpoints regarding this new development that it is difficult to predict whether the civic networks will usurp the informational function of the library, absorb it, or simply leave it alone. Although there appears to be some relationship between the activities of these networks and public libraries, there are also differences in the philosophies governing these organizations and the modes of thought of their respective custodians. Since the turn of the century, when public libraries instituted separate reference services, queries were accepted on matters as diverse as the price of Minnesota wheat in 1933, the number of states in the Confederacy, the date of the Shah's death, or the hours of opening of the local blood bank. Knowledge was not a province limited to geography. The statement, endlessly repeated, to the effect that any schoolchild can have access to the collections of the Library of Congress, if only she or he is connected to the Internet, has become a cliché repeated by many government officials, commentators, and reporters. Inherent in the statement is the assumption that electronic technology will even further the ability of libraries to transcend the boundaries of space and time.

But the original emphasis of the community networks was placed much more on the here and now. As Tom Grundner, founder of the Cleveland Free-Net, described it:

America's progress toward an equitable Information Age will not be measured by the number of people we can make dependent upon the Internet. Rather, it is the reverse. It will be measured by the number of local systems we can build, using local resources, to meet local needs. Our progress . . . will not be measured by the number of people who can access the card catalog at the University of Paris, but by the number of people who can find out what's going on at their kids' school, or get information about the latest flu bug which is going around their community.[77]

In her study of civic networks, prepared as her master's thesis in city planning, Anne Beamish reiterates this theme: "The most distinguishing characteristic of community networks is their focus on local issues. They emphasize local culture, local relevance, local pride, and community ownership."[78] At present, the community network movement is all inclusive, embracing many forms: the Free-Nets, InfoZones, bulletin board systems, televillages, and "smart" cities. In some localities the public library and the community network simply coexist, while in others, such as Cambridge, Massachusetts, there is considerable rapprochement between the two. The potential of these two entities to further their cooperation was discussed at a recent national conference where Patrick J. Finn of the LaPlaza Telecommunity Foundation observed, "It seems like libraries are trying to become community networks," to which Daniel E. Atkins, dean of Michigan's School of Information, replied, "It seems like community networks are trying to become like libraries." "Why can't they merge?" he asked.[79] At this point, it is an unanswerable question.

Another claimant to a community-information function emerged in 1994 in the now privatized United States Postal Service. That year, the White House asked the Postal Service to lead an interagency effort to provide electronic access to government information and services through the use of kiosks. Detailed in a Postal Service news release were some of the advantages of the "citizen kiosk" as a delivery vehicle: ease in filing applications for government services at all levels, the payment of fines or fees, the renewal of automobile registrations, and a category described as "help in solving real life situations such as: loss of job, retirement, health problems, births/deaths."[80] Speaking for the library profession, Arthur Curley, director of the Boston Public Library, and ALA president from 1994 to 1995, issued a response:

It's a great concept but a wasteful one if they don't take advantage of what's already there. Public libraries collect, organize and distribute information at more than 16,000 sites. We have more outlets than McDonald's. And we have staff to assist the public with their informational needs. . . . Our nation's libraries are the foundation of our nation's information infrastructure. . . . As librarians, we are concerned that [the] public's right to know be guaranteed through their public libraries.[81]

In January 1995, a seminar was convened by both the Postal Service and the library community in which the postal officials tried to illuminate their role and the librarians defended their profession. In all probability, neither side emerged the victor, but at least the Postal Service learned that librarians were familiar with electronic technologies and had considerable experience in fielding reference questions from the public. In April 1995, *The*

Kiosk Network Solution: An Electronic Gateway to Government Service was published by the Interagency Kiosk Committee, representing a coalition of federal agencies that was spearheaded by the Clinton administration's National Performance Review initiative. As a member of this coalition, the Postal Service in 1996 launched the WINGS (Web Interactive Network of Government Services) program, intended to provide an integrated gateway to combined local, state, and federal customer services. A component of this program was a kiosk pilot project conducted in Charlotte and Mecklenburg County (North Carolina), involving some twenty-five kiosks in libraries, the airport, shopping malls, grocery stores, the community college, the government center, and other sites. Although intended as a prototype for subsequent experiments elsewhere, the WINGS operation was discontinued by the Postal Service in May of 1998, even though the kiosks in North Carolina are still operational. In the opinion of several government officials, the WINGS experiment was useful, however, in that it clarified some of the issues and problems in providing electronic access to the information and services of all levels of government, national, state, and local. Said Frank McDonough, assistant commissioner for intergovernmental solutions at the General Services Administration: "We started talking about service to the citizen in 1988, and we don't have a lot to show for it. But there has been a lot of activity that allows you to see pieces of the future. This integrated service to the citizen is very difficult and will take longer than we thought. [But] the basic building blocks, like WINGS, are there."[82]

Stakeholders in the NII

As evidenced by the interest in community networks and information kiosks, interactive media are obviously with us. But the function of libraries has certainly never been solely linked to the provision of information, leaving both the ALA and the library profession in somewhat of a quandary as to just how far they should go in retaining their hold on the dissemination of a book-oriented culture while at the same time maintaining a viable presence on the data highway. In his iteration of the noncommercial stakeholders in the NII, William Drake defines three distinct categories. The first is reserved for organizations with specialized expertise in electronic issues, such as the Alliance for Community Media, Computer Professionals for Social Responsibility, the Electronic Frontier Foundation, the Benton Foundation, and the Center for Civic Networking. In the second tier are those organizations that have traditionally focused on other concerns but more recently have recognized the NII's importance to their objectives. Included are several organizations that deal with First Amendment issues, such as the American Civil Liberties Union and People for the American Way, and several with distinctive constituents, such as the National Association for the Deaf, the National Coalition for Black Voter Participation, and the United Cerebral Palsy Association. Also included here is the American Library Association, which represents not only a distinctive constituency but one that has taken strong positions on intellectual freedom. In the main, the third group comprises individuals, such as writers, teachers, academics, and artists, who may represent a constituency or merely themselves.[83]

Quite a few of the policy organizations in the first two categories came into being during President Reagan's administration in response to his privatization efforts at selling government information, previously distributed at either minimal or no cost to the American taxpayer. The American Library Association, however, represents somewhat of an exception. Founded during the nineteenth century when it was committed to the mission of furthering an institution devoted to a print-oriented culture, the ALA's current role is somewhat ambivalent, being at one and the same time the protector of older means of communication and the promoter of the idea that librarians were the first information professionals whose work in the organization of knowledge, both old and new, should still demand recognition and respect.

Federal recognition of the importance of libraries in the continuum of American education and of the potential role that they might play in a service-based economy has been achieved in two rather subtle but distinctive ways—the 1970 creation of the U.S. National Commission on Libraries and Information Science (NCLIS) and the 1979 and 1991 White House Conferences on Library and Information Services. The American Library Association vigorously lobbied for both of these initiatives and indeed inspirited the second. NCLIS resulted from a recommendation made by an ad hoc advisory commission, appointed by President Johnson, that a permanent national commission be appointed to oversee activities of the nation's libraries. Unfortunately, the legislation to legitimate this recommendation was introduced after Nixon had been elected. Few presidents, especially those who succeed presidents of another political party, feel much commitment to the priorities of their predecessors, and Nixon was no exception. Although he signed the legislation creating the Commission in July 1970, Nixon expressed vehement reservations about its necessity and indicated his opposition to the creation of new and separate agencies that are easily lost in "the vast machinery of government."

With only the most reluctant presidential acceptance of its mission, the Commission, composed of fourteen presidentially appointed members and one ex officio member (the Librarian of Congress or his designate), began its work. Throughout the quarter of a century of its existence, NCLIS has been on a somewhat seesaw course. With members appointed by the presidents of one political persuasion serving overlapping staggered terms with members named by those of another, the trajectory of this advisory body has been often uneven. Previous reference has been made to the strained relations in 1988 between the ALA and the National Commission over the latter's seeming endorsement of the FBI's Library Awareness Program, which sought information about foreign nationals using American scientific libraries for the use of Soviet intelligence. Incensed by what was perceived as a total disregard of the privacy rights of library patrons, the ALA Council called for a complete report of the Commission's effectiveness, and in a very fair-minded document the ALA Washington Office, although deploring the lapse, defended the Commission's overall contribution to library interests.[84] In recent years, chaired by attorney Jeanne Hurley Simon, the wife of former Illinois Senator Paul Simon, and directed until May 30, 1997, by Peter R. Young, a career librarian who is conversant with the newer technologies, the Commission has greatly enhanced its image and viability with the library and information professions. In future years, the Commission's role may be enlarged since provisions of the new Library Services and Technology Act require its members to advise the director of the newly established Institute of Museum and Library Services on policies relating to financial assistance for libraries and on the selection of joint projects involving libraries and museums.

The two White House Conferences, although important in raising grass-roots support in the selection of citizen delegates and in keeping the library agenda before federal officials, were not well covered by the national media, and both were undermined by the fact, unanticipated by the ALA, that they were held during the administrations of one-term presidents. Newly elected presidents do not necessarily undertake the implementation of recommendations afforded their predecessors, especially, as mentioned earlier, if those predecessors are of a different political party.

Not all the stakeholders affecting the role of libraries in the national information infrastructure are governmental in nature. One important aspect of the national scene is the proliferation of foundation activity bearing on the role of public libraries in the NII. Especially prominent in this regard is the work of the Benton Foundation, established in 1981 by Charles Benton, chair of the National Commission on Libraries under President Carter, with the legacy of his father, the late William Benton, senator from Connecticut, founder of Benton and Bowles, and owner of the Encyclopedia Britannica Corporation. Since the issuance of Clinton's agenda for action in the creation of the NII, the Benton Foundation has committed itself to a wide range of telecommunications issues, including digital television, spectrum allocation, discounted rates for schools and libraries, and many others.

The W. K. Kellogg Foundation, headquartered in Michigan, has funded a number of projects under the rubric Human Resources for Information Systems Management (HRISM). Designed to affect professional and institutional change in library and information science, this program pursued, through substantial grants and publications, three strategic goals—the reform of library and information science education, the redefinition of community library service, and the improvement of participation by library leaders in the public dialogue on information policy at all levels of government.

Libraries for the Future (LFF), a unique national nonprofit organization of public library advocates headquartered in New York City, specializes in funding exemplary projects that enhance the relationship between libraries and communities, particularly those lacking substantial resources. Through research and policy development, LFF aims to raise public awareness of the role of the public library as a site for individual and community development. As a joint author with the Benton Foundation, LFF recently issued a report profiling eight library technology projects serving a host of divergent constituents ranging from inner-city residents to rural households of no more than six hundred people. Other foundations contributing to the participation of public libraries in the NII include the Carnegie Corporation, the Andrew W. Mellon Foundation, the C. S. Mott Foundation, and the John D. and Catherine T. MacArthur Foundation, all of which, along with the Kellogg Foundation, support some of the activities of the Benton Foundation in the area of communications policy. Of more direct influence on the American Library Association were the grants made by the Kellogg Foundation and the MacArthur Foundation to the funding of the ALA Office for Information Technology Policy.

The John and Mary R. Markle Foundation, founded in 1927 to promote the "diffusion of knowledge . . . and the general good of mankind," has in recent years taken as its primary focus the advancement of new and innovative uses of communications and information technology, such as electronic voting. Its projects often lead to interesting findings, as in the case of a recent report on the so-called Internet dropouts, persons who originally used Internet services but later discontinued them.[85] The Gates Library Foundation, which has promised $400 million to support Internet access for public libraries, may ultimately have a role in influencing public policy, but it is too soon to assess its impact. Although not a foundation, mention should be made of the Urban Libraries Council, one of the three special interest groups shaping the parameters of the new Library Services and Technology Act. The Council seeks to identify and address problems relating to libraries serving populations of fifty thousand or more located in a Standard Metropolitan Statistical Area.

Although nongovernmental in nature, many special interest groups concerned with some aspect of interactive media also exist. Included here are organizations advocating proscription of the Internet (Family Research Council) and those opposing its proscription (People for the American Way); groups assuming oversight responsibilities for such governmental entities as the Office of Management and Budget (OMB Watch) and the National Archives (National Coordinating Committee for the Promotion of History); spokespersons addressing specific governmental policies toward national security (the National Security Archive), encryption technology (Electronic Privacy Information Center), copyright (the Information Industry Association), telecommunications deregulation (the Progress and Freedom Foundation), and many others. The list already seems interminable but is nonetheless growing.

With all these stakeholders shaping the policy of the national information agenda, questions naturally arise as to the staying power of the library profession and its viability in the policy debate. Writing in 1992, Thomas J. Galvin of the State University of New York at Albany (a past president of the ALA and its former executive director) commented that the "ALA has not yet fully established itself as a major organizational 'player' in the larger Washington arena of ongoing debate on the full range of issues of information and public policy. Its legislative and policy interests are still perceived in some quarters of the Washington community as narrowly partisan and as exclusively focused on traditional 'library' issues."[86] The past few years have eroded the validity of this statement: as its electronic listserv, ALAWON, and the printed version, *ALA Washington News*, reveal, the ALA Washington Office covers a host of information-related policy issues, including global intellectual property, high-speed wireless digital communication, the dissemination of electronically printed government information, the transmission of pornography, access to census data, and many others. In its legislative agenda for the years 1995 to 2000, the Association has placed first and foremost the category of "information policy" as a way to achieve its aim "to broaden its role and achieve full participation in the development of the national information infrastructure."[87]

Determinants that may hinder the ALA's full participation in the policy debate regarding the national information infrastructure do not necessarily include the efficiency of its lobbyists or the financial support allocated them. More to the point are the continuing stereotypical view of libraries and some evidence of a widening gulf between the aims of the national association and the practices of its members. In reference to the first of these factors, the public library in particular has suffered from a number of perceived limitations: with the exception of new or renovated buildings, its physical plant may not seem to connote a high-tech environment; as an institution, it may not appear as innovative or novel as the community networks or kiosks now being identified as disseminators of civic information; and, last, its personnel are largely female in an increasingly electronic environment in which men are popularly considered the custodians of technology. In commenting on this last point, Daniel J.Boorstin observes:

Until recently, when women were denied equal opportunities for fulfillment in other professions, they were perforce channeled into schoolteaching, nursing— and librarianship. They were refused access to the mechanical, engineering, and the high-tech professions. Movies still being replayed remind us of that stereotype—the unlipsticked librarian—lady with her hair in a bun, acting the gentle samaritan to the young and the lonely in the community. Computer technology, information technology, has offered a welcome opportunity to change this stereotype. . . . The librarian's work, no longer imprisoned in an obsolete gentility, has found its bold new place on the honorific frontiers of science and technology.[88]

Having championed the importance of the book during his administration of the Library of Congress, where he was responsible for the creation of the Center for the Book, Boorstin concludes somewhat reluctantly, "Ironically, this new technology has become a symbol of the liberation and invigoration of library science."

Finding its place on these new frontiers, however, has placed the library community somewhat at odds with its national association. Although paying considerable tribute to the nation's public libraries as society's "existing intellectual network," cultural historian Theodore Roszak has warned that countervailing forces that are not necessarily committed to the public good permit more and more information to fall into the hands of a profit-making industry, "turning what might be a public benefit into a private business."[89] Nonetheless, features of the private business world are being emulated as some public libraries, especially those in the larger metropolitan areas, assess fees, albeit modestly, for certain services. Officially, the posture of the American Library Association has opposed the institution of fees, deeming any infringement to access by electronic information, services, or networks a violation of the Library Bill of Rights.

A sense of the distance between the Association and some of its institutional members was reflected in a number of the interviews conducted during the course of this study. Neither the chief librarians nor their administrative staff expressed total dissatisfaction with Association policies, including those affecting the imposition of fees or the prohibition of filters, but an impression was conveyed that some of the interviewees felt that the activities of their national association were somewhat removed from their immediate concerns. There could be any number of reasons for this, but one that suggests itself here is the "institutionalization" of the federal role. In all probability, librarians of the present generation simply cannot generate the same excitement over federal aid that was exhibited by their professional predecessors during the early years of the LSCA's enactment. Then, too, the present managerial cadre of the nation's public libraries is constantly faced by a large tally of immediate and very localized problems, among them the need for greater effectiveness in their service and the constant demand to raise funds from either governmental or nongovernmental sources, or indeed both. Small wonder that the promulgations of a national organization located in Chicago may often seem of peripheral relevance to the daily lives of these active practitioners. Yet, at the same time, as they themselves acknowledge, the promotion of a public library presence in the national information infrastructure needs a strong voice on the national scene, and none of the highly articulate policy organizations and special interest groups abounding in Washington can represent that role better than the ALA. A greater convergence between the Association's leadership and that of its active practitioners is perhaps not the highest priority for either the Association or its membership, but in the long run its achievement is vital.

A further reflection on the ALA's own position in regard to its membership is in order here. Unlike many of the interest groups involved in the NII, whose officers and administrative staff set an agenda and follow it through, the ALA operates within a highly bureaucratized environment. ALA policy is established by the Council of the Association, which is made up of the Association's officers, members of its Executive Board, one hundred councilors at large, eleven councilors representing the divisions of the Association, and chapter councilors from each of the states, the District of Columbia, Guam, and the Virgin Islands. This somewhat unwieldy body meets twice a year. Elected from the Council are eight members of the Executive Board who, with the Association's officers, meet four times a year and because of their smaller size can be polled more easily by telephone or e-mail. Nonetheless, policies emanating from the Legislative Committee or the Intellectual Freedom Committee require in most cases Executive Board and Council endorsement, a process that must accommodate their prescribed meeting times. In this day of frequent, even frenzied, change, the time lags inherent in this procedure need to be rethought. Furnishing those responsible for setting the ALA's legislative priorities a more independent role and a quicker path to action would give a tactical advantage to the personnel lobbying on its behalf.

Political scientist Peter Woll has characterized the process of setting public policy in the United States as fragmented, specialized, and pluralistic.[90] Nowhere is this more true than in the establishment of a national information policy. Public libraries have a stake in that policy, because of both the intellectual content that they have historically represented and the process by which that content is disseminated, either through the circulation of the artifactual book or the transfer of digital data. Whether public librarians will achieve their goal of equity on the information superhighway will depend not only on their efforts to mobilize public opinion and support in their own localities but also on their ability to maintain a viable, visible, and persistent presence in the shaping of the national agenda for the information society.

5

The Institution: Services, Technology, and Communities

Vartan Gregorian, in an address to the American Academy of Arts and Sciences on reading in the computer age, observes that although the information revolution is "far from over," it is "about time for the enthusiasm and revolutionary fervor regarding the new technology to subside for a bit, while the methods of exploiting the technology are evaluated and integrated into the historical identity of institutions."[1] That evaluation and integration process does seem to have begun in public libraries. Piecemeal and pragmatically, and fairly rapidly, libraries are working out a place for themselves within the present information and communications environment, with the lines between the new and old (or traditional or classic) growing more tenuous. Librarians are learning to retain their identity and yet operate in a more complex media setting and move with some ease among information sources in different forms for different purposes. They are figuring out how to accommodate book and byte, the "yin and yang of knowing," as Marilyn Gell Mason, director of the Cleveland Public Library, expresses it.[2]

This is what library leaders, sometimes sounding as if they were whistling in the dark, have been bravely predicting over the past few years. In that scenario, librarians, trained to organize and evaluate information and help people find what they need, would function as organizers and navigators, consultants and guides in the new information age. A century ago, in another time of profound economic and industrial transformation, librarians collected and organized the products of mass publishing spawned by industrialized economies and brought these publications to a newly educated populace and expanding scholarly community. At the end of the twentieth century, librarians could, the argument went, act similarly in a new universe of global, evanescent, unmonitored digital information. Although the situation is fluid and not without problems, libraries are working at fulfilling this prophecy. "Disintermediation"—that is, the elimination of a helper or intermediary between information source and user—has no doubt occurred as people learned to find what they wanted by themselves (as some always did), but it has not occurred to the point of spelling the end of library service, as alternative scenarios projected. In fact, there is a growing demand for librarians to manage information systems, and in nontraditional (read *nonlibrary*) as well as traditional settings.

Not nearly everybody, furthermore, has or will have a computer and modem, although Internet connectivity is growing. Among those who do, not all can or will want to keep up with the constantly changing hardware and software that enable full use of the Internet or multimedia CD-ROMs. Most home systems do not have the wider bandwidths that institutions like libraries can have that enable fast Internet service. Not everyone can afford Internet connectivity, whose cost may rise or may decline, depending on the complicated and unpredictable economics of cyberspace. And not everyone can afford the expense of using commercial online databases on a private, individual basis. Libraries, even if they may charge for the service, can absorb some of the costs. Certainly not everyone knows how to use all this, in any case. A *New York Times* piece about Finland, the country with the most highly developed electronic culture and with the highest proportion of Internet connections per population (and where, another source claims, Helsinki City Library was the first public library in the world to put up a World Wide Web server), reports public libraries as key sites for people to use and learn to use the Internet.[3]

Is technology the driving force in public libraries today? Certainly it dominates much of the thinking of librarians and strains their budgets. On the whole, although libraries are moving ahead in using high technology, they appear to be taking a holistic view, trying to integrate new technology with classic services. But to say, as some librarians have done, that computers and telecommunications are just new tools in service of old purposes is a perhaps fatal understatement. Electronic technology may not be the only force at work in contemporary culture, but it is an inexorable, transformative force that is changing the way business is done, products are produced, and lives are lived. For libraries it brings new, never-before-available forms of communication and stores of information, both bibliographic and substantive, plus new modes of thinking about information and getting at it, and it offers new opportunities for service to individuals and communities. That is more than a mere tool, and no amount of nostalgia for the good old days of card catalogs and printed books can change that. At the same time, access to the Internet and online services does not and cannot define the public library. As more than one person told us, values define the public library. Hallmark of a democratic society, the public library is an open, community-based institution ensuring the public's right to know, a defender of the free life of the mind. Libraries remain complex, democratic, one-stop shopping and consultation centers for all manner of free (or mostly free) information, learning, cultural enrichment, and entertainment for people of all ages and persuasions. They still stock printed materials (as well as videotapes, audiorecords, maps, pictures, and so on), which continue to be produced and called for and not all of which will be in the near term, if ever, digitized. And as physical and intellectual presences they retain powerful symbolic as well as utilitarian importance in American society.

Public libraries have been given nationwide validation as important venues for public access to the electronic information highway. That they will not be unique in this respect is not unprecedented, granted that the magnitude of electronic information and ease of entry into it is new. In the age of print the library was never the sole source for current publications. There have been book shops, private book and magazine subscriptions, mail-order book clubs, and more recently big bookstore chains and video rental stores. People with money have always been able to purchase what they wanted on their own. The Benton report notes that some library leaders today see the spread of Borders, Barnes & Noble, and other super bookstores, with their easy chairs, coffee bars, and poetry readings, as posing a threat to middle-class use of libraries as dispensers of reading matter. The report also observes what the Public Library Inquiry documented in the 1940s and librarians have known for years—that frequent book buyers and frequent library users (and now computer owners) tend to be the same people: there is a self-selected, educated, media-savvy population that partakes of many cultural offerings, a population that may be larger today than ever given the spectacular growth in higher education that took pace when the baby-boom generation came of age in the 1960s and 1970s.

Furthermore, the superstores are not yet as ubiquitous as public libraries, if they ever will be, and the stores, in business to make money, offer relatively limited stocks of non-mass-market, nontrade materials. They tend to promote bestsellers and drive out independent bookstores, a trend both reflecting and influencing contemporary trade publishing and one that is much lamented in the literary community. And the superstore can go out of business quickly if profits decline (which is true of digital information companies as well). Capitalism is dynamic but unstable; knowledge and culture need both continuity and change. In any case, there are innumerable materials outside the current commercial book marketplace that people may be interested in and that have societal and archival value. The public library at its best remains a unique repository for non-mass-market publications, government documents, publications of nonprofit and alternative presses, extensive reference collections, runs of back issues of newspapers and periodicals, older and out-of-print books, and special collections. It is a comprehensive, stable, organized, open resource serviced by knowledgeable personnel and as such has few if any competitors. For digitized information the library also represents a durable commitment to public service and the public interest.

Modern libraries in the age of print always operated in a media market in the sense also of being dependent on what was available. Though exerting some direct influence in a few specific publishing sectors and indirectly through purchase of library materials, libraries seldom had control over the content of media. Neither did they, unlike ancient Alexandria's grand library or medieval monastic libraries, significantly engage in book production. They were first, consumers—buyers and recipients by gift, deposit, or exchange of books, magazines, and other materials—and second, distributors of those goods. The difference now is the scope, economic control, and technological transformation of information and its dissemination, as information has taken on a key role in the postindustrial global economy, and producers and vendors of information and its technology have become big business. These producers and vendors exert unprecedented control over electronic information because of its instantaneous availability on demand from a central source, so that in a way consumers are hostages to electronic technology and its corporate owners. At the same time, the hospitality and interactivity of the Internet and the ease so far of downloading, printing, or altering much of its contents can be seen as a certain democratizing of "publishing" and "consumption" of an immensely wide and ever-changing variety of data and expression. For authors wanting to protect and profit from their work, this new situation is problematic. The information industry perceives such easy access as threatening both copyright and the financial and intellectual investment in information. Librarians, for their part, worry that if copying of electronic materials is regulated too stringently, their traditional guiding principles of free access and fair use will be eroded. Then there is preservation—the library's classic responsibility—of this new elusive and alterable digital knowledge, a question that very much concerns librarians and that is beginning to be addressed seriously in the information community.

The Library and the Internet

Public libraries are not only providing Internet and other electronic resources; they are joining the Internet themselves. A 1996 survey of more than a thousand American public and academic libraries found that 62 percent of public libraries had home pages,[4] and as of this writing most large and prominent public libraries have them. (During fiscal 1996 the New York Public Library's site logged over 3.6 million hits; between December 3, 1996, and June 3, 1997, visits to the Denver Public Library home page nearly doubled, reaching more than eight hundred thousand, and by late October, they reached nearly 1.2 million.)[5] On these sites the libraries provide, in varying detail, information about their services, buildings, opening hours, rules and procedures for use, programs, mission, governance, funding, and history, plus various documents, databases, and links to their online catalogs and all sorts of bibliographic, textual, and graphic information. Some libraries accept reference questions and reservations for materials online. Perusal of a number of Web sites (including those from the largest public library systems in the United States) shows libraries proffering a raft of new electronic information and services as well as their classic activities. The Internet offers a wider outlet for libraries,

already more aggressive than ever before in their public relations, to promote their wares, show what they have, and indicate how to get it. Fairly
typical is the Miami-Dade Public Library System's home page, which
among its many links are those to materials about local county and municipal affairs, business and investment, information about Florida, multicultural resources, pictures of Old Miami, literacy services, and services for
people who are deaf and hearing impaired, visually handicapped, or
homebound. A special feature, reflecting the area's large Cuban-American
population, is a Spanish-language version of the home page. Another typical site is that of the Kansas City (Missouri) Public Library, which includes
links to job openings, HIV and AIDS resources, and local history resources
and special collections. The link "Cultural Mosaic: A Collection of
Resources Celebrating Human Diversity" points to sites for "African-
American; Blind/Visually Impaired; Gay/Lesbian/Bisexual; Latino;
Churches, Seminaries, & Religious Organizations; Women."[6]

Digitization allows presentation of contents of libraries' unique holdings, with graphics and sound, to a wide audience through the Internet. In
1994, in an effort to popularize and publicize its national role, the Library
of Congress started the National Digital Library. The aim is to digitize by
the year 2000 several millions of its original historical documents, many
of them graphic rather than textual, for use by students, teachers, and
researchers at school, in libraries, and at home. The program is now encompassing other libraries, historical societies, and archival institutions. To
enable such participation, Ameritech gave $2 million to the Library of
Congress to sponsor a competitive grant project, open to repositories,
including public libraries, that hold primary resource materials in American history. The first awards, announced in 1997, included two public
libraries out of a total of ten recipients—Denver Public Library, for a
collection of images illustrating the history of the American West from
1860 to 1920, and the New York Public Library, for "Small Town
America: Stereoscopic Views from the Dennis Collection, 1850–1910."
Among purely local initiatives there is, for example, the Carnegie Library
of Pittsburgh's "Bridging the Urban Landscape," a multimedia online
database of photographic images of Pittsburgh neighborhoods developed
in collaboration with a Pittsburgh coalition for technology in education
and with the support of a federal grant.

True to their professional creed, libraries are not offering the Internet without guidance. To greater or lesser degrees, types of information that users might be interested in are delineated, recommended sources are noted, and help is offered in navigating the Net, choosing and using search engines, and the like. The Cleveland Public Library, one of the first American public libraries to provide information sources through the Internet, did so selectively, in the Cleveland Public Electronic Library, which presented a "wide variety of carefully selected electronic information sources."[7] In Michigan an interesting experimental "virtual library," the Internet Public Library, composed of electronic resources, including full texts, organized by topic and interest, opened in 1995. Hosted by the School of Information of the University of Michigan (formerly School of Information and Library Studies) and supported by grants from the Andrew W. Mellon Foundation, the Kellogg Foundation, and an entity called "Friends of the Library," the project aims "to discover and promote the most effective roles and contributions of librarians to the Internet and vice versa" by "finding, evaluating, selecting, organizing, describing, and creating quality information resources."[8]

This project is among other things addressing the lack of quality control on the Internet, which is perhaps the ultimate postmodern artifact. Not only does the Net contain material that people may find morally or otherwise offensive or worthless, especially for children, but authenticating its contents, much less assessing its reliability, is difficult if not often nearly impossible. In the matter of offensive materials, the digital revolution, as we have already observed at length, presents new complexities for libraries trying simultaneously to adhere to the library profession's libertarian stance and, as public institutions, to accommodate a possibly conflicting sense of social responsibility.

Predicated on laws and court decisions in force at the time, libraries have been issuing disclaimers as to both the reliability and the propriety of Internet information. A typical disclaimer appears on the Web site of the Denver Public Library:

The Denver Public Library cannot control the information available over the Internet and is not reponsible for its content. The Internet contains a wide variety of material and opinions from various points of view. Not all sources provide information that is accurate, complete, or current, and some may be offensive.[9]

In its mission statement the Denver Public Library lists among its values "free and equal access to information."[10]

The Cleveland Public Library offers a more detailed "Internet Access Policy":

The Internet is a worldwide computer network which provides easy access to a massive body of information. The information and resources available on the Internet expand the Library's information services beyond traditional collections and electronic resources. Not all Internet sources provide accurate, complete, or current information, and some may be offensive. The Internet is a rapidly changing environment. The Library does not monitor and has no control over the information accessed over the Internet and is not responsible for its content. Users are responsible for determining that the information they access is acceptable, reliable, and suitable to their needs. . . .

As with all Library materials, parents, guardians and care givers are responsible for their children's use of the Internet. Library staff cannot control the databases that children may select on the Internet. Parents are encouraged to work with their children to develop acceptable rules for Internet use. Parents and children are also encouraged to read *Child Safety on the Information Highway*, jointly produced by the National Center for Missing and Exploited Children and the Interactive Services Association.[11]

Besides problems in offering free and unrestricted access, Internet use policy involves another intellectual freedom issue for libraries, one that had been more or less settled by state laws and intraprofessionally by acceptance of the Library Bill of Rights and the American Library Association Code of Ethics—the principle of protection of library users' confidentiality and privacy. The ease of tracking and discovering electronic transactions threatens this right, a serious problem not only in libraries. The ALA's interpretation of the Library Bill of Rights regarding electronic services urges libraries to uphold users' "right of confidentiality and the right of privacy" and that "few restrictions as possible" be imposed. But "because security is technically difficult to achieve," users should be advised that "electronic transactions and files could become public."[12] The Brooklyn Public Library's 1996 disclaimer on Internet use addressed this question: "The Brooklyn Public Library is not responsible for any patron misuse of copyright or any other violation. Patrons are advised NOT to type in their personal information or credit card number on any Internet site. The Library is not responsible for the security of the Internet . . . [and] specifically disclaims any warranty as to the information's accuracy, authoritativeness, timeliness, usefulness, or fitness for a particular purpose. The

Brooklyn Public Library shall have no liability for any direct, indirect or consequential damages related to the use of the information contained therein."[13] In general, as libraries gain more experience with the Internet, they are setting more explicit rules for use and requiring users to sign acceptable use agreements, although so far Internet use policies still vary a good deal.

Like censorship and confidentiality, matters of authenticity and quality control are not new ones for librarians. The task was more manageable, though, in the predigital age, when individual libraries could develop their collections on the basis of established criteria of quality and reliability. Furthermore, librarians, through the cataloging rules standardized at the turn of the nineteenth century, identified, verified, dated, and collocated varying editions of works and the works of particular authors. But at no time could libraries vouch for the accuracy and reliability of their entire contents, and they always faced the problems of inevitable obsolescence of information and keeping up with new editions and updated knowledge. As the number and kinds of publications proliferated, as libraries ranged more widely in collecting, and as postmodern cultural and intellectual relativism entered the picture, the idea of public library collections representing authoritative judgment and authenticated facts became attenuated. Still, best editions would be acquired and reference books chosen and consulted on the basis of standards of quality and reliability. The contents of each title remained in place and not capable of being easily changed at point of origin.

In cyberspace, by contrast—where any and all information and documents and opinions can be posted, are available on demand, and may be constantly changing—the old controls and relative stability are vitiated, if not obliterated. The ability of libraries to verify authorship and "publication" dates and to evaluate the reliability of the massive, ever-changing array of material claiming on the Internet to be information is problematic, as the disclaimers note. Nonetheless librarians may well more actively use their expertise to help users find their way to authoritative information, which the Internet does contain, as librarians have traditionally done in answering questions involving printed sources and in supplying reading lists. Many libraries are already recommending appropriate Web sites for various purposes, and librarians are answering reference questions online and helping to decide which medium—Internet, CD-ROM, online data-bases (not freely available on the Net), printed books and journals, audiorecords, videorecords, and so on—might best serve their clients' purposes.

The Library and the Community

One conspicuous component of public library Web pages is the display of all sorts of community and regional information—for example, directories and services of municipal and county agencies and cultural institutions, calendars of events, schedules of legislative bodies and sports teams, job banks, availability of child care, or subway and bus maps. While much of this kind of material has traditionally been available at public libraries in various forms, and most recently in the community information and referral systems of the 1970s, its packaging and promotion in online digital form and its extent are new. Technology has made possible an unprecedented expansion of digital civic information, including textual material, reachable through the Internet. The compilers of all this may or may not be the library staff. The information may represent the efforts, and initiative, of the library in cooperation with other community groups and government agencies or be entirely the work of such groups and linked to the library's Web site. Or the information displayed on the library's site may be gathered and maintained by a community or civic network. The goals of presenting community information are several—to supply the information, governmental and otherwise, for practical personal uses; to inform the public about governmental structures, rules, regulations, and actions; to enable more, and more informed, participation in civic affairs; and to promote a sense of community.

A current trend in public library rhetoric, and in practice in certain libraries, is to leverage resources and capabilities and strengthen community usefulness and status by entering into partnership with local community organizations and institutions to serve a variety of community needs, most notably through electronic information systems. This approach, as we have noted, also reflects the growth of communitarian thinking and of the new community networks and informs the attitudes of foundations and groups interested in public libraries, as is documented in several reports. The Benton Foundation's *Buildings, Books, and Bytes: Libraries and Communities in the Digital Age* concludes that public libraries, to remain viable, should be involved in creating "new life forms" in which they "team up with other public service information providers to form community education and information networks open and available to all" in a "seamless web of community information."[14] *Local Places, Global Connections: Libraries in the Digital Age*, produced in 1997 by Libraries for the Future and the Benton Foundation, notes that libraries, with their established physical spaces and knowledge about community information needs, "make natural partners for community networks" and that such partnerships "could be an answer to the financial threat faced by both institutions."[15] A Kellogg-funded Council on Library Resources report of case studies of twelve exemplary, innovative public libraries notes that "the central theme in each story is the use of technology to expand and enhance the public library's ability to serve the community's needs," albeit in different ways.[16] Contingent largely on local conditions and leadership, some public libraries have gone ahead to forge various alliances to provide community information, including collaborations with and in some cases management of community networks. Other libraries tend to pursue community-oriented goals largely independently. As the Council on Library Resources study found, not everything works everywhere, and "not every library has viewed its future as tied to the fortunes of the local community network or Free-net."[17]

Libraries are more than disseminators of community information or any other information per se. They serve communities as cultural and educational centers—as knowledge institutions—and by all accounts the public seems to expect them to go on doing so. (One of the best-regarded library systems and one characterized by partnership arrangements with many local agencies and businesses, Florida's Broward County Library, carries to a logical conclusion the old tradition of the public library as study place for students: it is the primary library for the Fort Lauderdale campuses of Florida Atlantic and Florida International Universities.) Public libraries still style themselves as multifaceted "windows on the world," to rephrase the Baltimore County Public Library's slogan, and, like the Chicago Public Library, exhort the public to "Read, Learn, Discover." Mission statements mention technology in relation to larger goals. Most library use remains borrowing of books and audiovisual materials (with audiotapes and disks very important in areas where residents spend a good deal of time in cars). Libraries still issue piles of reading lists (print and digital both) and notices of educational and cultural programs, exhibits, and services. Classic activities have not been abandoned. But when resources are limited and new technologies compelling and expensive, the emphasis becomes important. Recent nationwide increases in library budgets, according to *Library Journal* sample surveys, seemed to be expended mainly on technology, although proportions are really not known and there is evidence that spending on collections is up. This raises a question of balance, both fiscal and ideological. While cable lines are being laid and new computers and modems installed throughout library systems, librarians still need support to continue to hold children's story hours, help teenagers with homework, visit senior citizen centers or nursing homes, help visually handicapped persons with talking book equipment or enlargement machines, sponsor literacy tutoring and English as a Second Language (ESL) sessions, or plan exhibits, poetry readings, concerts, drama workshops, and film series.

Of course, new technology can assist in carrying out these traditional activities as well as publicizing them. There are, for example, computer programs for ESL and literacy students. (At one New York Public Library branch, 1,543 hours were logged in eight weeks for computer-assisted instruction in English for speakers of other languages.)[18] Homework help can involve data found on the Internet and in CD-ROM reference works; CD-ROM book lists describe and categorize contents of books for both adult and juvenile browsers; video and telecommunications devices serve the needs of visually or hearing impaired people;[19] and of course databases and the Internet can enormously enhance research on all levels.

Indeed, librarians are learning how to use all this. The prospect may be overwhelming on top of everything else they do, but they also find it exciting. A 1996 survey found that 59 percent of public library staff reported that their jobs had changed during the past year, mainly because of new technology; public librarians are participating heavily in staff training, mostly regarding the Internet.[20] Foundation money, most notably from the Kellogg Foundation, has helped by underwriting training programs in the field, and in 1996 Kellogg gave the University of Michigan School of Information, which worked on creating the Flint Community Networking Initiative with its strong training component, an additional $5 million for curriculum development. The Urban Libraries Council received Kellogg money to develop a video-based staff development series and is also engaged in technology training for systems staff of its member libraries. After a hiatus in the 1980s and a decline in the number of graduate library and information schools as universities sought to cut costs and downsize, there seems to be something of a resurgence in library and information school enrollment, apparently in response to the growth of the so-called information society and curricular changes to suit.[21]

At the same time as they undergo training in the new technology, librarians are trying to see how technology fits into their humanistic outlook. Historically, public librarians have been people oriented and not too concerned with the profession's technical aspects. The profession in general has traditionally suffered a split between the so-called technocrats and the public-service workers, albeit theoretically the ultimate goal of the technology is to serve the public. Today there is some unease among rank-and-file librarians about the wonderful new technology, a concern that its power, and expense, may overwhelm book-buying and programming budgets and undermine personal contact with clients as well as the intellectual and cultural essence of the library.

Librarians have classically seen community service and community empowerment as embodied in their commitment to helping individuals achieve positive personal goals. Communities are viewed as concentrations of persons with particular and varied cultural and intellectual interests as well as practical and political needs for information. In the words of the mission statement of the Los Angeles Public Library, the library "strives to inform, enrich, and empower every individual in its community by creating and promoting free and easy access to a vast array of ideas and information and by supporting lifelong learning in a welcoming environment." Many libraries have issued or are in process of developing strategic plans that analyze demographic and other local trends and prescribe library responses to them. The Queens Borough Public Library, in a highly diverse borough of New York City, now has a professional demographer on the staff. In some systems, like King County, Washington, the staff engage in continuous, detailed community analyses and needs assessment (at King County usually involving four constituent libraries a year), and the librarians, from the director on down, are deeply connected to their local communities. Many libraries' mission statements, strategic plans, and community studies, along with informal comments by librarians on all levels, express a broad concept of service.

Exemplary Services: Multilingual Populations

As examples of that concept in practice we point to two prime components of contemporary public library service, components that address urgent social concerns—service to multilingual populations and to children. Few libraries in large American cities and metropolitan areas have not felt the impact of the recent wave of immigration from all over the world. The percentage of foreign-born persons in the United States in 1995, the highest since 1940, nearly doubled that in 1970, and in 1994, 30 percent of population growth in the United States derived from net immigration, with the highest immigration rates among Hispanic and Asian peoples. According to the 1990 census 14 percent of the American population age five or more spoke a language other than English at home. The diversity is expected to increase.[22] A Public Library Association committee surveying services to multicultural populations in 1992 observed that "these days it is an unusual public library that serves a monolingual population of more than 50,000." The median number of languages spoken in the responding libraries' communities was twelve, the most frequent being Spanish, English, Vietnamese, Chinese, Russian, Japanese, and Korean, among hundreds of language populations across the country.[23]

Libraries can tell new arrivals about their civil rights, citizenship requirements, immigration regulations, business opportunities, and public services—in other words, community information. But public libraries are also apt places for immigrants to come to learn English, practice new language skills on reading materials, receive help for their children in school, or read books and magazines in their native languages.

In serving polyglot communities in a variety of ways, librarians display a nonpatronizing interest and a respect for the struggles of immigrants to adjust to a new country and a new culture. The 1992 PLA survey indicated that a number of libraries train staff in multicultural awareness and sensitivity and encourage contacts with relevant community groups and advisory committees.[24] During the first half of the 1990s there was a 40 percent increase in ethnic diversity among children and young adult public library users: 89 percent of public libraries stock multicultural materials for children, and 84 percent stock these materials for young adults.[25]

This concern seems to be a renewal of attention given in the 1960s and 1970s to serving "disadvantaged" minorities but is driven today mainly by results of changed immigration laws. It differs from that of many librarians (though not all and not everywhere) during the massive immigration at the turn of the nineteenth century. At that time the object was mainly, and quickly, to "Americanize" the masses of foreign-born working-class people crowding into American cities, not so much for the immigrants' own sake as for the preservation and protection of "American" culture. That meant initial resistance to or at least reservations about the idea of offering non-English reading matter. In the multicultural ideological climate of today, in many libraries foreign-language collections stand without apologies on shelves, along with the still substantial English-language collections. The missionary zeal is to give service as it is needed by the recipients, for their own purposes, but within a larger positive social purpose predicated on a liberal, inclusive concept of democracy. There does not seem to be public agonizing among librarians over possible conflicts between assimilation and multiculturalism. One librarian on the West Coast put it succinctly in discussing children's services: we want the children to read, to be educated, in whatever language. The vision statement of the Queens Borough Public Library expresses the ideology: "The Queens Borough Public Library represents a fundamental public good in our democracy. It assures the right, the privilege and the ability of individuals to choose and pursue any direction of thought, study or action they wish."[26]

In their decor, signage, publications, promotional materials, World Wide Web sites, collections, and multilingual staffs (albeit not enough of the latter), branch libraries take on the ethnic and linguistic flavors of their surrounding communities, both longstanding and recent. There are practical difficulties in finding and acquiring a wide range of non-English-language materials, but the major limitations of service to immigrants seem to be shortages of money and staff. A new American Library Association program, Spectrum Initiative, aims to attract more members of ethnic minorities to library and information schools and thus to bring more diversity to the profession and to cultivate "an inclusive, all-colors, professional cadre of expert knowledge navigators to provide new communities of new populations with quality library and information services. ⟨27⟩Of course, the money must be in library budgets to hire such personnel, and the library establishment in general is obliged to be not only responsive to the need to develop ethnically diverse staffs but sensitive to the problems, overt and subtle, that minority staff members face.[28]

Among libraries known for multicultural services, there is the example in New York, classic city of immigrants, of the Queens Borough Library, whose service area encompasses people of more than a hundred national origins. The library system, which boasts the highest circulation among American public libraries, offers language instructional materials in over seventy languages and reading material in forty-nine languages, including the country's largest Spanish and Chinese collections for general readers and substantial Korean and South Asian language collections. Demand for its ESL classes, said to constitute the largest library-sponsored ESL program in the United States, has been so great that a lottery system for registration was initiated in place of the lines of applicants that used to form at dawn (as also had to be done at New York Public Library branches across the East River). Queens has also developed its pioneering "World LinQ," with a $500,000 grant from AT&T, to offer multilingual access to electronic information and databases, including the World Wide Web; the project begins with Chinese, Korean, and Spanish, the languages of the largest ethnic groups in the borough. In spring 1997 the director, on a visit to China, worked out a collaborative program with the Shanghai Public Library signed later in the year that will involve exchange of staff, materials, technology, exhibitions, business and technical information, and access to their respective Web sites.

Newark Public Library runs a statewide Multilingual Materials Acquisition Center that supplies information and materials in eleven languages to all public libraries in New Jersey. In traditionally "ethnic" Chicago, the Public Library stocks materials in forty-five languages, including what the library terms the Midwest's largest Chinese and Spanish language collections; in 1995 the library system held a series of "conversations and public forums" on immigration and multiculturalism in collaboration with local television and radio stations. The advent of the new central building of the San Antonio Public Library inspired a community campaign to create therein a new reference collection, the Latino Collection; the library then also tried to acquire circulating copies of all the titles for the entire system, which serves a large Mexican-American population. The County of Los Angeles Public Library's multimedia, multilingual Chicano Resource Center is one of the largest in the United States and comparable, in the center chief's view, to the Chicano holdings at the University of California at Los Angeles. It is one of four centers established in the 1970s by the library system to document the African-American, American Indian, Asian Pacific, and Mexican-American (Chicano) experiences. The Los Angeles Public Library has, besides a central International Languages Department with a language learning center, branches with Latino materials and branches specializing in Japanese and Chinese resources that were developed with strong community support. In the 1990s photographic curators initiated a wide-ranging outreach program that resulted in Shades of L.A., an archive of photographs from ethnic communities.

Whether the passage in California of Proposition 187, which if implemented would cut off public services to illegal immigrants, will affect public libraries is an open question. Challenges to the constitutionality of the proposition are still going through the courts, but whatever the outcome libraries will likely not want to get into the business of questioning and reporting on their patrons. Taxpayers' ire, in California and elsewhere, seem so far to concentrate on immigrants' presumed disproportionate use of public welfare, public health, and public schools, not public libraries. Immigrants are not all poor and poorly educated, moreover, and many use the library knowledgeably as a vehicle for upward social mobility, for themselves as well as their children.

Exemplary Services: Children

During the heavy immigration a hundred years ago the children of immigrants constituted an important service group in urban libraries, where librarians sought to prepare them for life in America. Service to children generally was at that time becoming common all over the United States. Virtually every public library would eventually have a children's room, with small-scale furniture and lively decorations. Librarians saw public libraries as enjoyable alternatives to school regimentation as well as informal schools for citizenship. Besides helping with homework and school projects, especially when school libraries were scarce, librarians wanted to encourage reading for pleasure and inculcate a taste for lifelong learning. As time went on and young people began to go to secondary school rather than to work at the age of fourteen, public libraries extended their collections and club activities to meet teenagers' interests.

Service to children has remained a key component of public library programs, but not always with sufficient resources. Not only are there accumulated needs for new books as well as computers, but librarians report insufficient staff as the leading obstacle to expanding services to children and young adults. At the same time surveys show that more than half of adult Americans took their child to a public library at least once or twice monthly in 1993 and that the public perceives the library as eminently a place for children. Out of the 18 million people entering American public libraries during a typical week in the fall of 1993, 60 percent were estimated to be under age eighteen; more than 31 percent of reported total public library circulation in 1994 was for children's materials; attendance at children's programs stood at 39 million. The 1996 NCES survey of household use of public libraries found highest use in households with children. The American Library Association reports that more children were enrolled in summer reading programs at libraries than play Little League baseball.[29]

Children's services are receiving new focus today, as people worry about loss of reading skills and the shallowness of popular culture as well as the presumed necessity for computer literacy and the need to reach more poor children and youth. The Center for the Book in the Library of Congress, under the leadership of its director, John Y. Cole, has effectively worked nationwide and with publishers and the electronic media as well as other groups to stimulate interest in books, reading, and libraries among all ages. Among other programs, it sponsors, in partnership with more than eighty national civic and educational organizations, a national campaign to promote family literacy and lifetime reading. In her presidency in 1996 to 1997 of the American Library Association, Mary R. Somerville, director of the Miami-Dade Public Library, highlighted the urgency of reaching children, especially those at risk in their most crucial and vulnerable years—before school and during the years ten to fourteen. Major libraries are giving high priority to strengthening and promoting children's services and family-oriented programs. New central downtown library buildings express renewed commitment to children in charming and inviting children's centers furnished with computers as well as storytelling circles and reading nooks. Child-oriented computerized library catalogs have been devised (including one in the Spanish language), and the ALA and individual libraries are producing Web sites just for children and some for parents. The University of Michigan's Internet Public Library introduced in April 1997 "Culture Quest," a multicultural digital resource for children and young adults containing both content and links to available materials on the Internet.

Public libraries have also been receiving notable grants for work with children. In 1996 the William Penn Foundation, which decided to focus on improving life for Philadelphia area youngsters and gave $16.6 million to the city's parks, donated $18 million to the Free Library of Philadelphia for the modernization of children's services. This was the largest single gift the library ever received. Brooklyn Public Library obtained in 1997 $500,000 from the Vincent Astor Foundation to renovate its central children's room, and in 1998 the Uris Brothers Foundation announced a $3 million gift to the New York Public Library to create an endowment to buy children's books for the branches. On the other side of the country, the Contra Costa County (California) Library, which like other California county libraries has had its budget problems, received the Wilruss Children's Library Trust, which will yield some $100,000 annually. A good part of the Paul G. Allen Charitable Foundation grant to the Seattle Public Library Foundation was slated to be immediately spent on the children's collections. Omaha's Public Library Foundation gave $350,000 for "Kids Connection," a computer and homework project, and the Library Foundation of Los Angeles funds Grandparents and Books, an intergenerational reading program for children, and is financing the installation of homework centers, with computer and video workstations, in branch libraries. Money from the Chicago Community Trust, one of the largest community foundations in the country, enabled the Chicago Public Library to set up the Blue Skies for Library Kids program, which aims to turn a number of branches in poor neighborhoods into community centers; the new Mabel Manning Branch adopted by the Chicago Bulls includes a children's computer center financed by the team. Much of Microsoft's Libraries Online donations have gone toward bringing computer technology to children and youth, as will no doubt the project's successor, the new Gates Library Foundation, given Bill Gates's interest in young people's education.

Such gifts express not only the intense current concern about reading skills and effective education for the information age, but the classic modern view of libraries as good for children. Whatever else the public might think of libraries, their role as prime sites for children's reading is not in dispute. There also seems to be some recognition that libraries are a comparatively inexpensive investment in helping to save at least some children from a life of poverty and frustration and give them a sense of belonging to a broader, caring community. And even computer-obsessed people realize that computer literacy is predicated on traditional literacy—the ability to read and write—even if only to be able to chat with cyberspace pals.

In the context of the nationwide effort to prepare children for school and encourage effective parenting and early intellectual stimulation, preschoolers and then toddlers and infants, and their parents and caregivers, have received special attention. Storytelling and parenting workshops target the very young, and in a number of cities librarians collaborate with local clinics and hospitals to reach new mothers with children's reading material and information about the public library. Children's librarians work with Head Start on programming for preschoolers throughout the United States; libraries try to reach children in homeless shelters. The Association for Library Service to Children of the American Library Association sponsors, with foundation funding, a national project called Born to Read (with Hillary Rodham Clinton as honorary chair) that pairs library service with health-care agencies to help mothers, during pregnancy and afterward, understand their role as the child's first teacher and introduce them to children's books and to the library. The Queens Borough Public Library started in 1987 parent and child workshops to foster family literacy and cultivate in young children a love of reading; the New York Public Library has an Early Childhood Resource and Information Center; the Carnegie Library of Pittsburgh runs a children's literacy program called Beginning with Books in collaboration with other organizations working in low-income areas.

Public libraries traditionally functioned as complements to public schools, later as surrogates for school libraries, and in some places as suppliers of rotating book collections to classrooms. In the 1960s, with the general expansion of all educational enterprises in face of the baby boom, the promulgation of new standards by librarians and other educators for media centers in every school, and, most significantly, aid from Title II of the Elementary and Secondary Education Act, school libraries flourished. This prosperity was short lived. As the economic crisis in public education deepened in the 1980s and 1990s, the ax would often fall disproportionately on school libraries, especially in elementary schools. In a number of public libraries that we visited we were told that libraries in local schools were poor to almost nonexistent. Public library children's services have as a result taken on renewed importance as adjuncts to schools and as real or potential partners with them. The Chicago Public Library, in fact, bills itself as "the major provider of library service to Chicago's public and parochial schools which presently lack adequate school libraries."[30] Its Blue Skies for Kids program includes volunteer tutoring of local schoolchildren, and its new Project MIND aims particularly to make sure that school children and teachers have up-to-date electronic as well as other resource materials and skill in using them.

For years children in poor neighborhoods could escape from crowded and noisy homes and neighborhoods to do homework and read in peaceful, pleasant public libraries. Libraries fill this need today. It is estimated that one in seven libraries offers homework assistance programs, and more no doubt would if they had the money.[31] The library also takes on the role of safe place for so-called latchkey children who have no one to care for them after school because of changing family and working patterns. Undertaking this function can present a serious problem; it also can be taken as a challenge to set up activities for these children and encourage them to read, take up crafts, and use computers. A 1994 update of an earlier survey found that two-thirds of the exemplary public library programs for such children had been expanded or modified and a third had been discontinued, mostly for lack of money and staff; in a few cases other agencies took over the programs.[32] In response to a newer trend, home schooling, libraries are beginning to serve the needs of both the parent-educators and their children as one more client group in the community.

Although formal relationships between public libraries and public schools are not easy, not infrequently on account of bureaucratic bottlenecks in school systems, public libraries and schools have worked together informally for years. Public library children's specialists traditionally visit school classes, and classes visit the public library; school and children's librarians may consult with each other about duplicate purchases of expensive reference works; teachers may inform the public library about homework assignments needing substantial library resources. A recent instance of a formal program, begun in 1991, is the New York Public Library's initiation of Project CLASP (Connecting Libraries and Schools Project), funded at first by the DeWitt Wallace–Reader's Digest Fund (which is also funding the National Library Power Program to rejuvenate school libraries). The object of CLASP, which was extended to the two other New York City public libraries, Queens Borough and Brooklyn, is to develop effective cooperative programs between branch libraries and local schools, along with local advisory committees, and to create a community environment supporting children's reading and learning at school and at home. Broward County Library operates in cooperation with the county school board a professional library for educators and will be joining with a middle-school library in a new local community campus. A current nationwide trend in public library and school cooperation is electronic networking enabling public libraries to share resources and expertise with schools (many of which are not yet well equipped with computers). One notable example is CamNet, an electronic network managed by the Camden County (New Jersey) Library to connect public and private schools, one college, and the county library system to the library's catalog, online journals, and Internet resources. Also in New Jersey a public library consortium, the Bergen County Cooperative Library System, has similar connections with schools.

The new Gates Library Foundation, anticipating questions about why its intended recipients are public libraries, not school libraries, has offered the standard rationale for public libraries as separate and essential community institutions: "We chose to give to public libraries for several reasons. First, they provide an environment for lifelong learning. They are open to anyone, of any age, from any background. Second, they are open and accessible to children and adults outside of school hours, on the weekends, and over the summer. Third, they are staffed by information professionals whose mission it is—whatever the medium the information comes in—to help guide people to the resources they need."[33]

Social Symbol, Social Place

Clearly, the evidence points to the public library as having utilitarian and educational value to people and to communities. But its social significance runs deeper. It is a material symbol of civic culture and of society's cultural heritage. Public libraries are free, open, voluntary, neutral territory, and they do have something for everyone, from cradle to grave. They exemplify democratic freedoms and the American belief in the right to knowledge. In a library people are surrounded by human history—by the achievements, and failures, of human civilization. People need and want this environment and the sense of identity it sustains. Notwithstanding the historic American ambivalence toward the life of the mind and the existence of a certain anti-intellectualism, tinged with misogyny (which went far to inspire negative stereotypes of libraries and librarians), Americans do respect learning and cherish their libraries.

Libraries' unique characteristics take on special meaning today, when thoughtful people worry about the fragmentation of contemporary life and the apparent decline of the local activities that bound people together in the past. The work of social scientists like Robert N. Bellah and Robert Putnam on the value of communities, civic institutions, and participation in public life, of Amitai Etzioni on the new communitarianism, of Witold Rybczynski on the vitality of urban life, of Tony Hiss on *The Experience of Place* and Ray Oldenburg on *Great Good Places*[34] has focused interest on civic culture and along with it, civic space. We see new attention given to the meaning of *place*, to social interaction, not in anonymous commercial suburban malls or in chatting at home with computer buddies in the new communities of cyberspace, but in neighborhood institutions in real space. People are looking for social moorings. Libraries—stable, welcoming, venerable, but also modern—make good candidates. They are associated with education and culture and understood as communal property but not too associated with government. Although public opinion surveys indicate that people do not rank the library as a formal meeting place as highly as other roles, community groups do use library meeting rooms (quite heavily in the libraries we visited), and library programs do attract audiences (by the tens and hundreds of thousands annually in large cities and counties).[35] Current social comment often couples the renewal of civic culture with the need to revive civility and to offset the vulgarity and crass commercialism of much of American life. Libraries, of course, are classically civilized places (albeit not quite as hushed as they used to be).

The public library's essential value as social space inheres in its being a public facility for private contemplation in company with others. Reading itself, the initial, prime basis for the public library, is in our culture a silent and personal act. *Place* thus takes on an additional meaning: "The library," Vartan Gregorian observes, "always has provided and always will provide *a place elsewhere*—an imaginative retreat, an imaginative recreation, an imaginative rebirth."[36]

Rybczynski notes a "unique characteristic of the New World city: it was a setting for individual pursuits rather than communal activities."[37] Libraries span both: they ideally combine individualism with communality. People come there mostly as individuals, or in families, to choose books, locate information, or read (or, in our own time, listen to records or operate computers). This is all done mainly on a private, personal basis, in a public setting, surrounded by others doing similar things. People have their own reasons for reading or searching out information in libraries. They make of libraries what they will; they account to no one. Travel writer Kate Simon remembered her Bronx library branch of the 1920s: "The library made me my own absolutely special and private person with a card that belonged to no one but me, offered hundreds of books, all mine and no test on them, a brighter, more generous school than P.S. 59."[38]

Although unlike Gregorian the social scientists and commentators rarely mention public libraries, it is clear that people recognize them as agencies of civic culture, and they do occupy civic space, literally and figuratively. Public opinion polls support this, as does anecdotal evidence. The mayor of Utica, New York, one of the state's small cities experiencing serious fiscal shortfalls, announced with regret the elimination of city support for the public library: "Listen, a city is not a city without the library."[39] (Public outcry restored most of the cuts.) In Danbury, Connecticut, when an arsonist's fire destroyed the public library in 1996, the residents rallied to help, the *New York Times* reported, "in a way that has given the library's workers at least the consolation of knowing they had made the library a living center of the community." It was "the prime downtown gathering place in this city of 68,000: the reading room where old people leafed through newspapers in the morning, the nook where mothers brought children for story time, the desks where Literacy Volunteers tutored recently arrived immigrants, meeting rooms where Danbury's dozens of ethnic groups put on film and cultural festivals." The mayor, who gave the library administrators space in his office, said, "Community support built the library, and community support will rebuild it."[40] The city subsequently passed a bond issue that would pay for a rebuilt library.

This spirit is evident in the new central library buildings in metropolitan hubs around the country. The death of the American city has been somewhat exaggerated, though its problems remain grave enough. Certain core cities—New York, Chicago, Los Angeles, San Francisco—have renewed and expanded their status as global cities serving the global economy. Although not without persistent social and economic problems and desperately poor people, they remain vibrant centers. Even in the digital information age people with similar interests and special skills cluster together in real space. In the most highly automated, networked economies and the most global of cities, a critical mass of financial, commercial, legal, and technological experts and ancillary specialists—that is, the people themselves—still seems to be needed to conduct business and stimulate creativity. (William Mitchell, who predicted the "city of bits," commented a couple of years later on the trend among members of cyberspace communities to want to meet "in the flesh": "The more electronic communication expands and diversifies our circle of contacts, the more we're going to want to add the dimension of face-to-face.") Formerly small cities in the South and West have become thriving metropolitan centers, and cities elsewhere are, with some success, reinventing themselves as viable centers of postindustrial economic activity, including tourism and cultural offerings, in their metropolitan areas. Core cities left behind are struggling to see that local businesses survive and citizens can lead decent lives, as are certain suburban centers now facing the modern urban afflictions of crime, poverty, and flight from downtowns.[41]

Libraries are regarded as visible affirmations of metropolitan vigor. During the last decade costly new libraries, designed by distinguished architectural firms and replete with high technology and original art works, have gone up in Chicago, Phoenix, San Antonio, and San Francisco, with new ones planned for Las Vegas, Memphis, Miami, Oklahoma City, and Seattle. Extensive renovations and expansions in Boston, Brooklyn, Charlotte, Cleveland, Cincinnati, Denver, Los Angeles, Milwaukee, New York City, Pittsburgh, Portland (Oregon), and others have been completed or are in the works.

The journal *Architecture*, in a 1995 issue devoted to new city libraries, commented on the contemporary boom in library construction:

Intriguingly, this proliferation of book repositories is happening just as electronic media are revolutionizing access to information. But as Denver City Librarian Rick Ashton observes, the low-tech activity of reading a book is a fundamental path to knowledge that will never be supplanted by high-tech alternatives. Indeed, computers are taking their place alongside traditional book stacks and study carrels as integrated, indispensable reference tools. Furthermore, the social role of libraries is expanding with the inclusion of meeting rooms, day-care facilities, art galleries, and retail. No longer simple reference centers, these new libraries are being conceived as civic magnets—cornerstones of urban revitalization designed to bring people back downtown.[42]

Poignant expression of this latter goal emerged in the aftermath of the Oklahoma City bombing of 1995, which city officials, although of course lamenting the occasion, saw as an opportunity for the city to carry out their plans to refurbish the downtown and in the process help the community deal with its trauma. The future of the city, the *New York Times* reported, would lie "in stimulating growth through culture, sports and entertainment events to attract more people to an area that had begun to stabilize two years ago." The city manager said, "This will tie downtown into more of a cohesive area. If you accept the reality that you won't have Nieman Marcus or Bloomingdale's, those spaces are best used for other purposes. Libraries, museums and art centers give you a basis to have people back downtown." Major projects to be financed by a sales tax increase include renovating the civic and convention centers, constructing a minor league baseball park, an indoor sports arena and a new library, and digging a canal to link some of the projects, on the model of San Antonio's Riverwalk: "planning for the future of this community has to be based on the theorem that everybody has a part of this downtown."[43]

The current interest in constructing new library buildings and renovating old ones—and in edge cities and suburban library systems as well as central cities of metropolitan areas—can be seen as votes of confidence in libraries as monuments to cultural heritage, free exchange of ideas, public enterprise, the value of information in postindustrial life—and also architectural ambitions. In the future they may be viewed as shrines to a disappearing age (as some persons even now see them). But most people today are not ready to cede real civic space to flickering cyberspace, to yield the brick to the byte. Great civilizations have always created important public structures—if not, in a bourgeois and secular age, temples or cathedrals, then libraries, museums, and opera houses. Whether their monumental designs have always fully met functional requirements is another question.

The new library buildings become instant public attractions. Some eighty thousand people packed the new Los Angeles Public Library on opening day, five thousand people a day visit the new Denver Public Library, and three thousand people a day come to the new "enchilada red" San Antonio Public Library (designed by the well-known Legorreta Arquitecos of Mexico City); the numbers of new library users in San Francisco's New Main Library have been overwhelming. Registration and circulation figures at the new facilities have zoomed. The Phoenix Public Library is a stop in a new upscale Smithsonian study tour of Arizona Lifestyle and Architecture, and the June 1997 economic summit of world leaders was held at Denver Public Library in what the *New York Times* called "the quirky, turreted, copper-clad new wing [designed by Michael Graves and a Denver architectural firm] that looks out onto the lawns and classical architecture of the Civic Center."[44]

Most if not all of these buildings were no doubt initially proposed for practical rather than ideological purposes. Librarians and boards of trustees, though they would share and articulate in public statements the larger social purposes, were first of all dealing with practical problems of giving adequate, up-to-date service. They had usually been coping for years with the need for larger, more modern and workable quarters that would replace crumbling, crowded, obsolete structures and contain the infrastructure to support computers and modems and fax machines as well as air conditioning systems. (In Los Angeles the final stimulus was a devastating fire that destroyed much of the interior of the central library.) That communities, both public and private sectors, gave prominent sites and put up the money for monumental buildings no doubt evidenced understanding of the libraries' utilitarian needs. But not only that. Once the goal of new construction was decided on, the larger meanings counted probably more than anything. Otherwise inexpensive concrete and steel boxes planned by humdrum architects or construction engineers would have sufficed, and voters would not have approved huge bond issues. There would have been no gala celebrity studded openings, no successful capital fund campaigns, no international competitions for architects, no publicity in the national, library, and architectural press.

The opening of new central buildings also stimulated interest in citywide library service. Historically, city libraries grew from the center out, as cities expanded and the population moved, and branch library services would be separate from central library administration on organization charts. The central downtown libraries comprised often rather extensive general and special collections and had subject specialist librarians. Initially, before universities began to develop wide-ranging research collections and higher education became ubiquitous in the United States, urban public libraries served as loci for scholarly inquiry, advanced education, and intellectual work, as well as repositories of local archives, government documents, and rare materials. As high school and higher education expanded in the twentieth century, in some cities public libraries served in effect as college libraries for local students as well as resources for anyone needing extensive resources or complicated information. They still perform these functions. Local institutions of higher education, especially the newer ones, do not necessarily have strong libraries. In any case, they are not always fully open or helpful to unaffiliated visitors, although in some states and localities there are good reciprocal-use arrangements between academic and public libraries.

There seems still to be in the field an imperative to maintain and indeed enhance the central library, headquarters of the entire system and commonly with the largest collection. But people tend to live in the neighborhoods, and in some cities comparatively few residents may travel downtown very often. For ordinary purposes most branch libraries with well-chosen collections and good staffs might suffice, especially with efficient interbranch book delivery systems and the electronic union catalogs that became widespread in the 1980s and 1990s. One senses, though, that there has been competition between central and branches for funding, with central often winning out. A new generation of library directors and senior management, very community oriented and responsive to demographic changes, has been trying to change that. Branches are being strengthened through budget reallocations, construction and renovation programs, local fund raising, and efforts to install computers and telecommunications and eventually provide Internet services throughout entire library systems. Librarians and local officials recognize that a neighborhood library can be, as the Newark Public Library strategic plan states, "a safe haven, a community anchor, and a welcoming place for all."[45] Municipal branches, along with suburban libraries and county library branches, have perhaps closer ties to the people than central city main libraries. Cultivating local community support for neighborhood libraries is also politically wise: librarians' connections with local organizations and politicians can help to get budgets passed and construction projects under way.

Some city libraries have embarked on extensive branch building and rehabilitation programs. Los Angeles Public Library, for example, is in the midst of a branch construction, enlargement, and remodeling program encompassing more than two dozen projects. Denver's bond issue for its new central library also funded renovation and expansion of branches, and many of San Antonio Public Library's branches were renovated since the central library went up. The New York Public Library has been rehabilitating and constructing branches; in 1991 the badly needed up-to-date new quarters for its Andrew Heiskell Library for the Blind and Physically Handicapped opened. The Free Library of Philadelphia has launched a $50 million Changing Lives campaign to renovate branches and equip them technologically as well as increase the endowment; one part of this effort is Big Change, an initiative to develop community support to which the Pew Charitable Trusts gave $2.8 million. The Newark (New Jersey) Public Library aims to renovate and modernize all its branches by the turn of the century. Chicago opened a number of new branches since its new central library went up in 1991 and has raised money for branch collections. In 1996 the Chicago City Council approved a three-year, $50 million program, supported by a property tax increase, for construction of new branches and renovation of existing ones and for new equipment, furniture, and upgraded wiring for computers. An interesting new project is Green Branches, a collaborative effort to landscape the surviving Carnegie library branches in New York City's five boroughs. The plan was initiated by the Horticultural Society of New York, which will design the gardens and obtain the funds for them. The first garden, for which the Brooklyn Botanic Gardens is to provide technical assistance to local volunteers who will maintain it, was opened in June 1997 in Brooklyn.

Although the big-city libraries tend to get the most media attention, library refurbishing and construction programs have also been in progress in county systems and other communities. The voters of Charlotte and Mecklenburg County passed in 1995 a $9.7 million bond issue for new branch libraries, and the King County system has been carrying out an extensive building and renovation plan since the passage of a big bond issue in 1988. Older suburban cities like Evanston, Illinois, and newer edge cities have handsome, well-appointed new libraries. *Library Journal*'s annual lists of sites of new and renovated—and very attractive—public library buildings include numerous small city and town libraries in addition to branch buildings of large municipal and county libraries.

Success, Leadership, and the Future

The funds and pride and new users testify to the drawing power of fine library buildings. Finally, though, what will count most are the collections, the services, and the staffs therein, and the community's ability and commitment to maintain and enhance those elements. One case in point is a relatively small, autonomous institution, the Skokie (Illinois) Public Library. It is in a combined residential-business area in a suburb of Chicago with a population of nearly sixty thousand and in a state whose public libraries are almost exclusively independent institutions, most of them operating in single outlets and cooperating with each other regionally in systems of autonomous libraries. Skokie's attractive library building was designed by Skidmore Owings and Merrill, with an extension by Hammond Beeby Babka (design architects for the new Chicago Public Library), and is outfitted with classic modern furniture and interesting art works as well as, these days, computer terminals. Most impressive is the array of holdings, many special programs related to local interests and constituent groups, high per capita operating expenditures, high circulation of materials, and attention to the latest electronic resources. The library is an expression of community support, use, and respect—as well as the existence of a substantial tax base. Focal point of the community, it embodies the cultural center concept, which is valued by the education minded and technologically aware residents.

Or take King County's Bellevue Regional Library, also just outside a major city but operating within a different institutional framework from Skokie's library and in a more newly developed area of the country. Located in a hub of Seattle's mostly (but not altogether) prosperous, burgeoning suburbs, Bellevue Regional is a component of the popular and well-supported independent district library, King County Library System. The system, whose total circulation is among the highest in the country, has no central or flagship library, but Bellevue Regional is its largest unit and has the highest circulation. Bellevue, which became a city only in 1953 and now has a population of over a hundred thousand, has many new buildings, including office towers and a convention center. Its citizens, well educated and middle class, voted for the city to join the county library system as a full member in 1985, and the city, which had outgrown its existing library, shared in the subsequent bond issue to construct libraries in the county. The new building, whose square footage tripled the old, opened in 1993 with a wide-ranging collection of 325,000 volumes plus other media; there is a panoply of electronic resources and a backup reference center for the entire system. The building won an American Library Institute of Architects award for excellence in architectural design and planning. Its design was, as library brochures put it, "intended to express an image of civic importance and monumentality, coupled with a sense of intimacy in the interior, as well as efficiency and flexibility," an ideal which to our eyes was achieved in the façade and interior both.[46] In addition to permanent art works, there are changing art exhibitions mounted in cooperation with the Bellevue Art Museum. Patron use has been heavy and steady, including numerous bookings of meeting and study rooms. Although Bellevue Regional is the most extensive library in the system, other new and renovated smaller libraries that we saw in King County were equally impressive aesthetically and in their collections, levels of use, and responsiveness to their diverse communities.

In these instances we see an apt coalescence of significant factors—communities willing and able to support library service, governance and tax structures allowing for that support and for autonomy and flexibility, populations wanting and using libraries and information technology, and librarians alert to community interests and power structures and dedicated to public service.

We also see extraordinary accomplishment under more complex and less auspicious circumstances. Another service-oriented, well-used county system on the West Coast is the County of Los Angeles Public Library. This network of functionally designed libraries in dozens of ethnically and socioeconomically diverse communities sprawled over 3,000 square miles and containing more than 3 million people has had, as we have seen, to face the drastic budgetary cutbacks that hit most California county libraries in the state's economic downturn. Complicating the situation have been the now two-decades-long antitax environment, the recent shift of property tax funds from county to state, and, most recently, passage of the proposition requiring citizen referenda to approve new tax assessments. The Los Angeles County Library administration, pragmatic and inventive, searched for ways to raise money as well as to change the public funding mode to give the library system a tax base less dependent on state and county fiscal policy. In addition to internal cost cutting, the library promoted income-yielding projects like its fee-based research and information service (FYI) and audio books by mail, sought to market commercially its "good reads" database, and pursued grants and solicited private donations. Most important, the library mounted a strong public campaign, with the support of all the newspapers in the area and the help of the library's union, that won voter approval in June 1997 of a special library tax assessment in communities that encompass some half the library system's units. The additional revenue is expected to allow the County of Los Angeles Public Library maintain its current levels of service and avoid heavy staff layoffs. The victory, county librarian Sandra Reuben said, showed "very strong support of public libraries here in California. I think it's something that surprised elected officials everywhere, because they never thought we could pull this off."[47]

Not least in all these and other success stories is that vital element that pulls everything together—library leadership. If leadership was always important, it is perhaps more acutely so now. In the past, with all the challenges of establishing libraries from scratch and developing their services and collections, there was a sense of expansiveness and of continuity between present and future and within a fairly stable technological paradigm. Today we have an ensconced institution trying to adapt to a technological revolution that deeply affects its raison d'être. It is striving to avoid obsolescence without losing its essence, in an era of scarce resources for public enterprises and with many impinging forces to consider. In this environment leadership is pivotal. Effective libraries demand socially conscious, politically astute, proactive chief executives. These are men and women who know how to get things done and who can think strategically.

In the end, institutional accomplishment should be measured by the quality of service given by people in the field, the ultimate goal of any library. Achieving that goal, though, is very much determined by the quality of leadership in the organization, both chief executives and senior management. Each library, of course, has a particular culture that can be a force for positive change or negative inertia. Effective leaders manage that culture to implement a mutual vision of public service. Leadership styles may vary and personalities differ, but clarity of purpose and the ability to get others to share in its fulfillment are crucial everywhere.

Leadership is necessary but not sufficient. Aside from changing societal conditions, local circumstances—political configurations and struggles, state and local laws, economic conditions and levels of public revenues, or differing priorities for public services—may be such as to defeat the best intentions and professional abilities of librarians. There are the cases in which administrators whose libraries are caught in difficult, even dire situations can manage to save the day or at least survive to fight on another day. Still, at times and in some places, prospects just cannot be very rosy, given forces beyond the control of libraries and librarians.

In the long term, all libraries may be at the mercy of one overwhelming force—technology. The Benton Foundation report, while endorsing library "leaders'" concept of the public library in the digital age as combining cyberspace and real space in a traditional and innovative information agency, worried about "warning bells." The most alarming to the report's writers was a sense, especially among young adults, that libraries would become irrelevant in the future digital age. They would be reduced to the status of cobwebby museum. George Steiner, writing in the *New Yorker*, poses the issue in another way. He discusses the "fascinating question" of whether "the life of the book as we have experienced it . . . will persist much longer." We have come to the point where "the conception of the planet as a living book, as a single storehouse of information, record, entertainment, rhetorical argument—each special domain interrelated with all others via electronic synapses of recognition, classification, and translation (as in the human brain?)—is no longer a science-fiction fantastication." Milton, Steiner observes, "held a good book to be the 'lifeblood of a master spirit.' Doubtless this precious liquor will continue to flow, but, perhaps, in altogether different channels and test tubes. The boys and girls at their computer keyboards, finding, stumbling onto insights in logic, in fractals, may neither read nor write in any 'book sense.' Are they illiterate?"[48]

If the cobwebs do descend, the entire culture as we have known it will have changed, and libraries will have suffered the fate of "traditional" schools, colleges and universities, museums, bookstores, and who knows what else—as knowledge and communication all go virtual. If so, no efforts at institutional adaptation could succeed, no matter how charismatic the leadership. But the future may not turn out the way prognosticators think it will. Books may well remain a highly useful technology, alongside digital information. Traditional reading may retain its intellectual values and personal pleasures even among new generations raised with the cathode ray tube. (Indeed, if a recent *Time* article is to be believed, book reading is more popular than ever, even if hardcover sales are down.)[49] Institutions have great staying power, and information technology may not be all that determinative in society. We don't know. As Steiner says, "Periods of transition are difficult to make out. They are also intensely stimulating."[50]

We all have to live in this stimulating world, not the one fifty years from now or, for that matter, fifty years ago. We also have to believe that what people think and do today will matter for the future. The finest and most thoughtful librarians struggle to understand their own time and how to shape their democratic ethos and their institutions to meet complex and countervailing pressures and demands today and, as best they can, in the years ahead. It is intensely interesting.

Appendix

Site Visits and Interviews

Site Visits and Group Interviews

Site visits were made to various libraries and library-related agencies throughout the United States. These included individual interviews with chief executives and also, in many cases, group discussions with senior management staff, as well as conversations with individual staff members. Tours of the central library were also provided, as were visits to selected branch agencies. Names and positions listed here are those in effect at the time.

California
County of Los Angeles Public Library, July 1955
Sandra F. Reuben, county librarian, and staff
Norwalk Regional and East Los Angeles Libraries

Los Angeles Public Library, July 1995
Susan Goldberg Kent, city librarian, and staff
Goldwyn Hollywood Regional, Felipe de Neve, Benjamin Franklin, and Chinatown Branches

Illinois
Chicago Public Library, May 1995
Mary A. Dempsey, commissioner, and staff
Mabel Manning, Portage-Cragin, and Uptown Branch Libraries

Evanston Public Library, May 1995
Neal J. Ney, director

Skokie Public Library, May 1995
Carolyn A. Anthony, director

Maryland
Baltimore County Public Library, April 1996
Charles W. Robinson, director, and Jean-Barry Molz, deputy director
Cockeysville, Essex, Towson, and White Marsh Libraries

Enoch Pratt Free Library, April 1996
Carla D. Hayden, director, and staff

Maryland State Department of Education, Division of Library Development and Services, April 1996
J. Maurice Travillian, assistant state superintendent for libraries
Barbara G. Smith, Sailor project manager

Massachusetts
Boston Public Library, January 1995
Arthur Curley,* director and librarian, and staff
Dudley and South End Branches

New Jersey
Bergen County Cooperative Library System, December 1993
Robert W. White, executive director

Newark Public Library, March 1995
Alex Boyd, director, and staff
North End and Van Buren Branch Libraries and Business Information Center

New York
Brooklyn Public Library
Martín Gómez, executive director, April 1997
Judith M. Foust,* deputy director, November 1993

New York Public Library
Catherine Carver Dunn, director, governmental relations, November 1993
Paul Fasana, senior vice president and Andrew Mellon Director, The Research Libraries, April 1994
Edwin S. Holmgren, senior vice president and director, The Branch Libraries, November 1993
William D. Walker, associate director for the Science, Industry and Business Library and for Access Services, The Research Libraries, December 1993

Queens Borough Public Library
Constance B. Cooke, director, October 1993
Gary E. Strong, director, May 1997

Texas
Harris County Public Library, June 1995
Catherine S. Ensign, director, and staff
Baldwin Boettcher Branch

Houston Public Library, May 1995
Barbara A. B. Gubbin, director, and staff
David M. Henington, director emeritus
Lonnie E. Smith and Eleanor K. Freed–Montrose Branch Libraries

Washington, DC
The Library of Congress
John Y. Cole, director, The Center for the Book, November 1995
Frank Kurt Cylke, director, and John P. Cookson, head, Engineering Section, National Library Service for the Blind and Physically Handicapped, September 1995
Barbara R. Morland, chief, National Reference Service, September 1995
Robert Zich, associate director of communications; acting director, National Digital Library; director of electronic programs, September 1995

U.S. Department of Commerce, National Telecommunications and Information Administration, Telecommunications and Information Infrastructure Assistance Program (TIIAP), November 1996
Donald Druker and Sahon C. Palmer, program officers

U.S. Department of Education, Office of Educational Research and Improvement, Library Programs, November 1996
Robert Klassen, director, and Jane Heiser, program officer

Washington State
King County Library System, July 1995
William Ptacek, director, and staff
North Bend, Kirkland, Bellevue Regional, and Burien Libraries

Seattle Public Library, July 1995
Elizabeth Stroup, city librarian and chief executive officer, and staff

High Point, Beacon Hill, and Douglass-Truth Libraries
Jim Taylor, coordinator, Automated Services, July 1996

Wyoming
Albany County Public Library, August 1996
Susan M. Simpson, director

Individual Interviews

Positions listed are those in effect at the time.

Rick J. Ashton, city librarian, Denver Public Library, March 1994

John N. Berry III, editor-in-chief, *Library Journal,* September 1993

Charles M. Brown, director, Hennepin County Library (formerly director, Arlington County, Virginia, Public Library), March 1994

Sandy Dolnick, executive director, Friends of Libraries USA (FOLUSA), June 1996

Judith A. Drescher, director, Memphis-Shelby County Public Library and Information Center, March 1994

Ronald A. Dubberly, director, Atlanta-Fulton Public Library, March 1994

Ronald G. Dunn, president, Information Industry Association, November 1996

Keith Michael Fiels, director, Massachusetts Board of Library Commissioners, January 1995

June Garcia, director, San Antonio Public Library and Information Center, March 1994

Carol C. Henderson, executive director, ALA Washington Office, associate executive director, American Library Association, November 1996

Stanley N. Katz, president, American Council of Learned Societies, November 1993

Ruth Kowal, regional administrator, Eastern Massachusetts Regional Library, January 1995

Kozlowski, Ronald, administrator, Public Library of Annapolis and Anne Arundel County, Inc., Annapolis, Maryland (formerly director, Miami-Dade County Public Library System), March 1994

Nancy C. Kranich, associate dean, Elmer Holmes Bobst Library, New York University, November 1995

Judith F. Krug, director, Office for Intellectual Freedom, American Library Association, June 1995

Sarah Ann Long, system director, North Suburban Library System, Wheeling, IL, May 1995

J. Andrew Magpantay, director, Office for Information Technology Policy, American Library Association, November 1996

Elizabeth Martinez, executive director, American Library Association, May 1995

Marilyn Gell Mason, director, Cleveland Public Library, March 1994

George Needham, executive director, Public Library Association, American Library Association, May 1995

Paul Evan Peters,* executive director, Coalition for Networked Information, November 1996

Neil Postman, professor and chair, Department of Culture and Communications, New York University, November 1995

Eleanor Jo Rodger, president, Urban Libraries Council, May 1995

Saskia Sassen, professor, School of Architecture, Planning and Preservation, Columbia University, November 1995

Karen G. Schneider, library consultant on electronic resources, March 1995

Diantha D. Schull, executive director, Libraries for the Future, December 1995

Patricia Woodrum, director, Tulsa City-County Library, March 1994

Peter R. Young, executive director, National Commission on Libraries and Information Science, November 1996

---

* Each of these persons is now deceased.

Notes

Although the citations to Internet sources are as accurate and current as we could make them, the Internet addresses and even the sources themselves may have been changed or deleted by the time this book is published; e-mail addresses may also have changed.

Introduction

1. Robert D. Putnam, *Making Democracy Work: Civic Traditions in Modern Italy*, with Robert Leonardi and Raffaella Y. Nanetti (Princeton, NJ: Princeton University Press, 1993), ch. 6; also his "Bowling Alone: America's Declining Social Capital," *Journal of Democracy* 6 (January 1995): 65–78.

2. (Cambridge, MA: Harvard University Press, 1986), p. 394.

3. Haynes McMullen, "The Distribution of Libraries Throughout the United States," *Library Trends*, 25 (July 1976): 31; Haynes McMullen, "The Very Slow Decline of the American Social Library," *Library Quarterly* 55 (April 1985): 207–225; also survey in Boston Public Library, *Annual Report*, 1869, app. XXI–XXIII.

4. U.S. Bureau of the Census, *Historical Statistics of the United States, 1789–1945* (Washington, DC: 1949), pp. 319, 315 (price indexes on pp. 231, 235–236; data on wages, pp. 67–68); U.S. Bureau of the Census, *Historical Statistics of the United States, Colonial Times to 1970* (Washington, DC: 1975), pt. 1, pp. 162–164, 167.

5. Jon Teaford, *The Unheralded Triumph: City Government in America, 1870–1900* (Baltimore: Johns Hopkins University Press, 1984), p. 146.

6. Arthur E. Bostwick, *The American Public Library* (New York: Appleton, 1910), pp. 1–2, 19.

7. *Intellectual Freedom Manual*, 5th ed., comp. by the Office for Intellectual Freedom of the American Library Association (Chicago: American Library Association, 1996), p. 3.

8. U.S. Bureau of the Census, *Statistical Abstract*, 1950, p. 130; 1970, p. 133; 1980, p. 476 (cited hereafter as *Statistical Abstract*); *Libraries at Large: Tradition,*

Innovation, and the National Interest; the Resource Book Based on the Materials of the National Advisory Commission on Libraries, ed. Douglas M. Knight and E. Shepley Nourse (New York: Bowker, 1969), pp. 174, 214, 181, 183, 275; Richard B. Hall, "Trends in Financing Public Library Buildings," *Library Trends* 36 (Fall 1987): 423–453; Raymond M. Holt, "Trends in Public Library Buildings," ibid., 267–269; George S. Bobinski, *Carnegie Libraries, Their History and Impact on American Public Library Development* (Chicago: American Library Association, 1969), pp. 171–178.

9. Bernard Berelson, *The Library's Public: A Report of the Public Library Inquiry* (New York: Columbia University Press, 1949); Jim Scheppke, "Who's Using the Public Library?" *Library Journal* 119 (October 15, 1994): 36; Alan F. Westin and Anne L. Finger, *Using the Public Library in the Computer Age: Present Patterns, Future Possibilities*, a National Public Opinion Survey Report by the Reference Point Foundation, in Cooperation with the American Library Association (Chicago: American Library Association, 1991), p. 14; *Libraries at Large*, p. 273; "The Resilient Library," *U.S. News & World Report* 119 (December 11, 1995): 29. See also Donald J. Sager, *Research Report on the American Public Library*, Report No. OCLC/OPR/RR-82/1 (Dublin, OH: OCLC Office of Research, 1982), pp. 25–27, 30.

10. Joel Garreau, *Edge City: Life on the New Frontier* (New York: Doubleday, 1991).

11. Sam Roberts, *Who We Are: A Portrait of America Based on the Latest U.S. Census* (New York: Times Books, 1993), chap. 6; Charles Mahtesian, "The Civic Therapist," *Governing* 8 (September 1995): 24–27; Neil Peirce, *Citistates: How Urban America Can Prosper in a Competitive World*, with Curtis W. Johnson and John Stuart Hall (Washington, DC: Seven Locks Press, 1993).

12. William J. Mitchell, *City of Bits: Space, Place, and the Infobahn* (Cambridge, MA: MIT Press, 1995), pp. 55–57, 48–49. The electronic version is available at <http://mitpress.mit.edu/e-books/City_of_Bits>.

Chapter 1

1. William F. Poole, "Some Popular Objections to Public Libraries," *American Library Journal* 1 (November 30, 1876): 50.

2. Poole, "Some Popular Objections," 49.

3. William I. Fletcher, "Public Libraries in Manufacturing Communities," in U.S. Bureau of Education, *Public Libraries in the United States of America* (Washington, DC: U.S. Government Printing Office, 1876), pp. 410–411.

4. Melvil Dewey, "Book Selections," *American Library Journal* 1 (July 31, 1877): 391.

5. William S. Learned, *The American Public Library and the Diffusion of Knowledge* (New York: Harcourt, Brace, 1924), p. 12.

6. Robert D. Leigh, *The Public Library in the United States* (New York: Columbia University Press, 1950), p. [12].

7. Helen E. Haines, *Living with Books: The Art of Book Selection,* 2d ed. (New York: Columbia University Press, 1950), p. [15].

8. Ernestine Rose, *The Public Library in American Life* (New York: Columbia University Press, 1954), p. 170.

9. Bernard Berelson, "Reply to the Discussants," in *A Forum on the Public Library Inquiry* (New York: Columbia University Press, 1950), p. 62.

10. American Library Association, Student Use of Libraries: *An Inquiry into the Needs of Students, Libraries, and the Educational Process* (Chicago: American Library Association, 1964).

11. Kathleen Molz, "The Figure in the Carpet: A Report on the ALA Conference Within a Conference," *Wilson Library Bulletin* 38 (September 1963): 48.

12. Herbert J. Gans, "The Public Library in Perspective," in Ralph W. Conant, ed., *The Public Library and the City* (Cambridge, MA: MIT Press, 1965), p. 71.

13. Dan Lacy, "The Dissemination of Print," in Conant, *The Public Library and the City*, p. 128.

14. Carolyn F. Ruffin, "The Not-So-Silent Inner-City Branch Library," *Christian Science Monitor*, September 4, 1968, 15.

15. Carleton B. Joeckel and Amy Winslow, *A National Plan for Public Library Service* (Chicago: American Library Association, 1948), p. 105.

16. American Library Association, Public Libraries Division, *Public Library Service* (Chicago: American Library Association, 1956), p. 7 (emphasis in the original).

17. Ruth W. Gregory and Lester L. Stoffel, *Public Libraries in Cooperative Systems* (Chicago: American Library Association, 1971), p. 223.

18. American Library Association, Public Library Association, *The Public Library Mission Statement and Its Imperatives for Service* (Chicago: American Library Association, 1979), p. iii.

19. U.S. National Commission on Libraries and Information Science, "A New National Program of Library and Information Service," October 1, 1973, processed, pp. 16–17.

20. U.S. National Commission on Libraries and Information Science, *Toward a National Program for Library and Information Services: Goals for Action* (Washington, DC: U.S. Government Printing Office, 1975), passim.

21. Eileen D. Cooke, "Statement . . . before the Senate Subcommittee on Labor-HEW Appropriations on FY 1979 Labor-HEW Appropriations Bill," March 16, 1978, p. 2. Unpublished document.

22. John Holt, *Freedom and Beyond* (New York: Dutton, 1972), pp. 127–128.

23. Statement of John Brooks [1978], cited in Walter W. Powell, "From Craft to Corporation: The Impact of Outside Ownership on Book Publishing," in James S. Ettema and D. Charles Whitney, eds., *Individuals in Mass Media Organizations: Creativity and Constraint* (Beverly Hills, CA: Sage, 1985), p. 35.

24. Vernon E. Palmour and Marcia C. Bellassai, *To Satisfy Demand: A Study Plan for Public Library Service in Baltimore County* (Arlington, VA: Public Research Institute, a division of the Center for Naval Analyses, 1977), p. 9.

25. Baltimore County Public Library, Blue Ribbon Committee, *Give 'Em What They Want!* (Chicago: American Library Association, 1992), passim.

26. Kenneth C. Davis, "The Selling of the Library," *Publishers Weekly* 216 (August 13, 1979): 26–28.

27. Palmour and Bellassai, *To Satisfy Demand*, p. 10.

28. Murray L. Bob, "The Case for Quality Book Selection," *Library Journal* 107 (September 15, 1982): 1709.

29. George Ritzer, *The McDonaldization of Society* (Thousand Oaks, CA: Pine Forge Press, 1993), p. 4.

30. Stephen Akey, "McLibraries: The Serious Reader Gets Shelved," *New Republic* 202 (February 26, 1990): 12–13.

31. Vincent B. Leitch, *American Literary Criticism from the Thirties to the Eighties* (New York: Columbia University Press, 1988), p. 181.

32. Harold Bloom, *The Western Canon: The Books and School of the Ages* (New York: Harcourt Brace, 1994), p. 33.

33. King County (Washington) Library System, *The Year 2000 Plan* (Seattle: King County Library System, 1994), p. A–1.

34. Karl Shapiro, "Library, Asylum, Platform for Uninhibited Leaps," *Wilson Library Bulletin* 37 (April 1963): 669.

35. Mary Jo Lynch, "Foreword," in Vernon E. Palmour et al., *A Planning Process for Public Libraries* (Chicago: American Library Association, 1980), p. xii.

36. Palmour, *A Planning Process*, p. 52.

37. Allie Beth Martin, *A Strategy for Public Library Change* (Chicago: American Library Association, 1972), p. 49 (emphasis in the original).

38. George D'Elia, *The Roles of the Public Library in Society: The Results of a National Survey. Final Report* (Minneapolis, MN: University of Minnesota, 1993), ERIC #IR-054814; George D'Elia and Eleanor Jo Rodger, "Public Opinion about the Roles of the Public Library in the Community," *Public Libraries* 33 (January-February 1994): 23–28.

39. Leigh Estabrook and Chris Horak, "Public vs. Professional Opinion on Libraries: The Great Divide?" *Library Journal* 117 (April 1, 1992): 52.

40. Peter F. Drucker, *Managing in a Time of Great Change* (New York: Truman Talley Books/Dutton, 1995), p. 85.

41. Helen Woodhams, "A New Vision for Planning," *Public Libraries* 36 (September-October 1997): 270.

42. Charles R. McClure, John Carlo Bertot, and John C. Beachboard, *Policy Initiatives and Strategies for Enhancing the Role of Public Libraries in the National Information Infrastructure (NII): Final Report* (Syracuse, NY: Syracuse Univer-

sity, School of Information Studies [mimeograph], 1995), ERIC Clearinghouse, ED 386202. See also Charles R. McClure et al., "Enhancing the Role of Public Libraries in the National Information Infrastructure," *Public Libraries* 35 (July-August 1996): 232–238.

43. Lowell A. Martin, *The Public Library: Middle-Age Crisis or Old Age?* (New York: Bowker, 1983), pp. 15, 18.

44. American Library Association, Public Library Association, "Fees for Public Libraries: An Issue Statement" (June 1995).

45. Sue Curry Jansen, *Censorship: The Knot That Binds Power and Knowledge* (New York: Oxford University Press, 1991), p. 8.

46. Scott DeNicola, "What Lurks in the Library?" Focus on the Family, *Citizen*, 9 (September 18, 1995). The subtitle of this article is "The American Library Association believes children should have access to all material, no matter how violent or obscene."

47. Donna A. Demac, *Liberty Denied: The Current Rise of Censorship in America* (New Brunswick, NJ: Rutgers University Press, 1990) pp. 108–127; Jansen, *Censorship*, pp. 169–170.

48. Jansen, *Censorship*, p. 167.

49. Brooklyn Public Library, "Mission Statement for the Brooklyn Public Library" (March 3, 1989), p. [1].

50. American Library Association, *ALA Goal 2000* (Chicago: American Library Association, 1994), p. [3].

51. Eastern Massachusetts Regional Library System, *Plan of Service FY '96* (October 20, 1994), p. 6.

Chapter 2

1. Sources for statistics on library use, expenditures, and staff, and on attendance at other venues: U.S. Department of Education, National Center for Education Statistics, *Public Libraries in the United States: 1994*, NCES 97-418 (Washington, DC: U.S. Government Printing Office, 1997) (cited hereafter as NCES, *Public Libraries: 1994*); U.S. Bureau of the Census, *Statistical Abstract of the United States*, 1995, pp. 258–259, 263, 576–577; 1996, pp. 561, 257–258; American Library Association, Public Library Association, Public Library Data Service, *Statistical Report '96* (Chicago: 1996), pp. 21–22, 112, 108–110, 65–66 (cited hereafter as PLA, *Statistical Report '96*); "The Resilient Library," 29; U.S. Department of Education, National Center for Education Statistics, "Use of Public Library Services by Households in the United States: 1996," February 1997, <http://ed.gov/NCESpubs/97446.html> accessed March 26, 1997 (cited hereafter as NCES, "Use of Public Library Services"); *Arts Participation in America: 1982–1992*, prepared by Jack Faucett Associates, comp. John P. Robinson, National Endowment for the Arts, Research Division Report 27 (October 1993), pp. i–ii. In 1993 there were altogether over 105 million ticket holders at major league baseball, professional

basketball, and professional football games. The National Endowment for the Arts survey estimated that attendance in 1992 at museums was 164 million and at classical music concerts was over 60 million. It should be noted that the NCES figures, which depend on submissions through state library agencies, are neither consistent nor complete. As a gauge of general trends, however, they are useful, especially when supported by other data. In general, national statistics are difficult to evaluate and compare. For example, there are discrepancies among several sources. Not only do publication dates and dates of coverage of the statistics vary, but the bases for the data are different, as are the questions asked. The NCES figures purport to be for all libraries, but in some categories (like number of library visits) some states did not report data, and some data applied to the fiscal year previous to the one the total survey covered. The PLA figures are for a fairly large sample (791 American libraries plus thirty-two Canadian libraries in 1996). The annual *Library Journal* budget survey published in 1996 was based on 352 public library respondents. Evan St. Lifer, "Public Library Budgets Brace for Internet Costs," *Library Journal* 122 (January 1997): 44. The survey published in 1995 was based on 400 respondents. Evan St. Lifer, Julie C. Boehning, and Adam Mazmanian, "Public Libraries Face Fiscal Challenges," *Library Journal* 121 (January 1996): 40. A respected index of circulation and expenditures, done annually by the Library Research Center at the University of Illinois/Urbana–Champaign, was based on a survey of about fifty libraries until 1996, when the sample was doubled to 112. The index for 1996 is summarized in Lisa A. Wright, "Public Library Circulation, Spending Continue Upswing," *American Libraries* 28 (October 1997): 74–75. It shows a median circulation per capita for 1996 of 6.0, for 1995 of 5.6, and for 1994 of 5.7. The *Library Journal* budget survey for 1995 came up with a per capita circulation figure of 7.7.

2. NCES, *Public Libraries: 1994*, pp. iii, 19–27, tables 1, 1A, 1B, 2, 2A; definition of administrative entity, p. 103; quotation on definition of population of legal service area, p. 112; Jim Scheppke, "The Governance of Public Libraries: Findings of the PLA Governance of Public Libraries Committee," *Public Libraries* 30 (September/October 1991): 289–292.

3. Census regions are as follows: *Northeast*—Connecticut, Maine, Massachusetts, New Hampshire, New Jersey, New York, Pennsylvania, Rhode Island, Vermont; *Midwest*—Illinois, Indiana, Iowa, Kansas, Michigan, Minnesota, Missouri, Nebraska, North Dakota, Ohio, South Dakota, Wisconsin; *South*—Alabama, Arkansas, Delaware, Washington, DC, Florida, Georgia, Kentucky, Louisiana, Maryland, Mississippi, North Carolina, Oklahoma, South Carolina, Tennessee, Texas, Virginia, West Virginia; *West*—Alaska, Arizona, California, Colorado, Hawaii, Idaho, Montana, Nevada, New Mexico, Oregon, Utah, Washington, Wyoming.

4. Figures derived from *The World Almanac and Book of Facts*, 1997, p. 257; PLA, *Statistical Report '96*, pp. 21–22.

5. Figures derived from NCES, *Public Libraries: 1994*, pp. 68–69, table 13; PLA, *Statistical Report '96*, pp. 21–22, 38.

6. Carleton Bruns Joeckel, *The Government of the American Public Library* (Chicago: University of Chicago Press, 1935), p. 31.

7. NCES, *Public Libraries: 1994*, pp. iii, 84–85, table 17. The table actually shows all but four states with municipal libraries, including Maryland, where the Enoch Pratt Free Library in Baltimore has a separate legal status in the state but is classified as a county-parish library in the national statistics. The 5 plus percent "other" either did not report or reported another form of governance. In U.S. Department of Education, National Center for Education Statistics, *Public Library Structure and Organization in the United States*, Technical Report NCES 96-229 (Washington, DC: March 1996) (cited hereafter as NCES, *Public Library Structure*), whose figures are for 1993, there is a separate category that is subsumed under "other" in NCES, *Public Libraries: 1994*: "Native American Tribal Government." Comprising ten libraries, one-tenth of 1 percent of all public libraries, this category, "an organized local government authorized and established to provide general government to residents of a Native American reservation; includes native Alaskan villages" (pp. 3, 11). For a discussion of the complications of categorizing library governance and organization, see NCES, *Public Library Structure*, pp. 3–9; state-by-state summaries of the legal structure and organization of public libraries follow, pp. 13–40.

8. *Public Library Organization in California*, comp. Linda Wood, ed. Beverley Simmons (San Mateo, CA: Restructuring California Public Libraries: A Joint Task Force, 1994 or 1995).

9. NCES, *Public Libraries: 1994*, pp. 84–85, table 17.

10. Lowell A. Martin, James E. Bryan, and Mary V. Gaver, *Library Service for Baltimore County: A Report to the County Librarian and Board of Library Trustees* (n.p.: 1957).

11. NCES, *Public Libraries: 1994*, pp. 84–85, table 17; p. 108; NCES, *Public Libraries in the United States: 1993*, NCES 95-129 (Washington, DC: 1995), p. 82, table 17 (cited hereafter as NCES, *Public Libraries: 1993*); NCES, *Public Libraries in the United States: 1992*, NCES 94-030 (Washington, DC: 1994), p. 78, table 16; NCES, *Public Library Structure*, pp. 13–40. The NCES compilation for 1992 lists more special district libraries than for 1993 but fewer than for 1994, so the upward trend holds. The 1992 Census of Governments lists 844 "libraries" under the category "single-function districts" that are "directly providing program or service with own employees," which would seem to correspond with the category as used in NCES and in the library field (U.S. Bureau of the Census, *Census of Governments*, 1992, vol. 1, no. 1: Government Organization [Washington, DC: 1994], p. 25).

12. *Statistical Abstract*, 1996, p. 295; U.S. Bureau of the Census, *Census of Governments*, 1992, vol. 1, no. 1, p. 25.

13. Peirce, *Citistates*, especially the chapter on Seattle and King County.

14. David Rusk, *Cities Without Suburbs* (Washington, DC: Published by Woodrow Wilson Center Press, distributed by Johns Hopkins University Press, 1993).

15. Lee B. Brawner, "The People's Choice," *Library Journal* 118 (January 1993): 59–62. Brawner cites the need for a model library district law and suggests desirable provisions. A 1989 survey of public library governance indicates increases in

formation of such districts in five states over the preceding ten years and efforts to begin such formation in five other states (Scheppke, "Governance of Public Libraries," 291). See also *Balancing the Book$: Financing American Public Library Service*, ed. Jane B. Robbins and Douglas L. Zweizig for the Urban Libraries Council (Fort Atkinson, WI: Highsmith Press, 1993), pp. 20, 42–45; and Michael Madden, "Independent Library Districts," *ibid.*, pp. 127–137.

16. NCES, *Public Libraries: 1994*, pp. 92–93, 109, table 119.

17. Restructuring California Public Libraries: A Joint Task Force, *Report and Recommendations*, ed. Anne M. Turner (San Mateo, CA [1995?]), pp. 2, 4–5, 13–14.

18. In 1989, 76 percent of public libraries were reported by state library agencies as having governing boards, and many more unreported libraries probably did. Scheppke, "Governance of Public Libraries," 291, 293. A 1982 estimate was 95 percent. Alex Ladenson, *Library Law and Legislation in the United States* (Metuchen, NJ: Scarecrow Press, 1982), p. 31. The state-by-state summaries of the legal structure and organization of public libraries in NCES, *Public Library Structure*, include the provisions for board governance.

19. Teaford, *Unheralded Triumph*, pp. 75, 68; Joeckel, *Government*, pp. 22–24, chap. 8, and Ladenson, *Library Law*, pp. 4, 9, 29–31, 52; Arnold Miles and Lowell Martin, *Public Administration and the Library* (Chicago: University of Chicago Press, 1941), pp. 217–245; Oliver Garceau with C. DeWitt Hardy, *The Public Library in the Political Process: A Report of the Public Library Inquiry* (New York: Columbia University Press, 1949), pp. 32, 54, 58, 62–63, 238–239.

20. Some statistical research for 1988 suggested that the specific form of library governance correlated weakly in the aggregate with levels of financial support (Scheppke, "Governance of Public Libraries," 292).

21. The current roles of directors are discussed in Keith M. Cottam, "Directors of Large Libraries: Roles, Functions, and Activities," and David Henington, "Public Library Directors: Hierarchical Roles and Proximity to Power," *Library Trends* 43 (Summer 1994): 15–33, 95–103. Cottam's article is based on a survey of thirty directors, including eight public librarians, and Henington's article is based on conversations and correspondence with seven public library directors and his own long experience. The conclusions of both these articles are borne out by our own research and impressions several years later.

22. NCES, *Public Libraries: 1994*, p. 56, table 10.

23. Derived from *Statistical Abstract*, 1996, p. 315.

24. Statistics from NCES, *Public Libraries: 1994*, pp. 56–57, table 10; pp. 68–69, table 13; *Statistical Abstract*, 1996, p. 170.

25. NCES, *State Library Agencies, Fiscal Year 1994*, NCES 96-121, by Keith Curry Lance (Washington, DC: NCES, 1996), esp. pp. 14–19, 94–121, 126–127; "State Aid for Libraries (Fiscal Year 1994)," *The Book of the States*, 31 (1996–97) (Lexington, KY: Council of State Governments, 1996), p. 312; National Commission on Libraries and Information Science, *The 1996 National Survey of Public Libraries and the Internet: Progress and Issues; Final Report*, [by] John Carlo

Bertot, Charles R. McClure, and Douglas L. Zweizig (Washington, DC: NCLIS, 1996), pp. 9–13, 21–23 (cited hereafter as NCLIS, *1996 National Survey*).

26. For a more comprehensive summary of federal roles in supporting public libraries, as of 1990, see R. Kathleen Molz, *The Federal Roles in Support of Public Library Services: An Overview* (Chicago: American Library Association, 1990).

27. U.S. Library of Congress, Public Affairs Office, "Library of Congress Bicentennial to Spotlight Libraries and Creativity," press release, October 6, 1997.

28. U.S. Library of Congress, National Library Service for the Blind and Physically Handicapped, *Library Resources for the Blind and Physically Handicapped: A Directory with FY 1993 Statistics on Readership, Circulation, Budget, Staff, and Collections* (Washington, DC: U.S. Government Printing Office, 1994), p. 80.

29. Thomas J. Waldhart, "Resource Sharing by Public Libraries," *Public Libraries* 34 (July–August 1995): 220–224.

30. Percentages derived from NCES, *Public Libraries: 1993*, p. 32, table 4; NCES, *Public Libraries: 1994*, p.30, table 4.

31. The PLA 1996 survey found that 66.3 percent of public libraries reported having remote access online public catalogs, with percentages as high as 87.7 among libraries serving from half a million to a million people; a little over 19 percent offered Internet access through modem. PLA, *Statistical Report '96*, p. 142. As for circulation, in the latest Library Research Center of the University of Illinois/Urbana–Champaign Index of American Public Library Circulation, circulation for 1996 increased by 1 percent over 1995 and 2 percent over 1995 (which represents a return to the 1992 level after slight decreases in 1993 and 1994). See Wright, "Public Library Circulation, Spending Continue Upswing," 74.

32. Mark Smith and Gerry Rowland, "To Boldly Go: Searching for Output Measures for Electronic Services," *Public Libraries* 36 (May–June 1997): 168–172.

33. Frank W. Goudy and Ellen Altman, "Local Public Library Funding in the 1980s," *Public Libraries* 33 (January–February 1994): 37–39.

34. St. Lifer, "Public Library Budgets Brace for Internet Costs," 44–45; St. Lifer, Boehning, and Mazmanian, "Public Libraries Face Fiscal Challenges," 40–45; Evan St. Lifer, "Public Libraries Post Solid Gains," *Library Journal* 123 (January 1998): 48–51. See also Lisa A. Wright, "Public Library Circulation Rises Along with Spending," *American Libraries* 27 (October 1996): 57–58; Lisa A. Wright, "As Public Library Circ Falls, Spending Keeps Pace with Inflation," *American Libraries* 26 (October 1995): 912–913; Wright, "Public Library Circulation, Spending Continue Upswing."

35. Dennis P. Carrigan, "Public Library Spending for Materials: A Report Based on a Survey," *Public Libraries* 34 (January–February 1995): 29; Norman Oder, "Online Resources Emerge," *Library Journal* 121 (November 15, 1996, Supp.): S74–S76; Barbara Hoffert, "Book Report: What Public Libraries Buy and How Much They Spend," *Library Journal* 123 (February 15, 1998): 106–107.

36. NCLIS, *1996 National Survey*, pp. 23–30. Of those libraries that in 1996 did report percentage of technology related operating costs, the range among legal

service area categories by size ran from 1.7 to 6.1 percent, and by region ran from 6.1 to 3.4 percent, with the highest in the West and South. The 1997 survey information is from ALA, Office for Information Technology Policy, "The 1997 National Survey: Summary Results," November 1997, <http://www.ala.org/oitp/research/plcon97sum.pdf> accessed November 19, 1997, and from its "The 1997 National Survey of U.S. Public Libraries and the Internet: Final Report," by John Carlo Bertot, Charles R. McClure, and Patricia Diamond Fletcher, December 1997, <http://www.albany.edu/~/jcbert/ala97.html>.

37. Richard B. Hall, "A Decade of Solid Support," *Library Journal* 122 (June 15, 1997): 41–46; Richard B. Hall, "Back in the Black: Library Campaigns Pay Off," *Library Journal* 121 (June 15, 1996): 36–42; Richard B. Hall, "The Vote Is In: Undeniably Operational," *Library Journal* 120 (June 15, 1995): 40–45; *Keeping the Book$: Public Library Financial Practices*, ed. Jane B. Robbins and Douglas L. Zweizig for the Urban Libraries Council (Fort Atkinson, WI: Highsmith Press, 1992), p. 25. On public opinion surveys see American Library Association, *Library Advocacy Now! Quotable Facts About America's Libraries*, brochure (Chicago [1996?]); and Benton Foundation, *Buildings, Books, and Bytes: Libraries and Communities in the Digital Age—A Report on the Public's Opinion of Library Leaders' Visions for the Future* (Washington, DC: Benton Foundation, 1996), pp. 6, 18, 22–24, 29.

38. Henry S. Wulf, "State Government Finances, 1994," *Book of the States*, 1996–1997, p. 493.

39. *American Libraries* 27 (January 1997): 16; *American Libraries* 28 (October 1997): 32; *Library Journal* 121 (December 1996): 14–15.

40. Bette-Lee Fox with Corinne O. Nelson and Marcie Zwaik, "Everything Old Is New Again," *Library Journal* 120 (December 1995): 41–52; Bette-Lee Fox with Erin Cassin, "Beating the High Cost of Libraries," *Library Journal* 121 (December 1996): 43–53; Hall, "A Decade of Solid Support," 44.

41. In the absence of current statistics, it is hard to say how many public librarians and support staff are unionized and how many public libraries have recognized collective bargaining units. An outdated and incomplete 1984 survey of library staff organizations (including collective bargaining agencies) listed eighty public libraries as having staff organizations acting as collective bargaining agents, thirty-nine of them affiliated with a labor union. Frances M. Jones and Patrick L. Jarvis, eds., *Directory of Library Staff Organizations* (Phoenix: Oryx Press, 1986), pp. 4, 47.)

42. The study is discussed in both *Balancing the Book$* and *Keeping the Book$*.

43. NCES, *Public Libraries: 1994*, p. 56, table 10. For a discussion of the historic relationship of public libraries to philanthropy in the United States, see Phyllis Dain, "American Public Libraries and the Third Sector: Historical Reflections and Implications," *Libraries & Culture* 32 (Winter 1996): 56–84.

44. Bette-Lee Fox and Maya L. Kremen, "The Renovation Role Model," *Library Journal* 122 (December 1997): 49–60. The actual proportion of fiscal year 1997 projects receiving nonpublic financing was 57.3 percent. (The proportion of gift

funds was skewed to 21.4 percent in fiscal year 1996 because of one unusually large private contribution; see Fox, "Beating the High Cost of Libraries.")

45. Ronald J. Baker, "Outsourcing in Riverside County: Anomaly, Not Prophecy," *Library Journal* 123 (March 15, 1998): 34–37. For another view see Ronald A. Dubberly, "Why Outsourcing Is Our Friend," *American Libraries* 29 (January 1998): 72–74. Dubberly, a former library director, is a member of the advisory council of the management company running the Riverside County system. For the Jersey City situation see Robert Hanley and Steve Strunsky, "Jersey City Weighs Private Management of Libraries," *New York Times*, June 29, 1998, pp. B1, B6; "Jersey City Library to Get Private Management," *ibid.*, July 16, 1998, p. B4; Robert Larkins and Omar Alvarez, "Library Board Votes to Privatize," *Jersey Journal*, July 15, 1998, pp. A1, A14.

46. Thomas H. Jeavons, *Public Libraries and Private Fund Raising: Opportunities & Issues; a Report of the Urban Libraries Council* (Evanston, IL: Urban Libraries Council, 1994), pp. 5–6; St. Lifer, "Public Library Budgets Brace for Internet Costs," 45; St. Lifer, Boehning, and Mazmanian, "Public Libraries Face Fiscal Challenges," 40; St. Lifer, "Public Libraries Post Solid Gains," 49.

47. Jeavons, *Public Libraries and Private Fund Raising*, pp. 12–14; *The Foundation Grants Index, 1997: A Cumulative Listing of Foundation Grants Reported in 1995*, 25th ed. (New York: Foundation Center, 1996), pp. xiii, xx; *Foundation Giving: Yearbook of Facts and Figures on Private, Corporate, and Community Foundations*, 1996 ed. (New York: The Foundation Center, 1996), pp. 64–65, 76–77, 81, 89–91, 97–98; Libraries for the Future, "Philanthropy and the Public Library," LFF Research Brief, Draft, 18 July 1995; and Libraries for the Future, "Community Foundations and Public Libraries," LFF Research Brief (September 1995).

48. ALA, PLA, Public Library Data Service, *Statistical Report '93* (Chicago: 1993), p. 127 (cited hereafter as PLA, *Statistical Report '93*). On the Hawaii situation, see Norman Oder, "Outsourcing Model—Or Mistake? The Collection Development Controversy in Hawaii," *Library Journal* 122 (March 15, 1997): 28–31; *American Libraries* 28 (June–July 1997): 30; *American Libraries* 28 (August 1997): 15–18.

49. PLA, *Statistical Report '93*, p. 111.

50. PLA, *Statistical Report '93*, pp. 111, 127.

51. PLA, *Statistical Report '93*, pp. 111–127; Jeavons, *Public Libraries*, pp. 9–11.

52. Richard Steinberg, "The Theory of Crowding Out: Donations, Local Government Spending, and the 'New Federalism,'" in *Philanthropic Giving: Studies in Varieties and Goals*, ed. Richard Magat (New York: Oxford University Press, 1989), pp. 154–155; Lester M. Salamon, *America's Nonprofit Sector: A Primer* (New York: Foundation Center, 1992), p. 51; *Foundation Giving*, 1996 ed., pp. xi, 58–59.

53. Economist Bruce Kingma has been studying public library funding over a ten-year span in two states and over one year in a third state; data are strongest for New York State, where on average, annual public appropriations for public libraries

declined proportionately with the increases in unrestricted gifts each previous year; this zero-sum game did not take place in connection with restricted gifts. Telephone conversation of P. Dain with Professor Bruce Kingma, State University of New York at Albany, January 6, 1997. We do not know how representative this pattern is or whether it expresses a cause-and-effect relationship.

54. *American Libraries* 26 (June 1995): 501; *American Libraries* 27 (September 1996): 13; also various articles in the *Los Angeles Times*, May 3, 1995, June 25, 26, 30, 1996.

55. See Paul Demko and Susan Gray, "When Public Agencies Seek Private Funds," *Chronicle of Philanthropy* 9 (December 12, 1996): 1, 12, 15, 17.

56. Herbert Muschamp, "Room for Inspiration in a temple of Reason," *New York Times*, May 12, 1996, sec. 2, p. 54; John Berry, "A 'World-Class' Library: *LJ* Interviews SF City Librarian Ken Dowlin"; Peter Booth Wiley, "An Act of Political Will: SF's Quest for a New Central Building," both in *Library Journal* 121 (April 15, 1996): 32–34, 36–37; Nicholson Baker, "The Author vs. the Library," *New Yorker* 72 (October 14, 1996): 50–62; "San Francisco Public Library Challenges Accuracy of New Yorker's 'Author vs. the Library,' " press release, October 11, 1996; Demko and Gray, "When Public Agencies Seek Private Funds." Baker is exercised over the disappearing card catalogs of research libraries, against which he protested in "Discards," *New Yorker* 70 (April 4, 1994): 64–86; see also David Dodd, "Requiem for the Discarded," *Library Journal* 121 (May 15, 1996): 31–32. The San Francisco library controversy can be followed in the news columns of *Library Journal* and *American Libraries* and in the San Francisco papers; it has also been discussed over the Internet, and it reached the *New York Times* on January 26, 1997 (sec. 1, p. 10).

57. *Foundation Giving*, pp. 57–58.

58. PLA, *Statistical Report '93*, pp. 112, 127.

59. PLA, *Statistical Report '96*, pp. 161, 143–145; "Getting Down to Business: Public Library Services to Business," *Public Libraries* 36 (March–April 1997): 87–92.

60. Rodger commented to this effect at "The Transformation of the Public Library: Access to Digital Information in Networked World," a conference at the Library of Congress, December 8, 1995. Bowen spoke on April 27, 1996 at a "Summit of World Library Leaders" convened by the New York Public Library. His remarks appear in " 'Global Library Strategies for the 21st Century': Proceedings, April 25–April 27, 1996," *Biblion: The Bulletin of The New York Public Library* 5 (Spring 1997): 113–114.

61. Restructuring California's Public Libraries, *Report and Recommendations*, p. 15; California State Library, Institute for the Future, *Entering the 21st Century: California's Public Libraries Face the Future* (Menlo Park, CA: 1996), p. 101. An extended argument in favor of fee-based services by the director of the fee-based information service of the County of Los Angeles Public Library, Stephen Coffman, is "Fee-Based Services and the Future of Libraries," *Journal of Library Administration* 20 (1995): 167–186.

62. Economists' views on public library finance are summarized in Nancy A. Van House, "Public Finance and the Public Library," in *Balancing the Book$*, pp. 47–69.

63. Figures on Internet access and use of computers are in *Statistical Abstract*, 1996, pp. 561, 723, 423; and 1997, pp. 566–567, 728; also U.S. Department of Commerce, *Falling Through the Net: A Survey of the "Have Nots" in Rural and Urban America* (Washington, DC: 1995).

64. "Economic Barriers to Information Access: An Interpretation of the Library Bill of Rights," *Intellectual Freedom Manual*, pp. 60–63.

65. "Access to Electronic Information, Services, and Networks: An Interpretation of the Library Bill of Rights," Adopted by the ALA Council, January 24, 1996, p. 2.

66. "Draft Version 1.1: Questions and Answers: Access to Electronic Information, Services and Networks: An Interpretation of the Library Bill of Rights," (June 1996?), questions 17–18, <gopher://ala1.ala.org: . . . freedom/electacc.q%26a> accessed April 16, 1997.

67. Kirk Johnson, "Help for Inner-City Libraries," *New York Times*, October 9, 1996, p. B4.

68. Evan St. Lifer, "Born-Again Brooklyn: Gates Wires the Library," *Library Journal* 121 (November 1, 1996): 32–34.

69. "Gates Gives to L.A. Libraries," *American Libraries* 27 (January 1997): 17.

70. Quotations from Gates Library Foundation, "Foundation Background," <http://www.glf.org/background.html> and Gates Library Foundation, "FAQ," <http://www.glf.org/faq.html> accessed June 24, 1997.

71. We are grateful to Professor Philip Lane, formerly of the Columbia University Economics Department, for calculating the first values for us. A *Library Journal* estimate is similar to his: see Evan St. Lifer, "Gates Speaks to Librarians," *Library Journal* 122 (July 1997): 45. The 21 and 18 percent estimates are from calculations by the American Library Association (*American Libraries* 28 [August 1997]: 14).

72. Quotations and information on the Gates Library Foundation are from "Gates Library Foundation," <http://www.glf.org>; American Library Association press release, June 24, 1997, <http://www.ala.org/news/gatesfoundation.html>; Gates Library Foundation, "Foundation Background," <http://www.glf.org/background.html>; Gates Library Foundation, "FAQ," <http://www.glf.org.faq/html> all accessed June 24, 1997. Stonesifer's remarks quoted in Steve Lohr, "Gates to Help Libraries Acquire Gear to Go Online," *New York Times*, June 24, 1997, p. D18.

73. "MCI LibraryLINK Home Page: Facts at a Glance," 1997, <http://www.librarylink.com/facts.htm> accessed February 28, 1997.

74. Lohr, "Gates to Help Libraries," p. D18; St. Lifer, "Gates Speaks to Librarians," 45.

75. Witold Rybczynski, *City Life: Urban Expectations in a New World* (New York: Scribner, 1995), p. 49.

76. New Jersey State Library, *Libraries 2000: New Jersey's Technology Plan for Libraries in the 21st Century* (Trenton, NJ: New Jersey State Library, 1996), p. 3.

77. NCLIS, *1996 National Survey*, pp. 13–17, 33–34; ALA, Office for Information Technology Policy, "The 1997 National Survey." The PLA, *Statistical Report '96* (p. 142) lists 87.5 percent of its total sample of U.S. and Canadian public libraries as having Internet access within the library for staff only, 47 percent for patrons with intermediary, and 40 percent for patrons directly.

Chapter 3

1. James L. Sundquist with David W. Davis, *Making Federalism Work* (Washington, DC: Brookings Institution, 1969), p. 7.

2. Carleton B. Joeckel, *Library Service: Staff Study Number 11* (Washington, DC: U.S. Government Printing Office, 1938), pp. 5, 9.

3. Thomas McIntyre, in *Congressional Record,* vol. 109, pt. 17 (November 26, 1963), S22703.

4. Walter W. Heller, *New Dimensions of Political Economy* (Cambridge, MA: Harvard University Press, 1966), p. 145.

5. U.S. Advisory Commission on Intergovernmental Relations, *The Federal Role in the Federal System: The Dynamics of Growth—Federal Involvement in Libraries* (Washington, DC: U.S. Government Printing Office, 1980), p. 33.

6. U.S. Advisory Commission on Intergovernmental Relations, *The Federal Role in the Federal System: The Dynamics of Growth—An Agenda for American Federalism: Restoring Confidence and Competence* (Washington, DC: U.S. Government Printing Office, 1981), p. 16.

7. American Library Association, *ALA Washington Newsletter* 34 (February 9, 1982): 1.

8. American Library Association, *ALA Washington Newsletter* 47 (January 15, 1995): 2.

9. Library Services and Technology Act, 20 U.S.C.A., Section 9121(3) (1998).

10. Information about the Institute of Museum and Library Services was derived from that agency's Web site at <http://www.ims.fed.us/> accessed November 13, 1997. The current URL is <http://www.imls.fed.us>.

11. Joeckel, *Library Service,* p. 20.

12. Sources for these figures are U.S. Office of Education, *State Library Extension Services: A Survey of Resources and Activities of State Library Administrative Agencies, 1955–56* (Washington, DC: U.S. Government Printing Office, 1960), p. 24; *Book of the States* 31 (1996–1997): 312; "Federal Appropriations for Libraries," ALA Washington Office, unpublished handout. (The appropriation for LSCA for fiscal year 1994 includes both Hawaii and the District of Columbia.)

13. *Serrano v. Priest,* 5 Cal. 3d 584 (1971).

14. *Rodriguez v. San Antonio Independent School District,* 337 F. Supp. 280 (W.D. Tex., December 23, 1971).

15. *San Antonio v. Rodriguez*, 411 U.S.1 (1973).

16. Government Studies & Systems, Inc., *Improving State Aid to Public Libraries* (Washington, DC: National Commission on Libraries and Information Science, 1977), p. 2. See *ibid.*, p. 42, table 3, for comparative figures for public library and public education by governmental sources of funding, 1975.

17. Alec Ladenson, "Essential Now: Direct State Aid to Public Libraries," *Library Journal* 104 (April 1, 1979): 805.

18. NCES, *Public Libraries: 1994*, pp. 56–57, table 10; *Statistical Abstract*, 1996, p. 156, table 235.

19. Government Studies & Systems,Inc., *Alternatives for Financing the Public Library* (Washington, DC: U.S. Government Printing Office, 1974), p. viii.

20. "Public Library Services for a Diverse People," in American Library Association, *Issues and Challenges for America's Libraries* (Chicago: American Library Association, 1990), p. 4.

21. Don Sager, "In Retrospect: Public Library Service During the Past Fifty Years," *Public Libraries* 35 (May-June 1996): 167.

22. Brian Kahin, "The Internet and the National Information Infrastructure," in *Public Access to the Internet*, ed. Brian Kahin and James Keller (Cambridge, MA: MIT Press, 1995), p. 7.

23. Hugh Kenner, "Libraries and Glowlamps: A Strategy of Reassurance," *Scholarly Publishing* 18 (October 1986): 17.

24. Marc Uri Porot, *The Information Economy: Definition and Measurement* (Washington, DC: U.S. Government Printing Office, 1977), pp. 106–111.

25. William Z. Nasri, "Copyright," in *World Encyclopedia of Library and Information Services*, 3rd ed. (Chicago: American Library Association, 1993), p. 233.

26. U.S. Domestic Council Committee on the Right of Privacy, *National Information Policy* (Washington, DC: U.S. Government Printing Office, 1976), p. xii.

27. U.S. Commission on Federal Paperwork, *Final Summary Report* (Washington, DC: U.S. Government Printing Office, 1977), p. 21.

28. Gary Bass and David Plocher, *Strengthening Federal Information Policy: Opportunities and Realities at OMB* (Washington, DC: Benton Foundation, 1989), p. 7.

29. U.S. Office of Management and Budget, "Management of Federal Information Resources: OMB Circular No. A-130; final publication," *Federal Register* 50 (December 24, 1985): 52736.

30. Nancy Andes, "The Commodification of Government Information," *Government Publications Review* 15 (1988): 454, 457.

31. The figures for library expenditures during fiscal year 1970 to 1971 are cited in Government Studies & Systems, *Alternatives for Financing the Public Library*, pp. 34–35, table 3. These data were computed from U.S. Census worksheets and represent expenditures derived from governmental sources entirely; however, the 1.1 percent figure for the federal share of public library expenditures is derived

from NCES, Public Libraries: 1994, table 10, which includes 8.4 percent for "other" (that is, "nongovernmental") sources of total public library expenditures. Since the use of nongovernmental sources for public library revenue was not widespread in the early 1970s, there may be little discrepancy in the use of the comparative figures.

32. Libraries for the Future, "Philanthropy and the Public Library," pp. 8–9.

Chapter 4

1. Joseph Becker, "U.S. Information Policy," *Bulletin of the American Society for Information Science* 4 (August 1978): 14.

2. "The Freedom to Read," in American Library Association, *Intellectual Freedom Manual,* 5th ed. (Chicago: American Library Association, 1996), pp. 135–148; <gopher://ala1.ala.org70/00/alagophx/alagophxfreedom/40424020document>.

3. Dwight D. Eisenhower, letter to Robert B. Downs, June 24, 1953, in *The Papers of Dwight David Eisenhower* (Baltimore: Johns Hopkins University Press, 1996), vol. 14, p. 321.

4. Colin J. Bennett, *Regulating Privacy* (Ithaca, NY: Cornell University Press, 1992), p. 68.

5. Cited in R. Kathleen Molz, *Intellectual Freedom and Privacy* (Washington, D.C.: U.S. National Commission on Libraries and Information Science, 1994), pp. 25–26. ERIC No.: 100395.

6. *Intellectual Freedom Manual,* 5th ed., pp. 150–151.

7. U.S. Federal Bureau of Investigation, "The KGB and the Library Target, 1962–Present" (Prepared by the Intelligence Division, FBI Headquarters, January 1, 1988).

8. Tom DuHadway, "FBI Presentation to National Commission on Libraries and Information Science" (January 14, 1988). Transcript obtained through the Freedom of Information Act.

9. Launor F. Carter et al., *National Document-Handling Systems for Science and Technology* (New York: Wiley, 1967).

10. Albert Gore, Jr., *Congressional Record,* vol. 135, pt. 7 (May 18, 1989): S9887.

11. Al Gore, "Networking the Future," *Washington Post,* July 15, 1990, p. B3.

12. John Markoff, "Building the Electronic Superhighway," *New York Times,* January 24, 1993, sec. 3, p. 1.

13. Quoted in Markoff, "Building the Electronic Superhighway," p. 6.

14. U.S. Department of Commerce, Information Infrastructure Task Force, *The National Information Infrastructure: Agenda for Action* (Washington, DC, 1993): 3.

15. William J. Clinton, "Address before a Joint Session of the Congress on the State of the Union," *Weekly Compilation of Presidential Documents* 30, no. 4 (January 31, 1994): 150.

16. U.S. Advisory Council on the National Information Infrastructure, *A Nation of Opportunity: Realizing the Promise of the Information Superhighway* (Washington, DC: U.S. Government Printing Office, 1996); U.S. Advisory Council on the National Information Infrastructure, *KickStart Initiative: Connecting America's Communities to the Information Superhighway* (Washington, DC: U.S. Government Printing Office, 1996).

17. Edmund L. Andrews, "A Measure's Long Reach," *New York Times,* February 2, 1996, pp. A1, D6.

18. William Drake, e-mail message from William Drake, <drakew@gusun.acc.-georgetown.edu> to listserv <roundtable@cni.org>, January 31, 1997.

19. Mark Landler, "A Year of Law but Scant Competition," *New York Times,* December 23, 1996, p. D1.

20. Mark Landler, "AT&T Is Said to Break Off Merger Talks with SBC," *New York Times,* June 28, 1997, sec. 1, p. 35.

21. Mark Landler, "In Unusual Move, FCC Chief Criticizes a Possible Deal," *New York Times,* June 19, 1997, p. D1.

22. Mark Landler, "The SBC Deal Shelved, What Tack for AT&T?" *New York Times,* June 30, 1997, p. D6.

23. Campaign to Stop the Unconstitutional Exon/Gorton/Coats Communications Decency Act, "Frequently Asked Questions (FAQ) About the 1995 Communications Decency Act," August 26, 1995, <http://www.vtw.org/>.

24. Stewart Dalzell, District Judge, U.S. District Court for the Eastern District of Pennsylvania, *ACLU et al. v. Janet Reno* [No. 96–963]; *ALA et al. v. U.S. Department of Justice* [No. 96–1458]; June 12, 1996, <http://www.well.com/conf/liberty/cda/full_dec_text.html>.

25. Family Research Council, "Arrogant Decision Contradicts Prior Cases on Pornography Distribution to Minors, FRC Says," Press Release, June 12, 1996.

26. American Library Association News Release, June 12, 1996, e-mail message from Linda Wallace, <lwallace@ala.org> to listserv <alanews@ala1.ala.org>, June 14, 1996.

27. The National Law Center for Children and Families, et al., Brief filed in support of Janet Reno and the U.S. Department of Justice in the U.S. District Court for the Eastern District of Pennsylvania in Civil Action No. 96-963 and Civil Action No. 96-1458, <http://www.cdt.org/ciec/NLC_brief.html>.

28. Alan Boyle, "Resolving the Information Battle," 1997, <http://www.msnbc.com/news/59459.asp> accessed April 2, 1997.

29. "Baby-sitting the Internet," (editorial), *Washington Post,* January 2, 1997, p. A16.

30. Karen Jo Gounaud, "Family Friendly Libraries: Sense or Censorship?" presented at the Public Library Association 1996 National Conference, March 29, 1996, <http://pla.org/PLAConf/Papers/FamilyFriendly.html> (emphasis in the original).

31. *The Park Slope Paper* (February 28-March 6, 1997), p. 1.

32. Boyle, "Resolving the Information Battle"; Alan Boyle, "Court Questions Details of Decency Law," 1997, <http://www.msnbc.com/news/63001.asp> accessed April 10, 1997; Alan Boyle, "Libraries' Legal Ground Unsettled," 1977, <http://www.msnbc.com/news/59438.asp> accessed April 9, 1997.

33. *American Library Association v. Pataki,* 969 F. Supp. 160 (S.D.N.Y., June 20, 1997).

34. *American Library Association,* "ALA News," 2 (June 23, 1997), <alanews@a-la1.ala.org>.

35. *Janet Reno et al. v. American Civil Liberties Union et al.,* 117 S. Ct. 2329 (1997) in West's *Supreme Court Reporter* 117, no. 18 (July 15, 1997): 2347-2348. Justice Stevens does not mean, of course, the "card catalogue." His reference is intended to cover the digitized cataloging data in the library's online catalog.

36. American Civil Liberties Union, "Supreme Court Rules: Cyberspace Will Be Free!" press release, June 26, 1997, <http://www.aclu.org/news/n062697a.html> accessed June 27, 1997.

37. Office of the Press Secretary, "Statement by President Clinton," June 26, 1997, <http:www.ciec.org/SC_appeal/970626_Clinton.html> accessed June 26, 1997.

38. "A Framework for Global Electronic Commerce," prepared by an interagency working group under the leadership of Vice President Gore, July 1, 1997, <http://www.whitehouse.gov/WH/New/Commerce/> accessed July 1, 1997.

39. American Civil Liberties Union, "Fahrenheit 451.2: Is Cyberspace Burning?," <http://www.aclu.org/issues/cyber/burning.html> accessed September 3, 1997.

40. Milton Mueller of Rutgers University has prepared an historical account of "universal service," holding that it was initially promoted by Bell telephone interests to encourage connectivity among competing telephone exchanges and not to promote increased household penetration in sparsely populated or rural areas. Nonetheless, "the idea that the 1934 Communications Act mandated universal service" has become "an established part of telephone industry folklore." See Milton Mueller, " 'Universal Service' and the New Telecommunications Act: Mythology Made Law," <http://www.ctr.Columbia.edu/vii/univsvce/cacm.htm> accessed June 30, 1997.

41. U.S. National Telecommunications and Information Administration, "Clinton Administration Calls for Free Basic Telecommunications Connections to Every K-12 School and Library in the Country," news release, October 10, 1996.

42. Will Rodger, "Telcos to Clinton: No Such Thing as Free Access," *Inter@active* (October 28, 1996), distributed on October 31, 1996, to listserv <communet@list.uvm.edu>.

43. Reed Hundt, "Giving Schools and Libraries the Keys to the Future," January 27, 1997, <http://www.fcc/gov/Speeches/hundt/spreh704.html>.

44. John Simons, "There's No Free Lunch in Cyberspace," *U.S.News & World Report* 121 (December 9, 1996): 72.

45. American Library Association Washington Office Newsline, "American Library Association Responds to SBC Communications, Inc., Lawsuit on Library/School Discounts," vol. 6, no. 50 (June 29, 1997), <alawash@alawash.org>.

46. Kevin Taglang, "Universal Service Update," e-mail message to listserv <lists@-Benton.org>, November 17, 1997.

47. Courtney Macavinta, "Senators Slam FCC Over Net Fund," *The Net* (February 13, 1998), <http://www.news.com/News/Item/0,4,19151,00.html?st.ne.n-i.rel> accessed March 24, 1998.

48. Jeri Clausing, "Gore Defends Program to Wire Schools," *Technology/Cybertimes* (February 27, 1998), <http:/www,nytimes,com/library/tech/yr/mo/cyber/articles/27education.html> accessed February 27, 1998.

49. EdLiNC, Letter to William E. Kennard, chair, Federal Communications Commission, March 27, 1998, <http://www.itc.org/edlinc/press/kennardletter.html>, accessed April 5, 1998.

50. "Four Members of Congress Ask FCC to Halt E-rate Program," *Library Journal Digital* (June 8, 1998), <http://www.bookwire.com/ljdigital/leadnews.article$9416> accessed June 9, 1998.

51. Pamela Mendels, "Schools, Libraries Cope with Cut in Funding for Internet Plan," *Technology/Cybertimes* (June 17, 1998), <http://www.nytimes.com/library/tech/98/06/cyber/education/17education.html> accessed July 20, 1998.

52. Seth Schiesel, "FCC Slashes Budget of Plan to Wire Schools, Libraries," *The New York Times on the Web* (June 13, 1998), <http://www.nytimes.com.library/tech/98/06/biztech/articles/13fcc.html> accessed July 20, 1998.

53. John Berry, "Bad Government Costs Kids More," *Library Journal* 123 (July 1998) : 6.

54. Congress, Senate, "A Bill to Amend Section 223 of the Communications Act of 1934. . . . ," 105th Cong., 1st sess., S. 1482, <http://rs9.loc.gov/cgi-bin/query> accessed April 3, 1998.

55. Congress, Senate, "The Internet School Filtering Act," 105th Cong., 2nd sess., S. 1619, <http://thomas.loc.gov/cgi-bin/query/z?c105:S1619> accessed February 24, 1998.

56. "Filtering the Internet," *New York Times*, March 16, 1998, p. A24.

57. Courtney Macavinta, "Gore on Fence about Net Filtering," *CNET News*, March 23, 1998, <http://www.news.com/News/Item/0,4,20361,00.html> accessed March 24, 1998.

58. "Istook Acts to Protect Children from Internet Obscenity," *The Press Box: Press Releases*, June 23, 1998, <http://www.house.gov/istook/rel-obsc.htm> accessed June 30, 1998.

59. Jeri Clausing, "Senate's Internet Legislation Under Fire," *New York Times*, July 27, 1998, p. D5.

60. American Library Association Washington Office Newsline, "Action Alert: Amendments by Sens. McCain and Coats Attached to Appropriations Bill," vol. 7, no. 86 (July 22, 1998), <ala-wo@ala1.ala.org>.

61. American Library Association, "Guidelines and Considerations for Developing a Public Library Internet Use Policy," June 1998, <wysiwyg://2/http://www.ala.org/alaorg/oif/internet.html> accessed July 6, 1998.

62. American Civil Liberties Union, "Censorship in a Box: Why Blocking Software is Wrong for Public Libraries," [June 17, 1998], <http://www.aclu.org/issues/cyber/box.html#ExecutiveSum> accessed June 18, 1998.

63. Brian Hecht, "Net Loss," *New Republic,* 216 (February 17, 1997): 15.

64. U.S. National Science Foundation, Office of Legislative and Public Affairs, "Fact Sheet: The Next Generation Internet: Connections to the Internet," <http://www.nsf.gov/od/lpa/news/media/backgr3.htm> accessed June 10, 1997; U.S. National Science Foundation, "News: NSF Approves New Connections to High-Speed Computer Network," May 20, 1997, <http://www.nsf.gov/od/lpa/news/press/pr9739.htm> accessed June 10, 1997.

65. American Library Association Washington Office Newsline, "ALA Submits Comments on Draft Next Generation Internet Initiative Concept Paper," vol. 6, no. 35 (15 May 1997), <alawash@alawash.org>.

66. William J. Drake, ed., *The New Information Infrastructure* (New York: Twentieth Century Fund Press, 1995), p. 321.

67. Telecommunications Policy Roundtable, "Public Interest Principles," Attachment to memorandum to ALA Executive Board from E. J. Josey, September 17, 1993.

68. American Library Association, "Principles for the Development of the National Information Infrastructure," 1993, <http://www.ala.org/fulldoc.html>.

69. Joan Fanning and Doug Schuler, e-mail message to listserv<communet@uvm-vm.bitnet>, August 12, 1994.

70. <communet@list.uvm.edu>

71. U.S. National Telecommunications and Information Administration, *TIIAP: Telecommunications and Information Infrastructure Assistance Program, Fiscal Year 1994 Grant Awards; Fiscal Year 1995 Grant Awards; Fiscal Year 1996 Grant Awards* (Washington, DC: U.S. Department of Commerce [1995], 1996, [1997]).

72. <http://www.si.umich/edu/Community/libraries.html>.

73. Joan C. Durrance and Karen G. Schneider, "Public Library Community Information Activities: Precursors of Community Networking Partnerships," 1995, <http://www.laplaza.org/cn/local/durrance.html>.

74. National Public Telecomputing Network, "The Concept of Community Computing," April 24, 1996, <http://www.nptn.org:80/about.fn/whatis.fn>.

75. Scott London, "Civic Networks: Building Community on the Net," March 1997, <http://www.west.net/~insight/london/networks.htm> accessed March 21, 1997.

76. Michael Schuyler, e-mail message to listserv<communet@list.uvm.edu>, October 23, 1996.

77. Tom Grundner, "Seizing the Infosphere: Toward the Formation of a Corporation for Public Cybercasting," cited in Stephen Doheny-Farina, *The Wired Neighborhood* (New Haven: Yale University Press, 1996), p. 125.

78. Anne Beamish, "Communities On-line: Community-based Computer Networks" (master's thesis, Massachusetts Institute of Technology, 1995), <http://alberti.mitedu/arch/4.207/anneb/thesis/toc.html>.

79. Benton Foundation, *Buildings, Books, and Bytes* (Washington, DC: Benton Foundation, 1996), p. 39.

80. U.S. Postal Service, *Postal News*, "Service to the Citizen Kiosk Pilot Program," October 28, 1994, <http://www.usps.gov/news/press/94/kiosk.htm>.

81. American Library Association, "Library Association Calls for Libraries to Be 'Citizen Kiosk' Test Sites," news release, October 26, 1994. Distributed by George Needham to recipients of listserv <public-net@nysernet.org>, October 28, 1994.

82. Colleen O'Hara, "NPR to Take Flight After USPS Folds WINGS," *Federal Computer Week* (June 1, 1998). An e-mail copy of this text was sent by Ms. O'Hara to the authors, July 20, 1998.

83. Drake, *The New Information Infrastructure*, p. 321.

84. American Library Association Washington Office, "U.S. National Commission on Libraries and Information Science: A Report on Its History and Effectiveness," ALA Council Document no. 50 (1987-1988), passim.

85. James E. Katz and Philip Aspden, "Internet Dropouts: The Invisible Group" (New York: Markle Foundation, 1997), <http://www.markle.org/J96329pd9.html#1> accessed June 26, 1997.

86. Thomas J. Galvin, "Leadership in Legislation and Public Policy Development: The Case of the American Library Association," *Library Trends* 40 (Winter 1992): 454.

87. American Library Association, *Resolution Concerning the Committee on Legislation's Legislative Agenda,* adopted by the ALA Council, February 8, 1995, <http://www.ala.org/alaorg/washington/cd2095/html>.

88. Daniel J. Boorstin, *The Republic of Letters* (Washington, DC: Library of Congress, 1989), pp. 111–112.

89. Theodore Roszak, *The Cult of Information: A Neo-Luddite Treatise on High-Tech, Artificial Intelligence, and the True Art of Thinking,* 2nd ed. (Berkeley: University of California Press, 1994), p. 179.

90. Peter Woll, *Public Policy* (Cambridge, MA: Winthrop, 1974), pp. 14–20.

Chapter 5

1. Vartan Gregorian, "A Place Elsewhere: Reading in the Age of the Computer," *Bulletin of the American Academy of Arts and Sciences* 59 (January 1996): 58.

2. Marilyn Gell Mason, "The Yin and Yang of Knowing," *Daedalus* 125 (Fall 1996): 161–171.

3. Youssef M. Ibrahim, "Finland: Improbable Land for the Universal Use of Knowledge," *New York Times,* January 20, 1997, pp. D1, D6; the information about Helsinki is in St. Joseph County (South Bend, Indiana) Public Library, "SJCPL's List of Public Libraries with Gopher/WWW Services," October 17, 1996, <http://www.sjcpl.lib.in.us/homepage/publiclibraries/publibsrrsgpherwww.html> accessed January 27, 1997. A spring 1996 survey found 9.4 percent of adults in the United States had access to the Internet. The percentage rose with level of education (highest among college graduates) and income. More men than women had access, and more whites than other groups; old people had less than other age groups. Access rose to 16.4 percent in a similar survey in 1997 (*Statistical Abstract,* 1996, p. 561; 1997, pp. 566–567). Another source estimated in 1997 that only 41 percent of American households had a computer and that only one in seven of all households had Internet access (ALA Office for Information Technology Policy, "The 1997 National Survey: Summary Results"). Assessing the size of the anarchic and complicated Internet is difficult and controversial. A 1997 survey estimated a dramatic growth in the number of host computers permanently connected to the network, up to 26 million as of September 8, 1997, compared with 14.7 a year earlier. Another study indicated some subsequent slowing in the rate of Internet growth, from 12.8 million host computers attached to the Internet in July 1996 to 19.5 million in July 1997. John Markoff, "Internet Growth Continues," *New York Times,* September 15, 1997, p. D4.

4. *Library Journal* 121 (December 1996): 27–28; the survey was conducted by Opinion Technology Company of Palo Alto, California, for the Information Access Company. The summary of the NCLIS-ALA 1997 survey reported that about 10 percent of all public libraries had their own Web sites, with libraries in large cities more likely to have them than libraries in smaller towns. ALA Office for Information Technology Policy, "The 1997 National Survey: Summary Results."

5. New York Public Library, *Annual Report for 1996,* p. 20; Denver's figures appear on its home page: Internet: <http://www.denver.lib.co.us/> accessed December 3, 1996, June 2, 1997, October 27, 1997.

6. "Welcome to the Miami-Dade Public Library System," <http://cga.mdpls.lib.-fl.us/mdpl.mtm> (and links) accessed February 28, 1997; "Kansas City Public Library Home Page," <http://www.kcpl.lib.mo.us> (and links) accessed March 6, 1997.

7. Council on Library Resources, *Public Libraries, Communities, and Technology: Twelve Case Studies* (Washington, DC: 1996), pp. 64–66, 69. Examples of library guidance in using Internet, as of 1995, are also in Edward J. Valauskas and Nancy R. John, eds., *The Internet Initiative: Libraries Providing Internet Services and How They Plan, Pay, and Manage* (Chicago: American Library Association, 1995). Current examples may be found on library Web sites.

8. Internet Public Library, "Frequently Asked Questions About the IPL," June 7, 1996, <http://ipl.sils.umich.edu/about/iplfaq.html> accessed January 8, 1997.

9. "The Internet at the Denver Public Library," <http://www.denver.lib.co.us/ipolicy.html> accessed July 24, 1998.

10. Denver Public Library, "About the Library," <http://www.denver.lib.co.us/ dpl/aboutdpl.html> accessed July 24, 1998.

11. Cleveland Public Library, "Internet Access Policy," March 18, 1998, <http:// www.cpl.org/inetpol.htm> accessed July 24, 1998. *Child Safety on the Information Highway* (1994) is available on the Internet: <http://www.missingkids.org>, under links "Education and Resources" and then "NCMEC Publications." Other libraries also post their Internet use policies on their Web sites.

12. "Access to Electronic Information, Services, and Networks . . ." (January 24, 1996); "Draft Version 1.1: Questions and Answers: Access to Electronic Information" (June 1996?), questions 10–13.

13. Brooklyn Public Library, "Disclaimer," 1996, <http://www.brooklyn.lib.- ny.us/disclaim.htm> accessed March 4, 1997.

14. Benton Foundation, *Buildings, Books, and Bytes,* pp. 38–39. This approach is also expressed in California State Library, Institute for the Future, *Entering the 21st Century.*

15. Benton Foundation and Libraries for the Future, *Local Places, Global Connections: Libraries in the Digital Age* (Washington, DC: 1997), p. 3.

16. Council on Library Resources, *Public Libraries, Communities, and Technology,* pp. 3–4, 8. Valauskas and John's *Internet Initiative* also documents innovative Internet provision in public libraries.

17. Council on Library Resources, *Public Libraries, Communities, and Technology,* p. 8; see also Benton Foundation and Libraries for the Future, *Local Places, Global Connections* (pp. 14–39) for brief case studies of eight public libraries and state library agency projects offering public access to new technologies, three of which overlap with the Council's report.

18. New York Public Library, *Annual Report for 1996,* p. 20.

19. The 1996 PLA survey listed 57.9 percent of the reporting libraries as having telephone devices for the deaf (TDD), with much higher percentages among the larger libraries (PLA, *Statistical Report '96,* p. 142).

20. Evan St. Lifer, "Net Work: New Roles, Same Mission," *Library Journal* 121 (November 15, 1996): 26–28.

21. Prudence W. Dalrymple, "The State of the Schools," and Deanna B. Marcum, "Transforming the Curriculum; Transforming the Profession," both in *American Libraries* 27 (January 1997): 31–34, 35–38; see also Kate Murphy, "Moving from the Card Catalog to the Internet," *New York Times,* January 6, 1997, p. D5, and "Technology Sparks Demand for Cyber-Librarians," *National Business Employment Weekly,* February 16–22, 1997 (wherein a list of 1996 median salaries for libraries shows those in public libraries the lowest among thirty-two types of institutions, with librarians in the for-profit and government sectors earning considerably more).

22. Martha Farnsworth Riche, "A Profile of America's Diversity: The View from the Census Bureau, 1996," *World Almanac,* 1997, pp. 377–378; Martha Farnsworth Riche, "How America Is Changing: The View from the Census Bureau,

1995," *World Almanac,* 1996, p. 382; Katharine Q. Seelye, "The New U.S.: Grayer and More Hispanic," *New York Times,* March 27, 1997, p. B16; U.S. Census Bureau, press release, March 26, 1997, <http://www.census.gov/Press-Release/ cb97-48.html> accessed April 4, 1997; *Statistical Abstract,* 1996, pp. 52–53.

23. Lee Olivier, Robert Belvin, and Sylva Manoogian, "Survey on Services to Multicultural Populations," *Public Libraries* 33 (July–August 1994): 201.

24. Olivier, Belvin, and Manoogian, "Survey on Services to Multicultural Populations," 200.

25. Mary K. Chelton, "Three in Five Public Library Users Are Youth: Implications of Survey Results from the National Center for Education Statistics," *Public Libraries* 36 (March–April 1997): 104. The full report is U.S. NCES, *Services and Resources for Children and Young Adults in Public Libraries: A Statistical Analysis Report,* NCES 95-357 (Washington, DC: U.S. Government Printing Office, 1995).

26. Available at <http://www.queens.lib.ny.us/gstrong/mission.html>

27. Elizabeth Martinez, "Diversity: The 21st-Century Spectrum," *American Libraries* 28 (March 1997): 32.

28. A recent summary of findings on representation of minorities on professional library staffs and of attitudes toward such representation is Evan St. Lifer and Corinne Nelson, "Unequal Opportunities: Race Does Matter," *Library Journal* 122 (November 1, 1997): 42–46.

29. Virginia H. Mathews, *Kids Can't Wait . . . Library Advocacy Now! A President's Paper,* written for Mary R. Somerville, President, 1996–97, American Library Association (Chicago: American Library Association, [1996]), p. 15; Chelton, "Three in Five Public Library Users Are Youth," 104–105; Benton Foundation, *Buildings, Books, and Bytes,* pp. 28, 19; NCES, *Public Libraries: 1994,* p. 36, table 5; NCES, "Use of Public Library Services"; American Library Association, *Library Advocacy Now!*

30. Chicago Public Library Foundation, "Project Mind: Meeting Information Needs Democratically," <http://cpl.lib.uic.edu/003cpl/projectmind.html> accessed December 2, 1996.

31. Mathews, *Kids Can't Wait,* p. 15.

32. Frances Smardo Dowd, "Public Library Programs for Latchkey Children: A Status Report," *Public Libraries* 34 (September–October 1995): 291–295.

33. Gates Library Foundation, "FAQ," <http://www.glf.org/faq.html> accessed June 24, 1997.

34. Robert N. Bellah, et al., *The Good Society* (New York: Vintage Books, 1992); Putnam, *Making Democracy Work;* Putnam, "Bowling Alone: America's Declining Social Capital"; Amitai Etzioni, *The Spirit of Community: Rights, Responsibilities, and the Communitarian Agenda* (New York: Crown Publishers, 1993); Rybczynski, *City Life;* Tony Hiss, *The Experience of Place* (New York: Vintage Books, 1991); Ray Oldenburg, *The Great Good Place: Cafés, Coffee Shops, Community Centers, Beauty Parlors, General Stores, Bars, Hangouts and How They Get You Through the Day* (New York: Paragon House, 1989).

35. PLA, *Statistical Report* '96, pp. 68–86.

36. Gregorian, "A Place Elsewhere," p. 62.

37. Rybczynski, *City Life,* p. 109.

38. Kate Simon, *Bronx Primitive: Portraits in a Childhood* (New York: Viking, 1982), p. 44.

39. Steven Lee Myers, "Financial Crisis Is Gripping Smaller Cities of New York," *New York Times,* March 25, 1996, p. B6.

40. George Judson, "Its Library Crippled, Danbury Rallies," *New York Times,* March 12, 1996, pp. B1, B5.

41. U.S. Congress, Office of Technology Assessment, *The Technological Reshaping of Metropolitan America,* OTA-ETI-643 (Washington, DC: U.S. Government Printing Office, 1995); Steve Lohr, "The Internet as an Influence on Urbanization," *New York Times,* September 16, 1996, p. D1; Mitchell quoted in Carey Goldberg, "Face-to-Face Meetings Fill in Cyberspace Gaps," *New York Times,* February 25, 1997, p. A12.

42. "Vancouver, Phoenix, Denver, Paris, San Antonio: City Libraries," *Architecture* 84 (October 1995): 55.

43. David Gonzalez, "Wounded City Focuses on Redeveloping Its Core," *New York Times,* May 7, 1995, sec. 1, p. 37.

44. James Brooke, "What's Doing in Denver," *New York Times,* June 1, 1997, sec. 5, p. 10.

45. Newark Public Library, *Gateway to Information/Door to Learning: The Newark Public Library's Service Plan for 1994–1998* [Newark, NJ: 1993], p. 11.

46. King County Library System, "Bellevue Regional Library, Open House and Dedication Celebration, Saturday, July 17, 1993," and "The Art and Architecture of the Bellevue Regional Library," brochures, n.d.

47. Reuben quoted in *American Libraries* 28 (August 1997): 18.

48. George Steiner, "Ex Libris: A Love Letter Written to Reading," *New Yorker* 73 (March 17, 1997): 118, 120.

49. *Time,* April 21, 1997, pp. 102–106.

50. Steiner, "Ex Libris," p. 120.

Index

Truman administration, 124–125
trustees, boards of, 55–56
Tulsa Library Trust, 71

U.S. regions
 library services in, 47
United States Government. *See names
  of specific agencies, e.g.,
  Congress, Department of
  Education, etc.*
United States Postal Service
 and kiosk project, 173–174
universal service, 15, 155
 and Bell telephone, 240n40
 concept of, 135
 and fees for technology, 152
 impediments to, 157–160
 implementation of, 156–157
Urban Libraries Council, 178, 195
 survey of fundraising, 68–69
use figures. *See* circulation figures
user fees. *See* fees
Utica, New York
 and library role, 206
value-added services, 77. *See also* fees

War on Poverty, 19
western region
 and library development, 9, 47–48
 and library support, 48, 59
white flight, 9, 18
White House conferences on
  libraries, 175, 177
Wilson, Louis R., 47
Winslow, Amy, 22
Winsor, Justin, 12
women
 and librarianship, 12, 179–180
World Wide Web
 and CDA, 160
 libraries on, 85, 187–188
Wyoming
 library governance in, 50–51